AF653316

HOSPITALITY JOBS AND CAREERS

Ravi Sharma

CENTRUM PRESS
NEW DELHI-110002 (INDIA)

CENTRUM PRESS

H.O.: 4360/4, Ansari Road, Daryaganj,
New Delhi-110002 (India)
Tel: 23278000, 23261597, 23255577, 23286875

B.O.: No. 1015, Ist Main Road, BSK IIIrd Stage,
IIIrd Phase, IIIrd Block, Bengaluru-560085 (INDIA)
Tel: 080-41723429

Email: centrumpress@gmail.com
Visit us at: www.centrumpress.com

Hospitality Jobs and Careers

© Reserved

First Edition, 2013

ISBN 978-93-81293-99-7

PRINTED IN INDIA

Printed at Balaji Offset, Delhi.

Contents

Preface (*vii*)

1. Human Capital in Hospitality Industry 1
2. Human Resources Development in Hospitality 50
3. Training in Hospitality Management 87
4. Human Resources in Tourism Sector 150
5. Employment of Hospitality Professions 206
6. Trends and Opportunity in Hospitality Industry 227

Bibliography 245

Index 247

Preface

As lifestyle needs and services evolve, so new and different job positions are created. Indeed, when browsing the Classified Ads now, we encounter terms which didn't even exist just a few years ago. Terms like white collar jobs, blue collar jobs, and home based jobs. Also the newly popular term - 'hospitality management jobs'. But what exactly are hospitality management jobs? Jobs or professions that extend hospitality to the customer. Examples include hotels, restaurants, casinos, tourism, museaums & galleries, parks and fairs, and so on. The distinctive feature is catering services to other people so that they would feel more welcome - wherever the service is rendered. Thus, the core task is to be hospitable and accommodating to those you are serving. Even though this definition seems simple, it does not refer to just one specific job or activity. There are many ways to be hospitable and make someone feel at home. This is why there are numerous different fields of opportunity available under the general heading of "hospitality management".

In the field of hospitality, some workers serve the client face to face, but others do not. Many hospitality sector jobs entail work behind the scenes in the backstage arena - such as chefs, planners and other positions that involve planning and preparations. Positions with more direct exposure to customers are typically those which involve upfront services such as receptionists, waiters, waitresses, concierge, park administrators, and casino personnel. There is a vast range of options regarding where you might work in Hospitality. For instance, restaurants and cafes could be a good starting point. Alternatively, you might choose work in bed and breakfast accommodations and hotels. Casinos are also a good working environment where typically you could anticipate generous tips. Resorts and museums may also be of interest. You could even work in cruise ships and travel all over the world.

It is also possible to create your own business. This is especially relevant for specializing in the culinary arts. You could, for example, open your own restaurant, preferably after gaining practical salaried experience in several successful professional establishments. This is hard and demanding work but can be very rewarding and fulfilling. If you specialized on the tourism field, you might open your own travel agency. One advantage of this kind of career is that it can be very lucrative. Your effort is very much rewarded and reflected in your income.

However, how much you earn would definitely depend greatly on your position and specialty. Some enterprises pay by the hour. Others pay annually. Tips and bonuses may add a significant variable element to your package. Education Since there are many different job positions in this kind of career, there are also differing educational requirements. For instance, some positions don't require a diploma and accept high school graduates. Typically such posts would include hotel housekeeping services, cleaners, and the like. There are other positions, however, requiring thorough specialized training. For example, chefs will be expected to achieved a degree in culinary arts. You may consider taking Hotel and Restaurant Management courses to improve your prospects. This would be a significant advantage in your favour. Tourism courses are also worthwhile and are recommended if you want to specialize in a tourism oriented hospitality activity.

Each chapter in the book is self contained and is consistent with the general aim of the book. No doubt, the chapters given in this book shall help the teachers, students and social scientists to understand and explore more in the subject.

—*Author*

1

Human Capital in Hospitality Industry

Summer employees hired by local recreation departments or by amusement parks are often high school students or individuals with no education beyond a high school diploma. Specialized training in a particular field, such as athletics, music, or first aid, can be an asset when seeking employment in the recreation industry.

Getting the Job

High school students interested in careers in amusement and recreation should try to get summer, seasonal, or part-time jobs with local sports centers, amusement and theme parks, recreation centers, or other facilities offering recreation programs. It is best to inquire about positions at recreation departments or amusement parks well before the start of the summer season.

Advancement Possibilities and Employment Outlook

Employment in this industry is expected to grow faster than average for all occupations through 2014, although competition for full-time positions will be strong. Overall, about 30 percent of amusement and recreation positions are part time, and many jobs are seasonal.

Amusement and recreation attendants wishing to make a lifelong career in the industry should study the field at the college level. Specialized training, combined with experience in seasonal or part-time jobs, will improve a candidate's chances for landing a full-time position. Advancement opportunities within the field of amusement and recreation vary according to the needs of the population being served. Expect job growth within athletic clubs, camps, sports clinics, and commercial recreation enterprises.

Working Conditions

Amusement and recreation attendants typically spend most or all of their time outdoors in all sorts of weather. Most recreation attendants put in a forty-hour workweek, although many jobs do not feature typical 9-to-5 schedules. The work can be physically challenging, and park attendants are at risk for injury. Being responsible for the safety and well-being of participants can also place emotional stress on amusement and recreation attendants.

Earnings and Benefits

Recreation attendants earn less on average than attendants in other fields. According to the U.S. Bureau of Labour Statistics, the average wage for amusement and recreation attendants is $7.69 per hour. Self-employed attendants in the amusement and recreation industry are rare.

Bartender

Definition and Nature of the Work

Bartenders prepare alcoholic drinks for patrons of restaurants, bars, cocktail lounges, and other places where drinks are served. Alcoholic drinks are made up of many combinations of ingredients, and each drink may be made in several ways. The bartender's main job is to know the standard drink recipes and be able to mix them quickly and accurately. Occasionally, customers have their own preferences or recipes for a bartender to follow. Bartenders also check the identification of customers seated at bars to ensure that they meet the minimum drinking age.

Most bartenders take drink orders, serve drinks, and collect money for drinks. In restaurants bartenders fill drink orders placed by the diners, but the drinks are usually served by waiters. Bartenders may have additional duties. Sometimes they arrange bottles and barware, wash glasses, and clean the bar. Bartenders also remove empty bottles and trash and replace empty beer kegs. In large bars and restaurants they may be assisted by a bartender helper.

Bartenders stock the bar by bringing liquor bottles, mixed drink ingredients, and other bar supplies from the storeroom to the bar. They keep track of wines, beers, liquors, and other supplies. Some bartenders do the actual ordering of bar supplies. Others report what is needed to the owner or to a purchasing agent. In very large restaurants and bars the ordering of supplies is done by a wine steward or a beverage manager.

In addition to bars and cocktail lounges, bartenders work in hotels, in private clubs, aboard ships, and on trains. Many bartenders work in restaurants that have a liquor license. About one-fifth of all bartenders own their own bars.

Education and Training Requirements

Most bartenders learn their trade on the job. Some vocational schools offer courses in bartending. Working as a waiter is good experience for someone who wishes to become a bartender. Waiters can learn how to tend bar by watching the bartender work.

Bartenders must be aware of state and local laws concerning the sale of alcoholic drinks. In some states bartenders must have a bartender's license or a state health certificate. Bartenders usually must be at least twenty-one years old, but many bars prefer to hire individuals who are twenty-five or older. Bartenders must have a neat and clean appearance and a pleasant, agreeable manner. They often interact socially with the patrons, which works to their advantage as far as tipping is concerned.

Getting the Job

Many bars will train prospective bartenders who do not have bartending skills. Interested individuals can apply directly to bars in which they would like to work. Newspaper want ads often carry advertisements Bartenders work in a variety of locations where alcoholic drinks are served for bartending jobs. Many bartenders belong to labour unions. A union's local office can help candidates find out about jobs in the bartending field.

Advancement Possibilities and Employment Outlook

Many bartenders gain experience by working in small restaurants or bars. Then they look for jobs in large luxury hotels, restaurants, or cocktail lounges that offer higher wages. In hotels large enough to have many bartenders, one may advance to the position of head bartender. Skilled bartenders who have a knowledge of accounting can become wine stewards or beverage managers.

The employment outlook for bartenders is expected to grow as fast as the average through the year 2014. The overall number of bartenders is large and the turnover rate is high. There is always strong competition for positions in expensive restaurants where potential tip earnings are greatest. It is important to note that the consumption of alcoholic beverages outside of the home has been declining in the United States-a trend that is certain to affect employment. Opportunities will be best for bartenders with the most training and experience.

Working Conditions

Working conditions vary widely. Bars in luxury hotels, restaurants, and resorts offer more plush surroundings than do neighbourhood bars. Bartenders must be able to get along well with the public. They should also have good judgment and be willing to stop service to a customer who has had too much to drink. Bartenders must be prepared to work long hours on their feet and lift heavy cases and beer kegs.

Bartenders may work more than forty hours per week. They often work until very late at night and on weekends and some holidays. Some bartenders work split shifts; that is, they work for a few hours, take a long break, and return to work a few hours later. Part-time positions are often available. Many bartenders belong to labour unions.

Earnings and Benefits

According to the U.S. Bureau of Labour Statistics, bartenders earn a median salary of $7.42 per hour plus tips. Like waiters, bartenders who work in public bars may receive more than half their earnings as tips. Very popular bartenders, especially those who know their customers well and socialize with them at the bar, can make even more in tips. In some bars and restaurants workers contribute all or a portion of their tips to a tip pool, which is distributed among the staff. The tip pool allows workers who are not usually tipped to share the rewards of good service.

Some bars supply bartenders with jackets or uniforms. Bartenders who work in restaurants are usually given free meals while they work. Many bartenders receive paid holidays and vacations. Bartenders who work in large hotels and restaurants may receive health insurance, sick pay, and retirement benefits.

Cafeteria Attendant

Definition and Nature of the Work

Cafeteria attendants work in schools, colleges, clubs, hospitals, other institutions, and office buildings. Their main job is to serve food at a counter. Depending on the organization of the cafeteria, cafeteria attendants may serve all the items offered or only one or two items, including salads, soups, desserts, vegetables, or main dishes. Some attendants are in charge of beverage machines. Food servers must be careful to serve just the right amount of food to control the amount of waste.

Some cafeteria workers have specific tasks. Dining room attendants put out clean trays and silverware and refill napkin dispensers. After meals they may remove dirty dishes and wipe down tables. Food runners carry food from the kitchen to the serving line. They tell the cooks how many more people to expect.

Some cafeteria attendants are responsible for several tasks in the kitchen. They make coffee and tea, toast bread, cut pies and cakes, slice meat and cheese, or make sandwiches. They often cook foods to order such as eggs, bacon, and grilled cheese sandwiches. In some cafeterias attendants calculate the customer's bill, receive money, and give change; however, most cafeterias have cashiers who handle all of the money transactions.

Between serving hours, cafeteria attendants clean the kitchen, serving and dining areas, tables, and equipment. They may wrap and restock prepackaged items. They refill salt and pepper shakers, sweep, mop, vacuum floors, and get ready for the next meal shift.

Education and Training Requirements

Cafeteria attendants typically are trained on the job and need no special education; however, most employers prefer applicants who have a high school education. Cafeteria attendants should be patient and cheerful and able to get along well with other workers and the public. They should also have a neat, well-groomed appearance.

Many states require a health certificate stating that they have no communicable diseases. Cafeteria attendants who calculate customers' bills and handle money must have good mathematical skills.

Getting the Job

Interested individuals should apply to the cafeteria in which they would like to work. Office buildings, hospitals, and airports often have large cafeterias, and prospective cafeteria attendants can apply directly to the establishment's manager. Cafeteria jobs are frequently listed in newspaper want ads and at state and private employment agencies.

Advancement Possibilities and Employment Outlook

Experience in a small cafeteria may lead to a higher-paying job with more responsibility in a large cafeteria. In addition, cafeteria attendants Cafeteria attendants serve food at schools, colleges, clubs, institutions, and office buildings.

Although the work can be monotonous, attendants meet and interact with many people each day may become supervisors in charge of training workers. Some attendants become menu planners, cooks, or food and beverage managers. It has become increasingly necessary to take courses in cooking, nutrition, and food services to get these advanced jobs.

The employment outlook for cafeteria attendants is expected to grow as fast as the average through 2014. People who lead busy lives like the speedy and nutritionally balanced meals that cafeterias offer, so the demand for cafeteria attendants is expected to grow. There is a high turnover rate in this field, with many people using it as a short-term source of income.

Working Conditions

Cafeteria attendants work in clean, well-lighted kitchens and dining rooms. Kitchens usually are warm and noisy. Food servers stand almost the entire day and may often be pressured to work quickly. The work can get monotonous, although attendants are always meeting new people. Cafeteria attendants also have to do a lot of lifting, carrying, and bending. Most kitchens have modern equipment that is simple and convenient to use. It can be a pleasant job for those who like to work around food.

Cafeteria work can be either part time or full time. Some attendants work only during meal hours and go home between meals. Many workers belong to labour unions.

Earnings and Benefits

According to the U.S. Bureau of Labour Statistics, cafeteria attendants earned an average of $7.10 per hour in 2004. Unionized workers and those with experience earned more. Attendants often receive uniforms. Many workers are provided with health and accident insurance, retirement plans, paid holidays, and free meals while at work.

Dining Room Attendant

Definition and Nature of the Work

Dining room attendants, formerly called busboys or bussers, work in restaurants, cafeterias, and hotel dining rooms. Attendants clear tables and unload their trays in the kitchen, separating the dishes, silverware, and linen. Then they reset the tables, laying tablecloths, arranging the silverware perfectly, lighting candles if appropriate, and filling flower vases. Dining room attendants may have to arrange tables and chairs to make room for large groups. They are responsible for seeing that the dining room is well stocked with utensils, napkins, glasses, tablecloths, table decorations, and foods such as butter and crackers or bread.

Dining room attendants may also be expected to dust woodwork, wash mirrors, vacuum carpets, clean and wax floors, and help to clean up spills. They are usually assigned to a station, which consists of several tables, but may help other attendants whose stations get very busy. In addition to these duties, attendants act as assistants to waitresses and waiters. They get high chairs for children, help serve food, carry heavy trays, and fill water glasses. They clear dishes from tables between courses. Dining room attendants also act as messengers between the dining room staff and the kitchen staff.

Dining room attendants are usually supervised by other restaurant workers. Sometimes the supervisor is the waiter who works at the station with the dining room attendant. More often the supervisor is the headwaiter who manages the dining room. Sometimes the restaurant host instructs the dining room attendants.

Education and Training Requirements

Dining room attendants are not required to have a high school diploma. They typically receive on-the-job training, learning all about the operation of the kitchen and dining room. Their positions are considered starting points for other jobs in a restaurant, hotel, or cafeteria business. Some fine hotels offer training programs for all their employees, including dining room attendants, so that their customers receive the very best service. Many chain restaurants send their employees to a short training session. Dining room attendants should have a neat, clean appearance, a pleasant manner, and the ability to follow directions. Many states require a health certificate stating that the attendant has no communicable diseases.

Getting the Job

Prospective dining room attendants can apply directly to hotels, restaurants, or cafeterias and answer want ads in the newspaper. The opening of new restaurants provides more opportunities for work. Individuals interested in working during the summer months only should apply to resorts well in advance of the tourist season.

Advancement Possibilities and Employment Outlook

Dining room attendants may be promoted to other positions. They may become waiters or waitresses. If they are interested in preparing food, they may become kitchen helpers. Because of the expansion of the restaurant business, a good worker will have many opportunities for job advancement. Positions for dining room attendants are expected to grow about as fast as the average through 2014. There is one trend to note, however: although the number of restaurants is growing, waiters and waitresses are increasingly assuming the duties of dining room attendants.

Working Conditions

Dining room attendants work at a fast pace and often under pressure. They have to perform a variety of tasks quickly and efficiently. Their surroundings are usually pleasant, well lighted, clean, and comfortable. However, the area where they unload dirty dishes may be hot and noisy. Dining room attendants should have plenty of energy and strength to lift heavy trays and move furniture. In order not to disturb customers, they must work very quietly.

Candidates must be good multi-taskers, meaning they are capable of doing many things at once. They have an opportunity to meet many interesting people, both fellow workers and customers. Full-time attendants may work forty to forty-eight hours per week. Some work on a part-time basis. Many dining room attendants belong to labour unions.

Earnings and Benefits

According to the U.S. Bureau of Labour Statistics, dining room attendants earned a median hourly wage of $7.17 in 2004. New dining room attendants often begin at the minimum wage. Those who assist waiters or waitresses usually receive overtime pay. In some restaurants they may also receive a share of the wait staff's tips. Dining room attendants generally receive free meals while they work. Full-time workers may receive paid vacations and holidays, health and accident insurance, and retirement benefits.

Dishwasher

Definition and Nature of the Work

Sparkling glasses and clean silverware make a good impression on restaurant customers. A clean table setting suggests that the restaurant will offer good service and wholesome food. The person responsible for providing clean tableware is the dishwasher.

After customers have completed their meal, a dining room attendant takes the dirty dishes to the dishwasher. Dishwashers scrape, sort, and stack the dishes, and then load them into dishwashing machines. Dishwashers fill the machines with soap and turn them on. When the dishes are clean, dishwashers unload them and put them in their proper places so that other kitchen workers and waiters and waitresses can find them.

In very large establishments dishwashers may perform only one or two jobs. For example, one dishwasher may scrape plates, while another dishwasher may be in charge of washing large pots and pans. Dishwashers often are responsible for other cleanup jobs. Sometimes they clean floors, cabinets, sinks, and countertops. Occasionally they perform some of the tasks of dining room attendants such as clearing tables and assisting waiters and waitresses.

Dishwashers work in every establishment that serves food, including restaurants, buffets, hotels, coffee shops, hospitals, and schools.

Education and Training Requirements

Dishwashers learn all their duties on the job. Some states require that dishwashers have a health certificate stating that they are free of communicable diseases.

Getting the Job

The best way for an interested individual to get a dishwashing job is to apply directly to restaurants or other places where they would like to work. Newspaper want ads often have listings for dishwashers. The state employment office may also list job openings. Dishwashers must be strong enough to lift heavy dishes and pots and pans, and they must have enough stamina to stand or bend for long periods.

Advancement Possibilities and Employment Outlook

After obtaining some experience, dishwashers may advance to other jobs such as kitchen helper, dining room attendant, cook, or waiter or waitress. Taking courses in cooking and food service is helpful to those who wish to advance to a better job. The employment outlook for dishwashers is expected to be good through the year 2014. The turnover rate for dishwashers is very high because about half of all dishwashers are students who change jobs when they graduate. Prospective dishwashers can almost always find jobs.

Working Conditions

The dishwashing area in a kitchen is often hot, damp, and noisy. Sometimes the work gets hectic when the restaurant is busy. This job requires lifting heavy baskets of dishes along with heavy pots and pans. In addition to strength, dishwashers need stamina because they stand for long periods during the workday.

Restaurants are open for long hours to best serve the public. As a result dishwashers are often required to work evenings, weekends, and holidays. Sometimes they work split shifts, in which they work for a few hours, leave, and return to work a few hours later. Full-time dishwashers work from forty to forty-eight hours per week; however, about half of all dishwashers work part time. The average workweek for dishwashers is less than thirty hours. Many dishwashers belong to labour unions.

Earnings and Benefits

Dishwashers typically start out earning the minimum wage. They may make more money if they work in a large, upscale restaurant. Dishwashers who belong to labour unions generally earn higher pay. According to the U.S. Bureau of Labour Statistics, dishwashers earned a median hourly wage of $7.35 in 2004.

Doorkeeper

Definition and Nature of the Work

Doorkeepers are stationed at the entrances of most large city hotels, restaurants, and luxury apartment buildings, as well as country resorts. These uniformed greeters create a welcoming atmosphere for guests or tenants arriving at their doors. Doorkeepers must be diplomatic, courteous, and helpful to all guests. Their responsibilities include opening the doors of cars and taxicabs for guests who arrive at their establishment, helping the guests out of cars, shielding them from rain or snow with an umbrella, and opening the door of the building so that the guests can step inside. In exchange for these services, guests frequently tip doorkeepers.

Doorkeepers also hail taxicabs for guests and tenants, carry packages, and watch for unauthorized people who might try to enter the building. They report suspicious people to the building manager or the police. In addition, doorkeepers direct delivery workers to the delivery entrance of the establishment. Those who work in apartment buildings may notify tenants that visitors have arrived by calling the tenants on the telephone.

Education and Training Requirements

A high school diploma is not necessary for this position, but a good command of the English language is necessary to make the best impression on guests and tenants. Doorkeepers are usually trained on the job by experienced doorkeepers. They can start as bellhops in hotels or as kitchen helpers in restaurants. Doorkeepers must have a neat personal appearance and a pleasant and agreeable manner. They should also be polite, helpful, and responsible.

Doorkeepers assist hotel guests and apartment building residents who are in transit. They hail taxi cabs, carry packages, and open building and taxi cab doors for people.

Getting the Job

Interested individuals can apply directly to hotels, restaurants, and apartment buildings for a job as a doorkeeper. The want ads in local newspapers are also a good source for job listings. Candidates who are unable to find work as a doorkeeper can apply for a job as a bellhop or a kitchen helper and advance from that position.

Advancement Possibilities and Employment Outlook

There are very few advancement possibilities for doorkeepers; however, an experienced doorkeeper may be promoted to supervisor of all lobby employees, including bellhops, floor cleaners, and window washers. The employment outlook for doorkeepers is fair. Although openings develop quickly for many hotel and restaurant employees, most hotels and restaurants employ only a few doorkeepers. Turnover is low, so few job openings occur. Additional doorkeeper jobs will likely come from the development of new hotels.

Working Conditions

Doorkeepers typically work a five-day, forty-hour week. They sometimes work evenings or weekends and often work in shifts so that the door to an establishment is covered at all times. Most doorkeepers wear uniforms. Some doorkeepers are provided with uniforms or a uniform allowance. Others must purchase their own.

Since hotel and restaurant doorkeepers are stationed outside, they must endure all kinds of weather. All doorkeepers stand for long periods, which may be very tiring. In spite of physical discomforts, doorkeepers must remain cheerful and courteous at all times.

Earnings and Benefits

Doorkeepers generally start at minimum wage. Those who belong to unions may earn higher wages. Experienced doorkeepers earn an average salary of $17,000 to $19,000 or more per year. Doorkeepers in New York City earn much more-according to an April 19, 2006 article in the Christian Science Monitor, about twice as much as the average. Those who work night shifts generally receive extra pay. In addition, a large portion of doorkeepers' incomes come from tips given by patrons of the hotel, restaurant, or apartment that employs them. Doorkeepers generally receive benefits such as paid vacations, sick leave, health insurance, and retirement plans.

Fast Food Franchise Worker

Definition and Nature of the Work

Fast food franchise workers are employed by fast food restaurants throughout the country. The most popular restaurants of this type specialize in hamburgers, fried chicken, fried fish, roast beef sandwiches, and other easily prepared food items. Fast food franchise workers prepare and serve food, keep the restaurant clean, and make sure that the customers are satisfied with their service. In many fast food restaurants the food is prepared in an assembly-line fashion. Workers in some franchises are trained to do all of the jobs in the restaurant; in others each worker learns a specific task.

In a typical fast food chain, a counter worker takes the orders and gives them to the cook, who prepares the food and places the order on a plate or packages it in a box or paper wrapper. The counter worker then completes the order with beverages and processes payment. Some fast food restaurants have one counter worker who works as the cashier and takes all of the orders and another who fills them. A counter worker may also prepare sundaes and other ice cream dishes, cook french fries, and toast buns.

Dining room attendants are in charge of clearing and wiping the tables, filling the salt and pepper shakers, stocking packets of ketchup, mustard, and other garnishes, and making sure the napkin and straw dispensers are filled. They also sweep and mop the floors. Sometimes counter workers assist the dining room attendants by cleaning kitchen equipment, sweeping, mopping up spills, and carrying out trash.

All fast food franchise workers are supervised by a manager or an assistant manager. Sometimes the owner of the franchise acts as the manager. Managers hire Fast food franchise counter workers take customers' orders, receive payment, and make change. They deliver the order to the cooks, who prepare the food in an assembly-line fashion and fire workers as necessary, oversee the running of the franchise, and make sure the customers are satisfied. The majority of fast food franchise workers are students who work part time. Managers must set up schedules that cover all work shifts.

Education and Training Requirements

There are no formal educational requirements for fast food franchise workers. Most skills are learned on the job. Counter workers, however, should speak proper English and be able to do simple arithmetic. Most counter workers use a cash register or a computerized system for taking orders, totalling the check, and making change. Fast food franchises provide training in the use of these machines. It is helpful but not necessary for cooks to have some cooking experience. Dining room attendants need no special training.

Most fast food franchises have their own training programs in which they teach workers what to say when customers reach the counter and exactly how each food-related task should be done. This is the company's way of making sure that customers get fast, courteous service. In these training programs, cooks gain experience preparing the foods served by the franchise, counter workers practice greeting customers, using the cash register, and making change, and dining room attendants learn how to work efficiently. Training programs may last from two days to two weeks.

Counter workers must be able to get along with people and have a pleasant personality and a neat appearance. All positions require good health and physical stamina. State laws often require health certificates stating that workers are free from communicable diseases.

Getting the Job

Interested individuals should apply directly to fast food franchises in their area. Job listings often appear in newspaper want ads or on the windows or signs of franchises that are hiring. New restaurant openings are another source of job leads. The turnover rate for employees in the fast food business is very high, so potential workers are likely to find job openings.

Advancement Possibilities and Employment Outlook

Workers who show enough ability and enthusiasm can become assistant managers or managers. Some workers advance by taking other jobs in the food service industry.

Jobs for fast food franchise employees are expected to grow as fast as the average through the year 2014 because the lifestyle of many Americans is increasingly fast paced and because healthier items are being added to the menus of many fast food restaurants.

Working Conditions

Fast food franchise employees must work quickly and

efficiently. They rarely get a chance to rest, and they are always on their feet. The work can be monotonous. Job hazards include falls, cuts, and burns, although injuries are seldom serious. Fast food franchise workers typically have to work their share of weekends, evenings, and holidays. Students must arrange work schedules that allow them to attend classes. Most counter workers and dining room attendants work fewer than thirty hours per week. Cooks may work as many as forty-eight hours per week, although part-time work is available. Workers generally wear uniforms. Most employers provide uniforms or a uniform allowance, but some workers may have to purchase their own uniforms.

Earnings and Benefits

Earnings vary depending on the location of the franchise and the experience of the worker. According to the 2004 Occupational Employment Statistics survey, fast food franchise workers earn a median salary of $7.06 per hour. A few workers also receive tips. Many receive free meals during work hours. Full-time workers generally receive paid vacation time and other benefits.

Gaming Cage Worker

Definition and Nature of the Work

Gaming cage workers or cage cashiers count the money at casinos and other gaming establishments. They work in a secure place, known as the cage, which is the central depository for money, gaming chips, and casino paperwork. Cage workers exchange real currency for playing chips used in dice, card, and roulette games. They also buy these tokens back from patrons for cash, verify credit references for patrons who want to open a credit account at the casino, and cash checks.

Because the gaming industry is highly regulated, the cage cashiers must keep precise records. Transactions involving large sums of money must be reported to the Internal Revenue Service for tax purposes. Gaming cage workers use computers to calculate and keep track of all transactions. They must balance their money drawers at the end of each shift.

Education and Training Requirements

There are no formal educational requirements for the job, although most employers require a high school diploma or the equivalent. Casinos usually provide on-the-job training to acquaint cage workers with the establishment's procedures. They also may offer classroom training in rules and regulations. Employers expect applicants to speak clear and proper English and to have excellent math skills. Some employers administer a math test to job applicants. Experience in handling money or other employment in gaming establishments is helpful in getting a job as a gaming cage worker.

Gaming cage workers must be well organized, detail oriented, discreet, and trustworthy. They often handle confidential material. Good customer service skills are essential.

Gaming cage workers, like all casino employees, must have a license issued by a regulatory agency such as a state gaming control board or commission. To get this license applicants must show photo identification, provide proof of residency in the state in which they plan to work, and pay a fee. The fee may vary by geographical area. Age requirements for the job may vary by state as well. All gaming job applicants should expect a background check.

Getting the Job

People interested in casino work should contact the personnel offices of casinos directly for information on openings and entry-level requirements. Working part time or as a seasonal employee during major tourist seasons is a good way to move into full-time employment.

Advancement Possibilities and Employment Outlook

Gaming cage cashiers can advance to supervisory roles by maintaining spotless work records and by demonstrating professionalism and good customer relations skills. Additional education and training may be required for advancement.

The job outlook for gaming cage workers is only moderate through the year 2014, partly because of technology. All gaming establishments are finding ways to reduce the amount of cash handled by employees. Cash-out machines, change machines, and automated teller machines (ATMs) are common.

Some slot machines make payouts in tickets instead of coins. The tickets can be read by other slot machines and the amount on the ticket transferred to a new machine. By reducing the amount of cash needed to play, fewer workers are needed in the cage.

Gambling is legal in eleven states and the number of gaming establishments is growing. The largest growth will probably be in Native American-owned casinos and in racetracks that offer casino games. A fair number of openings for gaming cage workers should result from the continuous turnover in this occupation, which is usually due to the high level of scrutiny these employees receive.

Working Conditions

Most gaming cage cashiers work eight-hour shifts five days per week. Because casinos are typically open twenty-four hours a day, shifts are usually staggered, and cage workers are expected to work some nights, weekends, and holidays. Cage workers are on their feet throughout their shifts but are usually given two short breaks and a mealtime break.

They must work quickly and be able to concentrate for long periods in a noisy and hectic environment. Stress is particularly high for gaming cage workers because they are always being observed by supervisory and surveillance personnel. Cage workers must be tactful when dealing with unruly and frustrated patrons. In establishments that are not smoke free, they must also deal with exposure to cigarette, cigar, and pipe smoke. They are sometimes expected to lift and carry heavy bags of money.

Earnings and Benefits

Wages for gaming cage workers vary according to their level of experience, training, location, and the size of the gaming establishment that employs them. According to the U.S. Bureau of Labour Statistics, the median hourly salary of gaming cage workers was $10.74 in May of 2004.

Gaming Dealer

Definition and Nature of the Work

The most high-profile workers in casinos and other gaming establishments are the dealers, or croupiers, who run the games of chance. Dealers explain and enforce the rules and wagering guidelines for games, ask patrons to place their bets, conduct the games, make payoffs to the winners, and collect losing bets. Some games, such as dice, craps, baccarat, and roulette, require more than one dealer to run. Dealers are frequently moved from one gaming table to another during a shift and often switch between two or more games per day.

Education and Training Requirements

There are no formal education requirements for dealers, although employers do prefer to hire people with high school diplomas or the equivalent. They expect dealers to speak clear and correct English and to have strong mathematical skills. Some employers administer a math test to job applicants.

Gaming dealers are required to have a certificate or appropriate training from a dealer school. Some technical schools offer classes to train workers in specific games and skills. Other schools offer a Professional Casino Croupier certificate to students who have learned to run all of the games. Some colleges offer programs that include formal training for the casino industry. Casinos may provide dealer training, especially for employees who wish to change jobs.

Dealers, like all casino employees, must have a license issued by a regulatory agency such as a state gaming control board or commission. To get this license applicants must show photo identification, provide proof of residency in the state in which they plan to work, and pay a fee. The fee varies by geographical area. Age requirements for the job may vary by state as well. All gaming job applicants should expect a thorough background check.

Getting the Job

Individuals interested in working as dealers should contact the personnel offices of casinos directly for information on openings and entry-level requirements. Working part time or as a seasonal employee during major tourist seasons is a good way to move into full-time employment.

Advancement Possibilities and Employment Outlook

Dealers can advance by maintaining clean work records and by demonstrating professionalism and good customer relations skills. Dealers may be promoted to a higher wage table or to a more desirable work shift. With additional education and training, they may become supervisors.

The employment outlook for casino dealers is good, with jobs expected to grow faster than the average through the year 2014. As more states are legalizing casino gambling, more casinos are being planned and built, which will increase the number of dealer jobs. The largest future growth will probably be in Native American-owned casinos and in racinos, which are racetracks that offer some casino games. Part-time and seasonal positions will be most readily available.

Gaming dealers must work quickly and remain alert for long periods of time.

Working Conditions

Casino dealers usually work eight-hour shifts five days per week. Because most casinos are open twenty-four hours a day, shifts are usually staggered, and dealers are expected to work some nights, weekends, and holidays. Dealers are on their feet throughout their shifts but are usually given two short breaks and a mealtime break.

Casino dealing is a high-pressure job. Dealers must work quickly in a noisy, hectic environment; knowing that they are being observed by supervisory and surveillance personnel adds to their stress level. Dealers must be tactful when dealing with unruly and frustrated patrons and those who do not know when to stop gambling. They may be exposed to cigarette, cigar, and pipe smoke.

Earnings and Benefits

Casinos pay dealers a base salary that usually begins at

minimum wage. According to the U.S. Bureau of Labour Statistics, the median wage for dealers in 2004 was $14,340 per year; however, dealers earn a substantial portion of their income from tips. Gaming dealers generally prefer weekend, evening, and holiday shifts because those are the busiest times and often bring in the most tips. In some casinos dealers keep the tips they get; in others the tips are shared by all dealers. Casinos usually provide full-time workers with benefits that include health insurance, retirement plans, vacation time, paid sick days, and extra pay for working on holidays.

Hospitality Cashier

Definition and Nature of the Work

Hospitality cashiers are employed in many different establishments, including large resort hotels, restaurants, and small coffee shops. They are also employed in entertainment arenas ranging from Broadway theatres to amusement parks.

Cashiers are responsible for taking payments from customers, making change, and giving receipts. They generally operate a cash register or adding machine. Most modern cash registers automatically add the prices of items, total them, open the cash drawer, and provide a receipt. Some cashiers keep records of business transactions and prepare cash and checks for deposit in banks. Some also prepare sales tax reports.

Hospitality cashiers perform duties that relate directly to the kind of establishment for which they work. Cashiers who work for restaurants are called cashier checkers. They answer telephones, take reservations, and often serve as hosts by seating patrons. In addition, cashier checkers sell candy, cigarettes, and other items displayed at the cash register counter.

Cashiers who work for hotels generally keep track of charges to guests for room service, telephone calls, and valet service. Some sophisticated cash registers are linked to computer systems that can do all these things automatically. Sometimes cashiers assign and take care of safe-deposit boxes in which guests store jewellery and other valuables. They may also have front desk duties such as notifying hotel desk clerks when guests check out.

Those who work for theatres or amusement parks are generally called box office cashiers or ticket sellers. They sell tickets to customers, operate ticket dispensing machines, and answer telephones. In theatres they sometimes handle advance ticket sales and mail-order ticket requests. Cashiers come into contact with many customers throughout the working day. Some establishments, including restaurants and hotels, do a good deal of their business at night; therefore, hospitality cashiers often work evenings. About half of all cashiers work part time. Hospitality cashiers must be pleasant and agreeable and dress neatly. Above all they must be honest and trustworthy, since they often handle large sums of money.

Education and Training Requirements

Typically an individual needs a high school education to become a cashier. Some employers require that cashiers be at least eighteen years old. In high school prospective cashiers should take courses in business mathematics, bookkeeping, typing, and business machine operation.

Most businesses provide on-the-job training for newly hired cashiers. Large hotels and restaurants may have formal training programs that include classroom instruction. Smaller employers generally train beginners by having experienced cashiers supervise and instruct them.

Getting the Job

Interested individuals should apply directly to hotels, restaurants, theatres, and other businesses for cashier positions. Jobs are sometimes listed in newspaper want ads or job banks on the Internet. School placement offices may also be able to help candidates find cashiering jobs.

Advancement Possibilities and Employment Outlook

Cashiers have few opportunities for advancement unless they get additional education or training. Occasionally hotel cashiers advance to become hotel desk clerks. Those who show the ability to handle management responsibilities may be able to enter a management-training program. For example, a cashier in a restaurant may complete training and advance to the position of assistant manager.

The employment outlook for cashiers is mixed. Many hospitality establishments are installing self-service ticketing and checkout systems that eliminate some cashiering positions. Although growth in this field is expected to be slower than average through the year 2014, employee turnover is usually high enough to guarantee a steady number of job openings.

Working Conditions

Full-time hospitality cashiers generally work a five-day, forty-hour week, but only about half of all cashiers are considered full-time workers. Many work during the evenings and on weekends when the majority of people visit restaurants and movie theatres.

Cashiers often have to work quickly. They are under a great deal of pressure at peak periods of business such as lunch rushes in restaurants. It is important that they are efficient and accurate. Some cashiers have to work in small enclosed spaces such as ticket booths. Depending on where they work, they may have to stand for long periods of time, which can be very tiring.

Earnings and Benefits

Most cashiers start at minimum wage. Wages vary in different parts of the country. Cashiers typically earn more in the western and northern-central states. According to the U.S. Bureau of Labour Statistics, the median wage for cashiers was $7.81 per hour in 2004. Cashiers who belong to unions often receive higher salaries than non-unionized cashiers. Many full-time cashiers receive benefits such as paid vacations, sick leave, health insurance, and retirement plans.

Hotel Bellhop and Porter

Definition and Nature of the Work

Bellhops and porters usually work in hotels rather than motels. Like all employees in the hospitality industry, their main goal is to make sure that the guests enjoy their stay. In some hotels the duties of bellhops and porters are similar; however, bellhops usually work inside the hotel, whereas porters work outside.

Bellhops carry guests' luggage, show guests to their rooms, and make sure that everything in the room is in order. They check the lights, ventilation, and heating and show guests how to use the air conditioner, television, and telephone. If any equipment is not working properly, bellhops report this to the maintenance department so that it can be repaired as soon as possible. Bellhops may also give guests information about the hotel and local tourist attractions, deliver packages, run errands, and bring food and drink orders to guests' rooms. They also carry luggage for guests who are leaving. In large hotels bellhops are supervised by a bell captain. Bell captains give the bellhops their assignments, train new bellhops, record the bellhops' hours for payroll, and handle complaints made to their department.

Like bellhops, baggage porters handle baggage and suitcases. They deliver luggage to a guest's room on request and, when the guests are prepared to leave, arrange to have the bags shipped and carry them to the loading platform. Porters mail important papers and packages for guests and sometimes run errands that take them away from the hotel-buying tickets to a theater or sporting event, for instance.

Housekeeping porters do heavy work such as arranging furniture and rolling up rugs. They set up displays for conventions and sales meetings, sweep and mop floors, and dispose of trash.

The head porter's job is very similar to that of a bell captain. Head porters maintain employees' time records, conduct interviews, and hire and train employees. To ensure that all porters get a fair share of the work, head porters assign the calls equally among the employees.

Education and Training Requirements

Most employers prefer to hire individuals with a high school education. Beginners usually receive up to one month of on-the-job training. Physical strength is hail cabs, and perform other room service duties. Candidates should be able to get along well with people and take pride in providing services for others.

Many bellhops and porters start out as elevator operators. Most large hotels hire only experienced workers. Prospective bellhops and porters can gain that experience by starting out in a small hotel.

Getting the Job

In the hotel industry promotions usually come from within, meaning existing employees with a good work record have opportunities to advance from entry-level positions. Elevator operators and other entry-level hotel workers are often promoted to the position of bellhop or porter. Interested individuals should apply directly to the manager of a hotel that interests them. State employment offices may also provide job listings for bellhops and porters.

Advancement Possibilities and Employment Outlook

Bellhops and porters typically start out by working in small hotels to gain experience, then transfer to larger, more luxurious hotels where they will receive better tips. A good work record and a high school education increase the chances of advancing to other jobs within the hotel. Those who have clerical skills may become mail, room, or desk clerks.

A bellhop may become a bell captain, and a porter may advance to the position of head porter. Because there is usually only one bell captain or head porter in a hotel, the chances of becoming a supervisor are limited.

The hotel, motel, and resort industry is expected to grow faster than the average through the year 2014. Motels usually do not employ bellhops or porters; however, a number of large hotels are slated to be built throughout the United States by 2014. These new hotels and the growth in business travel and tourism should create an additional demand for bellhops and porters.

Working Conditions

The work bellhops and porters do can be exhausting. They must lift and carry heavy luggage, and they are on their feet all day. Bellhops are required to wear uniforms and must be well groomed when they are at work. In some hotels porters wear their own clothes. Bellhops and porters must be helpful and willing to do things for others. Not all hotel guests are easy to please, but bellhops and porters must be able to get along with all kinds of people.

Bellhops and porters usually work eight-hour shifts. Because their services are required twenty-four hours a day, they must be able to work evenings, weekends, and alternating shifts. Many bellhops and porters belong to labour unions.

Earnings and Benefits

It is difficult to determine how much bellhops and porters earn. Their salaries depend largely on the tips they receive from guests and the geographic location of the establishment in which they work. Those who work in large luxury hotels, including casino hotels and resorts, make more money than those who work in smaller hotels. According to the U.S. Bureau of Labour Statistics, bellhops and porters earn a median salary of $8.69 per hour before tips. Hotels usually offer benefits including insurance plans, paid vacations, and free meals during work hours. Hotels also furnish and maintain uniforms.

Hotel Housekeeper

Definition and Nature of the Work

Cleanliness is one of the most important features a hotel or motel can offer its guests. Housekeepers, also known as maids, are the staff members who perform cleaning duties in these establishments.

Housekeepers may be assigned specialized cleaning duties. For example, most hotels have laundry facilities for cleaning towels, linen, bedding, and workers' uniforms. Some housekeepers work only in the laundry area, washing, drying, and folding these items and then stocking the linen storage rooms.

Other housekeepers only clean guest rooms. An especially thorough cleaning is done after the occupants of a room check out. Using a large wheeling cart to hold supplies, guest room housekeepers bring clean linen, bedding, cleansers, and all other necessary cleaning equipment to the rooms.

The housekeepers replace soiled linen and towels; restock soap, tissues, and drinking glasses; disinfect bathroom surfaces;

dust and polish the furniture; remove all trash; vacuum the carpet; and wash any uncarpeted floors. Before leaving, they check to make sure that the room is spotless and ready for new guests. If housekeepers notice anything in a room that is not working properly, they report it to their supervisor, the executive housekeeper. They also send to the lost-and-found department any articles that previous guests may have left in the rooms when they checked out.

Aside from doing laundry and cleaning guest rooms, housekeepers replace light bulbs, wash windows, empty ashtrays, and clean hallways and stairs. Some housekeepers make sewing repairs or upholster furniture. Others work in lobbies, lounges, and conference and banquet rooms, where they clean carpets and move and set up furniture. In small hotels housekeepers usually perform several of these tasks.

Executive housekeepers supervise house workers, purchase supplies and equipment, and prepare budgets for the housekeeping department.

Education and Training Requirements

A formal education is not required to become a housekeeper, although employers prefer to hire people who have a high school education. Most hotels and motels provide on-the-job training. Hotel housekeepers must be able to work quickly and efficiently without invading their guests' privacy and should have a neat, clean appearance.

Getting the Job

The best way for prospective hotel housekeepers to find jobs is to apply directly to the hotels and motels in which they would like to work. Newspaper want ads and state employment offices often have listings for hotel housekeepers.

Advancement Possibilities and Employment Outlook

Housekeepers who have gained experience working in small hotels or motels can apply to luxury hotels that pay higher wages. Housekeepers in a large hotel or resort may be promoted to the position of executive housekeeper; however, since there is only one executive housekeeper in each hotel, advancement possibilities are quite limited.

Budgeting, inventory control, and staff selection are among the duties of executive housekeepers. Usually years of experience, a one-year internship, and/or college courses in institutional management, business administration, or hotel services are needed to advance to the executive position.

The hotel, motel, and resort industry is expected to grow faster than the average through the year 2014, so the job outlook for housekeepers is good. As more hotels and motels are built to accommodate increased business travel and domestic and foreign tourism, the demand for all hotel workers will rise. Existing hotels and motels are always looking for new members for their cleaning staff, and resort hotels typically hire more housekeepers for the vacation season.

Working Conditions

Modern hotels and motels have the best cleaning equipment for housekeepers to use; however, the work is demanding. Housekeepers must bend, stoop, climb, and reach to clean in corners and inside closets. Moving heavy equipment and furniture can be exhausting.

Housekeepers typically work forty to forty-eight hours each week. They may rotate from a morning to an evening or night shift and are expected to take their share of weekends and holidays. Most housekeepers wear uniforms. Some employers provide them with uniforms or a uniform allowance; others require housekeepers to purchase their own uniforms.

Earnings and Benefits

According to the U.S. Bureau of Labour Statistics, hotel housekeepers earned a median annual wage of $16,900 in 2004. Experienced workers may earn more. Executive housekeepers' salaries vary with training, experience, and most importantly the size of the hotel or motel. Their median annual salary in 2004 was $29,640, but some executive housekeepers in large luxury or resort hotels reportedly earned more than $40,000 per year.

Hotel housekeepers sometimes receive tips from guests at the end of their stay and may get free meals during work hours. Most hotels offer full-time housekeepers paid vacations, some paid holidays, health insurance, and retirement benefits.

Lodging Managers

Nature of the Work

A comfortable room, good food, and a helpful staff can make being away from home an enjoyable experience for both vacationing families and business travellers. While most lodging managers work in traditional hotels and motels, some work in other lodging establishments, such as camps, inns, boardinghouses, dude ranches, and recreational resorts. In full-service hotels, lodging managers help their guests have a pleasant stay by providing many of the comforts of home, including cable television, fitness equipment, and voice mail, as well as specialized services such as health spas.

For business travellers, lodging managers often schedule available meeting rooms and electronic equipment, including slide projectors and fax machines.

Lodging managers are responsible for keeping their establishments efficient and profitable. In a small establishment with a limited staff, the manager may oversee all aspects of operations. However, large hotels may employ hundreds of workers, and the general manager usually is aided by a number of assistant managers assigned to the various departments of the operation. In hotels of every size, managerial duties vary significantly by job title.

General managers have overall responsibility for the operation of the hotel. Within guidelines established by the owners of the hotel or executives of the hotel chain, the general manager sets room rates, allocates funds to departments, approves expenditures, and ensures expected standards for guest service, decor, housekeeping, food quality, and banquet operations. Managers who work for chains also may organize and staff a newly built hotel, refurbish an older hotel, or reorganize a hotel or motel that is not operating successfully. In order to fill entry-level service and clerical jobs in hotels, some managers attend career fairs.

Resident or hotel managers are responsible for the day-to-day operations of the property. In larger properties, more than one of these managers may assist the general manager, frequently dividing responsibilities between the food and beverage operations and the rooms or lodging services. At least one manager, either the general manager or a hotel manager, is on call 24 hours a day to resolve problems or emergencies.

Assistant managers help run the day-to-day operations of the hotel. In large hotels, they may be responsible for activities such as personnel, accounting, office administration, marketing and sales, purchasing, security, maintenance, and pool, spa, or recreational facilities. In smaller hotels, these duties may be combined into one position. Assistant managers may adjust charges on a hotel guest's bill when a manager is unavailable.

An Executive Committee made up of a hotel's senior managers advises the general manager, assists in setting hotel policy, coordinates services that cross departmental boundaries, and collaborates on efforts to ensure consistent and efficient guest services throughout the hotel. The Committee may be comprised of the department heads for housekeeping, front office, food and beverage, security, sales and public relations, meetings and conventions, engineering and building maintenance, and human resources. Executive committee members bring a different perspective of guest service to the total management objective reflecting the unique expertise and training of their positions.

Executive housekeepers ensure that guest rooms, meeting and banquet rooms, and public areas are clean, orderly, and well maintained. They also train, schedule, and supervise the work of housekeepers, inspect rooms, and order cleaning supplies.

Front office managers coordinate reservations and room assignments, as well as train and direct the hotel's front desk staff. They ensure that guests are treated courteously, complaints and problems are resolved, and requests for special services are carried out. Front office managers may adjust charges posted on a customer's bill.

Convention services managers coordinate the activities of various departments in larger hotels to accommodate meetings, conventions, and special events. They meet with representatives of groups or organizations to plan the number of rooms to reserve, the desired configuration of the meeting space, and banquet services. During the meeting or event, they resolve unexpected problems and monitor activities to ensure that hotel operations conform to the expectations of the group.

Food and beverage managers oversee all food service operations maintained by the hotel. They coordinate menus with the Executive Chef for the hotel's restaurants, lounges, and room service operations. They supervise the ordering of food and supplies, direct service and maintenance contracts within the kitchens and dining areas, and manage food service budgets. Catering managers arrange for food service in a hotel's meeting and convention rooms. They coordinate menus and costs for banquets, parties, and events with meeting and convention planners or individual clients. They coordinate staffing needs and arrange schedules with kitchen personnel to ensure appropriate food service.

Sales or marketing directors and public relations directors oversee the advertising and promotion of hotel operations and functions, including lodging and dining specials and special events, such as holiday or seasonal specials. They direct the efforts of their staff to purchase advertising and market their property to organizations or groups seeking a venue for conferences, conventions, business meetings, trade shows, and special events. They also coordinate media relations and answer questions from the press.

Human resources directors manage the personnel functions of a hotel, ensuring that all accounting, payroll, and employee relations matters are handled in compliance with hotel policy and applicable laws. They also oversee hiring practices and standards and ensure that training and promotion programs reflect appropriate employee development guidelines.

Finance (or revenue) directors monitor room sales and reservations. In addition to overseeing accounting and cash-flow matters at the hotel, they also project occupancy levels, decide which rooms to discount and when to offer rate specials.

Computers are used extensively by lodging managers and their assistants to keep track of guests' bills, reservations, room assignments, meetings, and special events. In addition, computers are used to order food, beverages, and supplies, as well as to prepare reports for hotel owners and top-level managers. Managers work with computer specialists to ensure that the hotel's computer system functions properly. Should the hotel's computer system fail, managers must continue to meet the needs of hotel guests and staff.

Working Conditions

Because hotels are open around the clock, night and weekend work is common. Many lodging managers work more than 40 hours per week, and may be called back to work at any time. Some managers of resort properties or other hotels where much of the business is seasonal have other duties on the property during the off-season or find work at other hotels or in other areas.

Lodging managers experience the pressures of coordinating a wide range of activities. At larger hotels, they also carry the burden of managing a large staff and finding a way to satisfy guest needs while maintaining positive attitudes and employee morale. Conventions and large groups of tourists may present unusual problems or require extended work hours.

Moreover, dealing with irate guests can be stressful. The job can be particularly hectic for front office managers during check-in and check-out times. Computer failures can further complicate processing and add to frustration levels.

Training, Other Qualifications, and Advancement

Hotels increasingly emphasize specialized training. Postsecondary training in hotel, restaurant, or hospitality management is preferred for most hotel management positions; however, a college liberal arts degree may be sufficient when coupled with related hotel experience or business education. Internships or part-time or summer work experience in a hotel are an asset to students seeking a career in hotel management. The experience gained and the contacts made with employers can greatly benefit students after graduation. Most degree programs include work-study opportunities. Community colleges, junior colleges, and many universities offer certificate or degree programs in hotel, restaurant, or hospitality management leading to an associate, bachelor, or graduate degree.

Technical institutes, vocational and trade schools, and other academic institutions also offer courses leading to formal recognition in hospitality management. In total, more than 800 educational facilities provide academic training for would-be lodging managers. Hotel management programs include instruction in hotel administration, accounting, economics, marketing, housekeeping, food service management and catering, and hotel maintenance engineering. Computer training also is an integral part of hotel management training, due to the widespread use of computers in reservations, billing, and housekeeping management.

More than 450 high schools in 45 States offer the Lodging Management Program created by the Educational Institute of the American Hotel and Lodging Association. This two-year program offered to high school juniors and seniors teaches management principles and leads to a professional certification called the "Certified Rooms Division Specialist."

Many colleges and universities grant participants credit towards a post-secondary degree in hotel management. Lodging managers must be able to get along with many different types of people, even in stressful situations. They must be able to solve problems and concentrate on details. Initiative, self-discipline, effective communication skills, and the ability to organize and direct the work of others also are essential for managers at all levels.

Persons wishing to make a career in the hospitality industry may be promoted into a management trainee position sponsored by the hotel or a hotel chain's corporate parent. Typically, trainees work as assistant managers and may rotate assignments among the hotel's departments—front office, housekeeping, or food and beverage—to gain a wide range of experiences. Relocation to another property may be required to help round out the experience and to help grow a trainee into the position.

Work experience in the hospitality industry at any level or in any segment, including summer jobs or part-time work in a hotel or restaurant, is good background for entering hotel management. Most employers require a bachelor's degree with some education in business and computer literacy, while some prefer a master's degree for hotel management positions.

However, employees who demonstrate leadership potential and possess sufficient length or breadth of experience may be invited to participate in a management training program and advance to hotel management positions without the education beyond high school.

Large hotel and motel chains may offer better opportunities for advancement than small, independently owned establishments, but relocation every several years often is necessary for advancement. The large chains have more extensive career ladder programs and offer managers the opportunity to transfer to another hotel or motel in the chain or to the central office. Career advancement can be accelerated by the completion of certification programs offered by various associations. These programs usually require a combination of course work, examinations, and experience. For example, outstanding lodging managers may advance to higher level manager positions.

Employment

Lodging managers held about 58,000 jobs in 2004. Self-employed managers—primarily owners of small hotels, motels, and inns—held about 45 percent of these jobs. Companies that manage hotels and motels under contract employed many managers.

Job Outlook

Employment of lodging managers is expected to grow about as fast as the average for all occupations through 2014. Additional job openings are expected to occur as experienced managers transfer to other occupations or leave the labour force, in part because of the long hours and stressful working conditions. Job opportunities are expected to be best for persons with college degrees in hotel or hospitality management.

Renewed business travel and domestic and foreign tourism will drive employment growth of lodging managers in full-service hotels. The numbers of economy-class rooms and extended-stay hotels also are expected to increase to accommodate leisure travellers and bargain-conscious guests. An increasing range of lodging accommodations is available to travellers, from economy hotels which offer clean, comfortable rooms and front desk services without costly extras such as restaurants and room service, to luxury and boutique inns that offer sumptuous furnishings and personal services. The accommodation industry is expected to continue to consolidate as lodging chains acquire independently owned establishments or undertake their operation on a contract basis. The increasing number of extended-stay hotels will moderate growth of manager jobs because these properties usually have fewer departments and require fewer managers. Also, these establishments often do not require a manager to be available 24 hours a day, instead assigning front desk clerks on duty at night some of the responsibilities previously reserved for managers.

Additional demand for managers is expected in suite hotels, because some guests—especially business customers—are willing to pay higher prices for rooms with kitchens and suites that provide the space needed to conduct small meetings. In addition, large full-service hotels—offering restaurants, fitness centers, large meeting rooms, and play areas for children, among other amenities—will continue to provide many trainee and managerial opportunities.

Earnings

Median annual earnings of lodging managers were $37,660 in May 2004. The middle 50 percent earned between $28,640 and $51,030. The lowest 10 percent earned less than $22,680, while the highest 10 percent earned more than $72,160. Median annual earnings for lodging managers in traveler accommodations were $37,420.

Salaries of lodging managers vary greatly according to their responsibilities and the segment of the hotel industry in which they are employed, as well as the location and region where the hotel is located. Managers may earn bonuses of up to 25 percent of their basic salary in some hotels and also may be furnished with meals, parking, laundry, and other services. In addition to providing typical benefits, some hotels offer profit-sharing plans and educational assistance to their employees.

Motel Hotel and Resort Desk Clerk

Definition and Nature of the Work

Desk clerks, also known as front office clerks or room clerks, are part of the front office staff of hotels, motels, and resorts. They are responsible for checking guests in and out, giving information about rates and the kinds of services their establishment provides, and assigning guests to rooms. Of all lodging employees, desk clerks have the most contact with the public; therefore, it is especially important that they make a good impression and ensure that guests' needs are being met.

There are many kinds of desk clerks in the hospitality industry. Key clerks issue and receive room keys. Reservations clerks handle reservations that guests make by mail, by telephone, or via the Internet and inform the room clerks when the guests plan to arrive. Rack clerks keep track of which rooms are occupied and unoccupied and oversee the work of the housekeepers and maintenance crew.

Mail clerks are in charge of the guests' mail and messages. Information clerks tell guests about local places of interest and provide directions. However, only in the very largest hotels are the clerks so specialized. Usually one hotel desk clerk performs several duties such as handling reservations, checking guests in or out, and giving them directions to local sites.

Desk clerks work throughout the country in all kinds of hotels, motels, and resorts. The differences in these types of lodgings lie in their location and needs of their clientele. Hotels are typically found in cities; residential hotels serve people who desire hotel service on a long-term basis. Most motels are located along highways rather than in large urban areas. Because they are designed to serve motorists who are driving a long way, motels are sometimes referred to as motor lodges. Resort hotels are usually located in vacation areas. In addition to providing rooms, many resort hotels provide recreational activities such as horseback riding and swimming.

Most hotels, motels, and resorts are open twenty-four hours every day of the year. There is almost always a desk clerk on duty to take care of the guests' needs. The desk clerk has the most contact with hotel guests. It is important for the desk clerk to be friendly, helpful, and well groomed.

Education and Training Requirements

Managers of lodging establishments like to hire people who have at least a high school education. Some large hotels prefer hiring individuals with some college experience. On-the-job training is provided. It is helpful to be good at typing, bookkeeping, and office machine and computer operation. Clerks should also have strong interpersonal and problem-solving skills.

Many desk clerks begin as bellhops, switchboard operators, or key clerks. After they gain some experience these workers may be promoted to desk clerk. Desk clerks must have a neat appearance and be able to get along well with people.

Getting the Job

Prospective desk clerks can learn about job openings from state employment agencies, newspaper want ads, or job banks on the Internet. They can also apply directly to hotels, motels, and resorts in which they want to work. Students attending training schools that specialize in hotel work should check for job listings with the school's placement office.

Advancement Possibilities and Employment Outlook

Lodging managers generally prefer to promote their employees rather than hire people from outside the staff. Desk clerks who do their jobs well can move up to the position of assistant manager or front office manager. Education beyond high school is useful in getting a promotion. Many colleges and junior colleges now offer courses and programs in hotel management. The hotel, motel, and resort industry is expected to grow faster than the average through the year 2014. An increase in business travel as well as in domestic and foreign tourism will create a demand for all lodging workers. Also, the turnover rate for desk clerks is high so jobs open up regularly.

Working Conditions

Hotels, motels, and resorts are pleasant places to work. They are usually open seven days a week, twenty-four hours a day. Desk clerks may be asked to work nights, weekends, and holidays. They often put in a five-or six-day forty-to forty-eight-hour week. Employees are usually given extra pay for working irregular hours. Most room clerks rotate their shifts with other workers. Front desks are generally clean and well lighted and the work is not strenuous. However, clerks may be on their feet much of the time, and their work can become quite hectic, especially in busy hotels and resorts; desk clerks in the hospitality industry need to be patient and tolerant even when guests are unreasonable.

Earnings and Benefits

According to the U.S. Bureau of Labour Statistics, hotel, motel, and resort desk clerks earned a median salary of $17,700 per year in 2004. Those working in large metropolitan areas usually earn more. Benefits for full-time workers include paid vacations and holidays, health insurance, life insurance, and retirement plans. Educational assistance is sometimes available as well.

Motion Picture Projectionist

Definition and Nature of the Work

Motion picture projectionists operate all of the equipment in the projection booths of indoor cinemas and drive-ins. They use movie projectors, audio equipment, and machines that rewind film to provide film entertainment for the theater's customers.

Projectionists must inspect films before they are shown. To do this they place each film reel on a hand rewinding machine and look for holes, worn places, or other defects. If necessary they repair any defects found in the film.

In most cases full-length motion pictures are recorded on several reels of film so projectionists must operate two projectors at a time. When one reel of film is ending, projectionists must have the other projector and film reel ready for showing. Projectionists know when to change projectors by watching for cue marks on the movie screen. When the cue marks appear, they close the shutter of the first projector, open the shutter of the second projector, and then rewind the first reel on a rewinding machine. The first projector is then ready for threading the next reel of film. An average reel runs about twenty minutes. This process is repeated until the entire film is shown. Some projectionists are assisted by a motion picture projectionist's apprentice.

Projectionists also clean and oil the equipment, check for defective parts, and make repairs. For major repairs they are assisted by a service repair worker.

Education and Training Requirements

There are no specific education requirements for motion picture projectionists, although a few cities and states require that they be licensed. Projectionists must have good mechanical ability because the equipment they use and repair is complex. Excellent hearing, eyesight, and manual dexterity are also important.

Many projectionist jobs are unionized. To qualify as a union projectionist a candidate must serve a one-to two-year apprenticeship and pass a union examination. Apprentices must be at least eighteen years old and have a high school diploma. They learn to operate projectors and other equipment by working on the job with experienced projectionists. Some do not get paid while they are learning; others do and they may also hold other jobs in the theater. Some projectionists learn their skills at vocational or technical schools or on the job at small, nonunion theatres; however, theatres with union contracts will not hire nonunion projectionists.

Getting the Job

In large cities projectionists who have served an apprenticeship usually find jobs through their union. Nonunion members can apply directly to local nonunion theatres. Projectionist positions are also listed in the want ads of local newspapers.

Advancement Possibilities and Employment Outlook

Motion picture projectionists who work in large multiscreen

theatres may advance to the position of chief operator. Some projectionists become service repair workers who fix sound equipment and projectors. Occasionally an experienced projectionist becomes a theater manager. The job outlook for motion picture projectionists is poor. Although the number of theatres is expected to grow slightly through the year 2014, increasingly sophisticated projection equipment does much of the work automatically. Most openings will occur as workers retire or change jobs.

Working Conditions

Both indoor and drive-in theatres are usually nice places to work. Most projection rooms are comfortable, clean, well lighted, and well ventilated. Projectionists must be able to work independently and be willing to view movies over and over again. Many motion picture projectionists work part time. Full-time projectionists work forty hours a week, including days and evenings. Their hours may be split over six days of the week instead of five. Some work in more than one theater, especially in multiscreen complexes.

Earnings and Benefits

Generally theatres in cities pay better wages than suburban or drive-in theatres. According to data from the 2004 Occupational Employment Statistics survey, motion picture projectionists earn a median salary of $8.32 per hour. Benefits for full-time workers may include paid vacations and health insurance as well as retirement plans.

Restaurant Host or Hostess

Definition and Nature of the Work

Restaurant hosts and hostesses serve as personal representatives of the restaurant for which they work. They are in charge of making reservations and greeting guests when they arrive at the restaurant. They also seat the guests and make sure that they enjoy their meal.

Hosts and hostesses try to give guests a good impression of the restaurant by greeting them in a warm, friendly manner. If guests have to wait to be seated, hosts and hostesses make them comfortable while they wait. The guests are given an idea of how long they will have to wait and are seated in a waiting area. Sometimes hosts and hostesses suggest that the diners wait at the bar and have a drink. Hosts and hostesses locate a table that is the right size for the guests, take the guests to the table, and give them menus. They may also assist guests in seating small children, or fill their water glasses.

While greeting incoming guests, hosts and hostesses must take care of guests who are leaving. Some hosts and hostesses receive the money for the guests' food and make change. To do this they must know how to operate a cash register. Restaurants sometimes have a candy or cigarette counter. If guests want to buy these items, hosts and hostesses add their cost to the guests' checks. In some restaurants this work is done by a cashier.

At the end of their work shifts, hosts and hostesses record the transactions that have taken place and total all guest checks to determine how much money has been received. These records are used to balance the accounts at the end of the day. The records are then turned in to the restaurant manager for inspection. The host and hostess stand near the restaurant entrance so they can greet guests as they arrive and then seat them at tables.

Education and Training Requirements

Individuals interested in becoming a host or hostess should take courses in business, arithmetic, bookkeeping, family and consumer science, and public speaking. Hosts and hostesses should be friendly and outgoing people who can remain calm and courteous during rush periods. They also must be neat and well groomed. Most restaurants prefer to hire people who have a high school education. Some vocational schools have programs in food service that can help prepare students for this kind of work; however, most restaurant hosts and hostesses are trained on the job.

Getting the Job

Prospective hosts and hostesses should apply directly to restaurants in which they would like to work. Newspaper want ads sometimes have listings for these positions, as do state employment offices. Previous restaurant experience is helpful in landing a hosting job.

Advancement Possibilities and Employment Outlook

Hosts and hostesses advance by transferring to more expensive restaurants that pay higher salaries. Experienced and responsible restaurant hosts and hostesses may become restaurant managers.

One big trend in the twenty-first century was an increase in the number of Americans dining out. With the restaurant business growing, the job outlook for hosts and hostesses is good, with positions expected to grow about as fast as the average through the year 2014.

Working Conditions

Because restaurants serve the public, they are usually attractive places in which to work. Expensive restaurants often provide elegant work surroundings. Hosts and hostesses are usually stationed near the restaurant entrance and are on their feet throughout their shifts.

They must maintain a neat appearance and always be courteous to guests. Full-time hosts and hostesses work forty hours a week and may rotate shifts, but there are many part-time workers in this field as well. Hosts and hostesses must work their share of weekends, evenings, and holidays. Many of these workers belong to labour unions.

Earnings and Benefits

Earnings depend on the restaurant, with expensive restaurants generally paying higher salaries. According to the U.S. Bureau of Labour Statistics, hosts and hostesses earned a median wage of $7.52 per hour in 2004. Their wages tend to be higher than that of waitpersons because they usually do not receive tips. (In some restaurants, however, they are included in a tip pool that gives them a small share of the day's tips.) Restaurants often offer full-time employees paid holidays and vacations, health insurance, and retirement plans. Most hosts and hostesses receive free meals when they are at work.

The Staff of Hotels

Background and Significance

This is a pilot study designed to help in the development of a large-scale research project on the future of work in the hospitality industry. The hospitality industry has experienced a wave of restructuring, consolidation, and new practices to cut costs including lean staffing and greater performance demands on the workforce.

The study will explore the impact of these and related changes on the health and quality of life the largest occupational group within the hospitality industry, room cleaners. Jobs in housekeeping (and food and beverage) operations of the hospitality industry represent the future of work in this growing service sector with jobs characterized by increasing repetitive physical workloads, low income, low skill utilization, low job control, and virtually no prospects for training and career advancement.

There is compelling evidence that this kind of low-income jobs result in a disproportionate high burden of illness, injury, and disability. Unlike other services, businesses in the hospitality industry, cannot be moved across the borders but will remain a fast growing sector in industrialized countries, creating increasing societal costs including disproportionate workers' compensation and health care utilization costs. Working conditions in the hospitality industry are representative for a growing number of workers of colour, working women, and former welfare recipients. The hospitality industry has become a major target for welfare-to-work and job training programs in cities throughout the country. An aging workforce is faced with increasing job demands in a competitive industry constantly upgrading services. Few studies have been done on this growing workforce and little is known about their specific working conditions and health risks and how they could be addressed.

This study will take a broad view at physical and psychosocial job factors, health, including general self-rated health, musculoskeletal disorders, work-related injury, and health-related quality of life. Further, this study will investigate which innovative organizational strategies can help to reduce the burden of illness and disability in the service sector by comparing hotels in different market segments, different degrees of unionization, and hotels with innovative joint labour management health and safety programs, negotiated child care/elder care benefits, and a multi-employer worker training project.

San Francisco is expected to provide several union and non-union cases for comparison to similar cases in low union density markets and to a selected number of additional cases in other high union density markets that highlight organizational innovations (such as training and career laddering in Las Vegas or work redesign in New York to avoid sub-contracting). The pilot study focuses on housekeeping since it is the largest occupational category in the industry and is the central focus of a larger study including hotels in other cities. The study combines qualitative and quantitative research methods and is participatory in design and implementation thereby laying the groundwork for sustainable efforts in understanding and improving health and safety of service workers.

Cooperative Setting

The pilot study is administered by the director of the Labour and Occupational Health Program (LOHP) at UC Berkeley Robin Baker, in collaboration with Niklas Krause, physician epidemiologist from the School of Public Health at UC Berkeley. Funding is provided by the United Way of the Bay Area and Local 2 of the Hotel Employees and Restaurant Employees International Union (HERE).

The level of union density in San Francisco is among the highest in the country. The largest union is HERE Local 2 which represents 8,000 workers or around 70 % of the industry's non-supervisory workforce. In San Francisco the multi-employer bargaining agreement with about 50 hotels in the city has taken wages and benefits out of competition.

The starting wage for non-tipped jobs is $11 per hour plus comprehensive portable benefits. San Francisco presents a special opportunity for comparisons of work conditions in the industry and for future workplace interventions because of a unique partnership with twelve first class hotels that is designed to improve customer service and job quality in the industry.

The San Francisco Hotels Partnership Project has implemented a core-training program throughout much of the industry, and developed pilot projects to resolve conflicts at the lowest possible level within an organization. The parties have also worked to establish joint decision making processes for redesigning work in the food and beverages and housekeeping operations.

Objectives

The objectives of the proposed study are:

1. To identify key changes in technology and organization in the hospitality industry that affects the future of work for room cleaners.
2. To explore the impact of industry changes on the health, injury rates, and well being of room cleaners.
3. To develop potential strategies for enhancing the future health and well being of room cleaners.
4. To demonstrate the utility of a participatory research methodology that actively involves room cleaners in every aspect of the study, and that results in the ability of participants to effectively advocate for health-promoting changes in their work.
5. To explore the relevance of the findings to similar low wage populations, particularly in the service sector.
6. To widely disseminate study findings and recommendations to encourage further study and action by academic researchers, labour, management, policy makers, and advocacy groups.

The pilot consists of establishing an advisory group of participants, focus groups with room cleaners, the development and administration of a survey instrument, analysis and discussion of results with participants, and dissemination of results in a final report.

Although designed for comparisons with other cities, the pilot will allow for comparisons between high quality and low quality (in terms of labour relations and customer service) hotels in San Francisco.

In addition, the use of some standardized instruments will enable comparisons of working conditions of housecleaners with jobs in different industries. Finally, future studies are planned to investigate the effects of changes in work conditions and labour-management collaboration on injury incidence, health and functional/quality of life outcomes.

Progress

A 30-member advisory group of room cleaners participated in the planning and implementation of this pilot study. Ten focus groups have been conducted with about 20-25 housecleaners at each meeting recruited from different San Francisco hotels.

A survey instrument has been developed and tested in a focus group of 25 roomcleaners. The revised survey has been translated into Spanish and Chinese languages. The survey includes standard instruments such as Karasek's Job Content Questionnaire, Siegrist's effort/reward balance scales including measures of intrinsic and extrinsic effort, SF36 health-related quality of life/functioning, general health status, and specifically developed questions to measure physical workload, musculoskeletal symptoms, work injury, and demographic variables. Depending on reading and language skills it takes 30 to 75 minutes for workers to complete the survey with assistance available from researchers and translators.

139 out of 397 roomcleaners from 4 selected hotels completed the survey during the first wave of data gathering in December 1998.

Plan

A second wave of data gathering among 258 non-responders is planned for February. Intensive efforts of personal recruitment at the workplace and telephone follow-up is planned for a random 50% sample of 130 non-responders. Data management and basic analyses limited to descriptive statistics and comparisons between four hotels are planned for March and April. A draft report will be prepared for the union by May 15 and will be available for joint labour management focus groups preparing for upcoming bargaining of five-year contracts. Further analyses including comparisons with national survey data, discussions with participants, and a final report will be completed by December 1999. Publications in peer reviewed scientific journals may be prepared simultaneously or thereafter but no funds have been allocated yet for this purpose.

Specific Aims

(1) Establish cooperative relationships between researchers and stakeholders

(2) Select 2-6 hotels (with a total of about 400 employees) representing "good" and "bad" overall work conditions as perceived by union representatives and key senior employees

(3) Conduct a series of focus groups with room cleaners from different hotels which are not selected into the pilot survey, to (a) gain a detailed understanding of their job tasks, workload, working conditions, and work-related health problems, (b) to discuss the scope and goals of the research project, and (c) to invite further participation in design and execution of the study (e.g. development and administration of survey instrument, organization of meetings with roomcleaners at participating hotels)

(4) Develop draft survey instrument

(5) Discuss draft survey instrument with union representatives and other key informants

(6) Pre-test survey instrument in focus group with 25 roomcleaners

(7) Revise survey instrument

(8) Translate survey instrument into Spanish and Chinese languages

(9) Obtain names and addresses of current employees at selected hotels

(10) Invite employees of selected hotels by mail to fill out the survey in off-site meetings

(11) Conduct first wave of survey under supervision of University researchers and with assistance of translators at different times and locations in San Francisco

(12) Create database for data entry using Microsoft Access software

(13) Enter data from questionnaires and check for completeness

(14) Follow-up of workers with incomplete responses by telephone in their first language

(15) Update list of employees and draw random 50% sample from survey non-responders

(16) Obtain contact information including telephone numbers for non-responders

(17) Invite all non-responders by mail to fill out the survey in off-site meetings

(18) Invite 50% random sample of non-responders by telephone and/or personal contact to fill out the survey in off-site meetings

(19) Conduct second wave of survey

(20) Provide follow-up meetings with research team for workers willing to participate but unable to attend the pre-scheduled survey meetings

(21) Enter data into database

(22) Check data for missing information and inconsistencies

(23) Prepare final data set with variable labels for all data fields and create scales for work conditions based on theoretical and/or empirical approaches

(24) Analyze survey data and (a) prepare frequency tables for all questionnaire answers and scales stratified by hotels, (b) compare responses of first wave responders with second wave of responders in 50% sample intensively followed up, (c) compare responses between "good" and "bad" hotels, (d) compare work conditions with reports from studies in

other industries, (e) investigate the association between work conditions and self-reported general health, musculoskeletal symptoms, quality of life, and work injury

(25) Gather OSHA 200 logs in selected hotels for 1998 and enter in separate database

(26) Replace employee names by ID code in injury data set and merge with survey data

(27) Analyze merged injury (OSHA 200 log) and survey data, and, specifically (a) compare frequency of self-reported and formally reported work injuries, (b) examine self-reported reasons for not reporting a work-related injury, (c) investigate associations between working conditions and both self-reported and OSHA 200 log based injury frequency

(28) Prepared draft report on May 15, 1999

(29) Present report to stakeholders in joint labour management meetings

(30) Prepare final report by December 1999

(31) Prepare peer-reviewed journal article(s)

(32) Integrate results of pilot study into proposed larger study comparing working conditions and health outcomes across different US cities representing different organizational settings and labour markets in the hotel industry.

2

Human Resources Development in Hospitality

Employment and Globalization in the Hotel, Catering and Tourism Sector

This report has been prepared by the International Labour Office as the basis for discussions at the Tripartite Meeting on Human Resources Development, Employment and Globalization in the Hotel, Catering and Tourism Sector.

At its 273rd Session (November 1998) the Governing Body of the International Labour Office decided that the Meeting would be included in the programme of sectoral meetings for 2000-01. At its 274th Session (March 1999) the Governing Body decided that the purpose of the Meeting would be to exchange views on policies and methods of human resource development, employment creation and globalization in the hotel, catering and tourism sector; to adopt conclusions that include proposals for action by governments, by employers' and workers' organizations at the national level and by the ILO; and to adopt a report on its discussion.

The Meeting may also adopt resolutions. The Governing Body also decided that the Meeting should be tripartite, that it should be composed of 75 participants and that the following 25 countries should be invited: Austria, Barbados, Brazil, Canada, China, Costa Rica, Dominican Republic, Egypt, France, Greece, India, Italy, Japan, Kenya, Republic of Korea, Lebanon, Mauritius, Morocco,

Netherlands, Poland, Portugal, South Africa, Spain, Switzerland and the United States. In the event that a government declines the invitation, an alternate will be invited from the reserve list which was established at the same time: Argentina, Chile, Croatia, Hungary, Mexico, Namibia, New Zealand, Philippines, United Republic of Tanzania, Thailand, Tunisia, Turkey, Viet Nam, Zimbabwe. The Governing Body also decided that 25 Employer and 25 Worker participants would be appointed on the basis of nominations made by the respective groups of the Governing Body. They do not necessarily come from the above list of countries.

The Meeting is part of the ILO's Sectoral Activities Programme, the purpose of which is to facilitate the exchange of information among constituents on labour and social developments relevant to particular economic sectors, complemented by practically oriented research on topical sectoral issues.

This objective is being pursued inter alia by holding international tripartite sectoral meetings with a view to : fostering a broader understanding of sector-specific issues and problems; promoting an international tripartite consensus on sectoral concerns and providing guidance for national and international policies and measures to deal with the related issues and problems; promoting the harmonization of all ILO activities of a sectoral character and acting as the focal point between the Office and the sectoral ILO constituents; and providing technical advice and practical assistance to the latter in order to facilitate the application of international labour standards.

The report attempts to illustrate how the issues of globalization, employment and human resources development in the hotel, catering and tourism sector are linked to the strategic objectives of the ILO and to its overall conceptual framework of decent work. At its 87th Session (June 1999), the International Labour Conference agreed that in future the ILO should focus its work on four strategic objectives:

- to promote and realize fundamental principles and rights at work;
- to create greater opportunities for women and men to secure decent employment and income;

- to enhance the coverage and effectiveness of social protection for all; and
- to strengthen tripartism and social dialogue.

All of the ILO's strategic objectives are closely linked to strengthening the social dialogue framework. Promoting a participatory process that gives a voice to those most directly involved in the world of work is an essential part of the conceptual framework of decent work. More especially, it provides the means of integrating the strategic objectives into a coherent approach for decent work initiatives with the full involvement of the social partners at the country level.

The report points to recent developments in the hotel, catering and tourism sector and highlights factors driving the internationalization of tourists' travel and of tourism services, including information technologies, as well as the internationalization of hotel and tourism enterprises. Without neglecting the huge subsector of small and medium-sized enterprises, it describes typical features related to the composition of the labour force and to working conditions. It raises questions concerning the difficulties faced by the sector in attracting and retaining skilled workers in enhancing the skills of newcomers to the labour market in order to stabilize the sector's labour force, while increasing the productivity of enterprises and the quality of services. Particular emphasis is put on new forms of management entailing new skills requirements, with a general tendency towards increased worker responsibility in an environment of flat hierarchies, multiskilling and teamwork. Some institutions, achievements and shortcomings of social dialogue in the hotel, catering and tourism sector are described in a perspective which also points to opportunities for increasing its scope and effectiveness. As for the causal relationships between globalization, employment and human resources development, it would be difficult on the basis of the available information to draw conclusions concerning such relationships more than is done here. On the other hand, other factors such as technological and educational progress or changes in tourism demand have also been highlighted.

Hard data on the hotel, catering and tourism sector are not easy to come by as it is rarely singled out from the services sector in general. Data specifically on tourism depend on accounting which covers a broad range of economic activities geared towards consumption by tourists. Only a few countries can provide systematically collected tourism data and little attention is given to labour issues.

The report draws on a wide variety of sources for information, including government institutions, intergovernmental organizations, trade unions, employers' organizations, companies, international non-governmental organizations, and individual scholars. The sources used are certainly not exhaustive but probably quite representative.

The report was prepared by an ILO team composed of Dirk Belau, Senior Specialist on Hotels, Catering and Tourism, Sectoral Activities Department (coordinator), Tom Higgins and Rajendra Paratian, with contributions from external experts, Lionel Becherel, Chris Cooper, Auliana Poon, Laennert Rijken and Klaus Weiermair. Editorial assistance was provided by Bill Ratteree, Sectoral Activities Department. The report is published under the authority of the International Labour Office.

General Developments in the Sector

Delimitation of the Hotel, Catering and Tourism (HCT) Sector

When the ILO Governing Body created the ILO Industrial Committee for the Hotel, Restaurant and Tourism Sector, which subsequently became the Committee for the Hotel, Catering and Tourism Sector, the sector included:

a. hotels, boarding houses, motels, tourist camps, holiday centres;

b. restaurants, bars, cafeterias, snack bars, pubs, night clubs, and other similar establishments;

c. establishments... for the provision of meals and refreshments within the framework of industrial and institutional catering (for hospitals, factory and office canteens, schools, aircraft, ships, etc.);

d. travel agencies and tourist guides, tourism information offices;
e. conference and exhibition centres.

Statistics are being organized according to the International Standard Industrial Classification of all Economic Activities (ISIC), the latest edition of which is ISIC Rev. 3. In that classification, the sectors most relevant for the ILO definition of the sector are Hotels and restaurants (division 55) and Activities of travel agencies and tour operators, Tourist assistance activities (class 6304).

Other organizations concerned with tourism, including governments, intergovernmental organizations and NGOs, often use much broader definitions of the term than that used by the ILO. They subsume under it all services and products consumed by tourists, including transport. In the ILO denomination of the sector, the part referring to "tourism" only covers travel agencies and tour operators. Hotels and catering, including restaurants, are considered by most organizations to belong to the "tourism characteristic industries" and therefore subsumed under tourism, although in some countries only a small part of their services is for tourists. However, the fact that the ILO definition of the sector thus differs considerably from the concept of tourism used by other organizations does not prevent most concerns about the development of tourism from being shared by those organizations. One such concern is the sector's potential to provide employment. Nevertheless, the ILO's focus on labour issues is unique as it includes all working and employment conditions in the HCT sector.

Tourism Satellite Accounts

As an economic concept, tourism is defined in "demand side" terms, as it comprises all services and goods consumed by tourists as well as all investments made to satisfy that consumption. A tourist has been defined by the United Nations as a traveller or visitor. The credibility and international comparability of "tourism statistics" depend heavily on: (1) a consensus regarding the choice of "tourism characteristic industries", i.e. those industries on which tourism demand has the most important direct impact, and an estimation of the "tourism ratio" of their output; as well as (2) the methods used to calculate the indirect effects on the output of many other industries. Statistical presentations differ in whether they include such indirect or induced effects in the measurement of tourism in the economy. Probably the most inclusive choice of industries is the one adopted by the World Travel and Tourism Council (WTTC), a private organization. It takes into account industries whose "tourism ratio" is low but whose products and services represent high value, such as the construction and operation of transport infrastructure.

The demand side nature of tourism is the basis of a methodology for Tourism Satellite Accounts (TSAs) developed by the World Tourism Organization and OECD and adopted by the United Nations Statistical Commission early in 2000. The ILO has been cooperating with those organizations in accordance with the mandate given to it by the Tripartite Meeting on the Effects of New Technologies on Employment and Working Conditions in the Hotel, Catering and Tourism Sector in 1997, with a view to providing a methodology for the production and presentation of tourism-relevant labour statistics to supplement the TSAs. A proposal has been formulated by the ILO for a tourism labour accounting system (TLAS) within that framework, based on its work on a general labour accounting system. A detailed "employment module" presenting labour-related issues was already attached to the TSA by the OECD, but this module does not provide the necessary framework for linking the different units, variables and classifications used when collecting labour statistics from many different sources.

Some early efforts towards TSA presentations have already been made by a number of pioneer OECD countries on the basis of figures from national accounts systems as required in the methodology adopted by the United Nations Statistical Commission in 2000. The World Travel and Tourism Council (WTTC) has been producing Tourism Satellite Accounts using a simulation method and based on a non-systematic variety of statistical sources. Relevant figures from some pioneer countries are presented in box 1.1. Because of differing definitions only very broad comparisons can be made between countries.

Tourism Economy

The Caribbean is the most tourism oriented region in the world. It is estimated that in 2000, tourism employed 3.1 million people either directly or indirectly, thus accounting for 13.4 per cent of total employment. Direct employment in the tourism characteristic industries alone amounts to 5 per cent of total employment. Visitor expenditures contributed an estimated US$17 billion, or 18.4 per cent, to export revenues. Countries whose international tourism receipts exceed 5 per cent of GDP or 10 per cent of export revenues are considered to be "tourism countries" for the purposes of the World Trade Organization.

Tourism is expanding in almost all countries including the developing countries. In fact, mass tourism involving domestic and regional travel is becoming an important phenomenon in several developing countries of Asia, Latin America, the Middle East and Africa, where the proportion of the population actively participating in domestic and regional tourism is predicted to grow considerably. In particular, regional tourism originating from China is expected to change the Asian tourism industry profoundly within the next one to two decades.

Employment in Hotels and Restaurants

This reflects a large number of small entrepreneurs and their non-remunerated family members. In some countries, this proportion is increasing as paid employment is growing more slowly than total employment, although in general growth rates for both are high.

Importance of International Tourism

Tourism across national borders represents a variable but generally large proportion of total tourism. Especially in a number of developing countries a significant proportion of gross domestic product is generated by activities designed to satisfy international tourism, which thus represents an important export activity in many countries. Globally, the World Tourism Organization (WTO) predicts that the number of international tourists will reach almost 1.6 billion by the year 2020 (as opposed to 565 million in 1995), and that international tourism receipts will exceed US$2,000 billion.

The estimated growth of world international tourism arrivals of 4.5 per cent per annum will pose enormous challenges and opportunities for those regions and countries seeking to benefit from tourism while avoiding its negative impacts.

The top ten tourism destinations in the world in terms of tourism receipts are the United States, Spain, France, Italy, United Kingdom, Germany, China, Austria, Canada and Greece. Eventhough tourism is a global industry, the majority of receipts still accrue to the Americas and Europe, reflecting both the fact that closeness to origin of the travellers still matters and the fact that countries in these regions have had the time, resources and demand needed to develop their tourism industries.

For many countries, international tourism is an indispensable source of foreign currency earnings. According to the World Tourism Organization, tourism is one of the top five export categories for 83 per cent of countries and the main source of foreign currency for at least 38 per cent of them.

In 1998, international tourism and international fare receipts (receipts related to passenger transport of residents of other countries) accounted for roughly 8 per cent of total export earnings from goods and services worldwide. Total international tourism receipts, including those generated by international fares, amounted to an estimated US$532 billion, surpassing all other international trade categories.

As a by-product of the rapid fall in the real costs of long-distance travel, the developing regions of the world participate fully in the worldwide growth of international tourism. However, market shares vary strongly from one county to another and within very short periods, reflecting the economic or security crises affecting different countries or regions.

A Changing Tourism Industry

Mass tourism in and from the industrialized countries is a product of the late 1960s and early 1970s. Since then a number of interrelated developments in the world economy, such as overall economic growth and various other socioeconomic changes, government policies, technological revolution, changes in production processes and new management practices, have converted part of the industry from mass tourismto so-called "new tourism". The latter connotes the idea of responsible, green, soft, alternative and sustainable tourism, and basically refers to the diversification of the tourism industry and its development in targeted, niche markets. Competition in the new tourism is increasingly based on diversification, market segmentation and diagonal integration.

The identification and exploitation of niche markets has also proven to be a great source of revenue within new tourism, suggesting that further diversification and customization can be expected in the years to come. Market segmentation – as exemplified by ecotourism, cultural tourism, cruise and adventure tourism – is clearly in evidence and is experiencing great success. New niche markets are constantly being identified in an attempt to diversify the industry further.

Customization has also begun to play an important role in the industry. Tourism players are attempting to gain a competitive edge by catering for the individual needs of clients. The tourism product has thus been transformed over time from being completely dominated by mass tourism to an industry that is quite diversified and caters more to the individual needs of its participants.

Changing Consumer Preferences

Today, new consumers are influencing the pace and direction of underlying changes in the industry. The "new tourists" are more experienced travellers. Changes in consumer behaviour and values provide the fundamental driving force for the new tourism. The increased travel experience, flexibility and independent nature of the new tourists are generating demand for better quality, more value for money and greater flexibility in the travel experience.

The new consumers also reflect demographic changes – the population is ageing, household size is decreasing and households have greater disposable income.

Changing lifestyles of the new tourists are creating demand for more targeted and customized holidays. A number of lifestyle segments – families, single parent households, "empty nesters" (i.e. couples whose children have left home), double-income couples without children – will become prevalent in tourism, signalling the advent of a much more differentiated approach to tourism marketing.

Changing values are also generating demand for more environmentally conscious and nature-oriented holidays. Suppliers will therefore have to pay more attention to the way people think, feel and behave than they have done hitherto.

In recent years the niche market has become an important factor in the tourism industry reflecting the need to diversify and customize the industry and ensure the sustainability of the product. The main niche markets (sports travel, spas and health care, adventure and nature tourism, cultural tourism, theme parks, cruise ships, religious travel and others) hold great potential and are developing rapidly.

The growth of the cruise tourism sector is an interesting case in point. Between 1980 and 1999, the cruise industry grew at an average annual rate of 7.9 percent. The Caribbean is the most important geographic market for the cruise industry, accounting for over half of all cruises taken in 1996. Since 1984, cruise visitor arrivals have increased every year except 1987 and 1989. In addition, between 1996 and 2000, the growth rate for cruise arrivals is expected to far exceed that of stay-over arrivals.

The rapid growth and development of the cruise tourism industry opens key opportunities but also poses a number of threats to their Caribbean destinations. The environmental and economic impacts of cruise tourism are increasingly the subject of discussion. Moreover, given the pace and magnitude of its development, the cruise industry is directly competing with land-based tourism and, as a result, poses a growing threat to hotels and other land-based resorts and businesses in the Caribbean.

Technology in Tourism

On the demand side, consumer preferences for flexible travel and leisure services provide a strong impetus for new tourism. On the supply side, technology plays an important complementary role in engineering new tourism. The applications of technology to the travel and tourism industry allow producers to supply new and flexible services that are cost-competitive with conventional mass, standardized and rigidly packaged options. Technology gives suppliers the flexibility to react to market demands and the capacity to integrate diagonally with other suppliers to provide new combinations of services and improve cost effectiveness.

In the travel and tourism industry a whole range of interrelated computer and communication technologies is being introduced. The system of information technologies (SIT) comprises computerized reservation systems, teleconferencing, video text, videos, video brochures, computers, management information systems, airline electronic information systems, electronic funds transfer systems, digital telephone networks, smart cards, satellite printers, and mobile communications. Each technology component identified in the SIT – for example, computers – can be and usually is fully integrated with the other components. For example, computer-to-computer communications allow hotels to integrate their front offices, back offices and food and beverage operations. This internal management system for hotels can in turn be fully integrated with a digital telephone network, and they then together provide the basis for linkage with hotel reservation systems which can be accessed by travel agents through their computerized reservations terminals (CRTs). Computerized reservations systems have emerged as the dominant technology among others being diffused throughout the travel and tourism industry.

In the United States, travel agents are using satellite printers at corporate offices to issue tickets directly at the point of demand. Interactive automated ticket machines (ATMs) have also been introduced. These consist of a computer with an attached printer that enables passengers to research schedules and fares, make reservations, purchase tickets and obtain boarding passes without the intervention of a human agent.

The Internet is a global network connecting millions of computers. As of 1999, the number of Internet users was above 200 million worldwide, and that number is growing rapidly, involving more than 100 countries. It is estimated that there were 63 million World Wide Web users in Europe in 1999. The United

Kingdom, with almost 13 million Internet users, currently registers the highest number of users among the European countries. Use of the Internet for travel booking and planning is increasing rapidly. The rapid diffusion of information technologies throughout the travel and tourism industry is expected to improve the efficiency of production and the quality of services provided to consumers, and to generate increasing demand for new services.

Globalization

The driving forces of globalization impacting upon travel, hospitality and tourism.

Liberalization of Air Transport

The air transport industry, which is located mainly in the industrialized regions and in the newly industrialized countries, is a key determinant in the development of tourism. It is expanding twice as fast as the general output of the world economy, with further growth potential expected over the next two decades. In the developing countries, air transport accounts for nearly 80 per cent of international tourist arrivals. In 1998, the industry provided 28 million jobs worldwide, and by 2010 the number of people travelling by air could exceed 2.3 billion each year, with over 31 million jobs provided.

Today, liberalization of air transport largely means market access for private carriers and cabotage rights. The liberalization of air transport, traditionally pursued at the bilateral level, is now being carried to the level of multilateral trade agreements. The recent trend towards the liberalization of air transport notably through the proliferation of open skies agreements, has thus raised the issue of air transport liberalization as a discipline to be debated in the framework of the General Agreement on Trade in Services (GATS).

Multi-bilateral negotiations are already under way on an open skies agreement between the European Union and the United States. If they succeed, 70 per cent of the world's international air traffic will be covered by the agreement. It is expected in that case that the agreement will serve as a model for other international air services agreements.

The formation of international alliances is an important development in the field of aviation. Airline alliances have become widespread and are still evolving, with partnership relationships becoming more intertwined and complex. The major airlines in the Americas and Europe are the most active in securing alliance agreements.

The main motivation behind such alliances is the need to minimize costs while maintaining the quality of global services and extending connections throughout the world. Alliances can take various forms including: cooperative arrangements; wide-ranging strategic alliances, most notably the so-called "megaalliances"; groupings and concentrations at national level, as in the case of the United States; purchase or franchising of small regional companies by major operators to carry their customers to hub airports; and regional civil aviation markets.

Other trends which characterize the changes under way in the context of airline liberalization include: partial or full privatization and restructuring of government-owned airlines; partial foreign ownership of airlines; equity investment in foreign carriers; updating of airline alliances by cancelling outdated or non-performing agreements; airline consolidations at the national level; joint ventures, either between airline companies or between airline companies and equipment manufacturers or independent maintenance companies; and outsourcing with no provision of maintenance service.

Some Results of Airline Liberalization

Recent privatization initiatives have ended the protection of national airlines by governments in a number of developing countries. However, the possibility of the market becoming dominated by a single private company is perceived as a serious risk. In some cases, developing countries that have liberalized their air transport sectors as part of a policy to promote tourism have found themselves dominated by one or two foreign airlines. Some bankruptcies and closures have taken place in countries where distressed national airlines were not or could not be rescued by governments. In this context, a review of the GATS annex on air transport services is intended to draw international attention to the need to design a system that enables developing countries to compete effectively in the world market for air transport.

With regard to the liberalization of air transport as a whole, the trend is increasingly for each State to choose its own pace of change, using bilateral, regional or multilateral mechanisms. In developed countries there has been a clear tightening of competition policies to prohibit governments from providing subsidies. It is well known that many bilateral agreements have resulted in inefficiency as they were based on market access restrictions, price control and protection of money-losing carriers.

Full liberalization of air services as implemented in 1997 in Europe boosted the development of "low-cost" services and their integration in the European aviation scene. Although these services still account for a rather small share of the passenger market, their marketing impact is increasingly being felt throughout the industry. It is estimated that around 25 per cent of passengers on United States domestic services use "low-cost" airlines, as compared to approximately 5 per cent in Europe. Another result of liberalization is that new route opportunities have opened up, stimulating new demands without tampering with major carriers' shares and therefore creating new opportunities for fare reductions. Some major European flag carriers have already created their own "low-cost" airline subsidiaries (examples are British Airways/Go and KLM/Buzz).

The low-cost market as it stands has considerable growth potential. Europe's low-cost airlines are finding plenty of untapped markets. Both Ryanair and easy Jet have placed orders for significant numbers of additional aircraft to almost double their capacity over the next four years to meet this new demand. The challenge for low-cost carriers is to strike the right balance between maintaining low costs, low prices and high aircraft utilization and establishing a presence at a certain minimum number of airports. A further development of the concept of the low-cost airline sector has been the advent of "seat-only" sales on charter airline flights, rather than as part of a package holiday. This has resulted, for example, in the formation of the European Leisure Group (ELG), an alliance of European charter and scheduled airlines.

Liberalization of Trade in Services

Negotiations on tourism services and existing commitments under the GATS.

The General Agreement on Trade in Services (GATS) became part of the "New World Trade Order" under the aegis of the World Trade Organization as established by the Uruguay Round in 1994. The functioning of GATS is based on the interplay of fundamental standards in commercial law, procedural regulations for their implementation and specific commitments in which member States document sector-specific limitations or concessions. GATS has universal coverage and includes a comprehensive definition of trade in services comprising four "modes of supply". They are: cross-border movement of services; movement of consumers; commercial presence; and the presence of natural persons, and to these modes the three principles of liberalization enshrined in GATS as shown in box 2.1 are to be applied. GATS thus provides a framework for the progressive liberalization of trade in services through commitments made by the World Trade Organization member countries concerning the abovementioned principles and their applications to one or more modes of supply. Future negotiations under GATS will provide an opportunity for developing countries to address trade barriers to their services. The tourism sector had already undergone various forms of liberalization before the Uruguay Round. It is also considered to be one of the service sectors most liberalized through sector-specific commitments made by signatory States. The number of commitments by the World Trade Organization members made so far in tourism under the GATS is rated as the highest of all sectors. Of 127 GATS signatory States, only eight have not made commitments in tourism and travel-related services. In the hotels and restaurants subsector, which offers the greatest potential for far-reaching liberalization within tourism, it is mostly low and lower-middle-income economies (LIEs and LMIEs according to the World Bank classification) in Africa and Latin America that have liberalized market access for foreign investors in the *"commercial presence"* mode: 64 per cent of all signatory States belonging to the group of LIEs and 75 per cent of LMIEs, but only about half (48 per cent) of the group of high-income economies

(HIEs) have "no restrictions" to that mode. On the other hand, it is not surprising that *"presence of natural persons"* is the least liberalized mode of supply: in 117 of the 119 countries signing commitments in travel and tourism-related services, there are restrictions on the movement of hotel staff. Sixty-eight countries refer to their non-sector-specific commitments which mostly offer only temporary stay for business visitors, intra-corporate transferees and professionals. This mode is the key starting point for future moves to shift liberalization away from declaring countries' restrictive measures towards removing those measures. It is expected that the next round of GATS talks will have important repercussions on destinations in terms of tourism marketing, investment and ownership, training and other aspects affecting the structure of the industry.

The case for a more specific treatment of tourism services under the GATS has been the subject of debate since the conclusion of the Uruguay Round. Significantly, UNCTAD has come up with conclusions and recommendations with regard to the future round of negotiations on trade in tourism under the GATS, including a recommendation and a proposal for an annex on tourism services called for by the World Trade Organization. So far, tourism is not among the specific sectors referred to by the six annexes of the GATS and other related instruments. Only an ancillary service to tourism (airline computer reservation services), is included in an annex on air transport services.

Possible impact of GATS on air traffic services, tourism services production, free movement of people, market access and labour markets.

Most air traffic services are not covered by the Agreement's disciplines. The main organizations responsible for air transport are now examining ways in which the GATS could contribute to future air transport liberalization.

The GATS provides a framework for negotiating temporary entry of service personnel into the territory of other parties. The movement of natural persons is a necessary condition for developing countries' participation in the world market for services. Developing countries have given priority to making commitments under the GATS relating to the movement of natural persons (mode 4 of the GATS), partly taking into account their competitive labour cost advantage. However, commitments in this mode are largely linked to commercial presence, and firms without such commercial presence are discriminated against by having to face visa restrictions such as the so-called economic needs test, which is discretionary and non-transparent. Those restrictions are serious barriers to trade in services and negate the opportunities for market access otherwise extended in the commitments. Increased movement of natural persons also raises the question of the need to strengthen international standards regarding the licensing, accreditation and certification of service providers. The World Tourism Organization, for example, is developing a range of quality standards to be applied at tourism destinations.

Recognition of diplomas and professional qualifications is another precondition for the movement of natural persons abroad. This calls for the harmonization of diplomas and mutual recognition agreements between countries. Several countries have notified mutual recognition agreements under GATS Article VII.4. It is hoped that the GATS will increase the recognition of qualifications across borders.

Considerations within the framework of the GATS may also become relevant for the migration to the richer countries of persons who overstay their tourism visas and take up work. Many of them work in hotels or restaurants where in some countries they form a significant proportion of the labour force. Globalization will give rise to increased migration pressures in the years ahead, as a recent ILO study has shown. The increased scale and diversity of global communications systems and their declining costs, which are rapidly narrowing telecommunications gaps, have helped to make international migration easier.

With regard to the movement of consumers, tourism is an example of the services sector where consumption abroad is particularly relevant. Nevertheless, the movement of tourists is in some instances constrained by the difficulties associated with the delivery of visas, hard currency regulations and insufficient availability or inadequacy of air transport services to and from tourist-receiving countries. GATS negotiations are expected to address these problems.

Specific commitments made under the GATS to encourage greater participation by developing countries in world services trade relate to three main areas: first, the strengthening of the domestic services capabilities of developing countries through access to technology on a commercial basis, which is normally achieved through the employment and training of local personnel in foreign-owned hotels; secondly, improving the access of developing countries to distribution channels and information networks.

In the tourism sector, this means access to computerized information and reservation networks managed and owned by entities in the industrialized countries; thirdly, the liberalization of market access in sectors and modes of supply of export interest to them (GATS, Article IV). According to GATS Article XIX., developing countries can attach additional conditions to such access aimed at achieving the development objectives of Article IV, namely the strengthening of their domestic services capacity and improvement of their access to distribution channels and information networks. The liberalization of services is likely to have both positive and negative impacts on the labour force in relation to wages and employment. Increased competition by better equipped hotel and restaurant companies from abroad may in the short term lead to job losses in local enterprises. However, foreign firms will employ local people, increasing local employment and contributing to a higher standard of living.

Economic Integration

The world economy is currently witnessing two distinct trends – globalization and regionalization – and within this context States as well as companies are pursuing a variety of different strategies in order to become more competitive. Shifting patterns of production and consumption across the world are also reflected in the rise of new international tourism destinations, particularly in the East Asia and Pacific region. This has given rise to increasing regional, intra-regional and interregional competition and to new challenges in terms of investment needs and human resources development, especially with regard to training and labour mobility.

The impact of trade blocs on the hotel, tourism and catering sector can be gauged by the strategies adopted to create an environment conducive to tourism development. The European Union has launched a wide range of initiatives and activities through a variety of programmes in such broad areas as sustainable development, dissemination of information, training and enterprise promotion.

The main thrust of social policy in the European Union is the improvement of labour market conditions with a special focus on those excluded from the labour market and the unemployed. European Union labour laws and social policy are having a positive impact on the tourism sector. Of importance here is the Maastricht Social Protocol which has benefited seasonal and part-time workers and small businesses. Other policies that have proved beneficial to the development of tourism include the free movement of workers across Europe, harmonization of qualifications and tax incentives for education and training.

The North American Free Trade Agreement (NAFTA) benefits the travel and tourism industry in many ways. It promotes demand for direct air and charter/tour bus travel in the region, guarantees that tourism companies will receive national treatment in all three countriesand maintains high quality of tourism services by encouraging the expansion of telecommunications links between the United States and Mexico.

Mercosur is, in economic terms, the world's fourth largest trade bloc, covering a population of 205 million people. Economic integration, through the practice of free trade with no tariff or pre-tariff restrictions between the member States of the bloc, has led to increasing cross-border flows of labour, goods and investment. MERCOSUR's concern is to tackle labour relations, employment and social security issues and the short-term negative effects of integration on labour in the member States.

Tourism development is a priority on the agenda of the Association of South-East Asian Nations (ASEAN). Its development strategy incorporates: promotion of sustainable tourism development; preservation of cultural and environmental resources; provision of transportation and other infrastructure; simplification of immigration procedures; and human resources development. A plan of action on ASEAN cooperation in tourism shows the emphasis that is being placed on investment in human resources development, with a special focus on tourism education and training with a view to upgrading the skills needed to meet the demand for improved service quality and professionalism in the tourism and travel industry and thereby sustain ASEAN's overall competitive advantage. Cooperation in tourism education and training is being intensified through the sharing of resources, skills and training facilities provided by tourism training institutions through technical assistance and experts.

Information and Communication Technologies in the HCT Sector

Computerized reservation systems (CRSs) have been developed by large air carriers since the 1970s to process flight reservations, but have evolved and expanded over time to provide other air transport-related services. Each airline has its own CRS and they are interconnected through global distribution systems (GDSs). A huge number of Internet on-line reservation systems act as a kind of virtual agent, most of them having direct links to one or several CRS/GDS.

The CRS and GDS systems have become the main distribution and marketing tool in the international tourism trade and have greatly enhanced the efficiency of travel agents' business operations. They cater to the needs of different market segments, including management of air and land transport services, the hospitality sector and entertainment services, as well as other ancillary services which make commercial transactions and risk coverage feasible. As a result, they have become increasingly important and are extensively used by all suppliers of tourism services.

There is some concern that developing countries' suppliers may well be left out because GDSs can present major barriers to entry owing to their unfavourable access conditions (their operational costs, problems of access for small service suppliers, the fact that they are owned by large air carriers).

A number of African and south Asian countries are poorly represented in these systems because of structural handicaps such as the low level of tourism development in general and their underdeveloped hospitality sector. The poor representation of small service suppliers in GDSs adversely affects the dissemination of information on their tourism products, thereby holding back their sale and marketing of tourism services. This leaves such suppliers, especially SMEs, at a competitive disadvantage compared with those who are represented in the major GDSs. GDSs in many developing countries, particularly in Africa, are established in the form of joint ventures with local partners – for example, the national carrier – but operate within a de facto monopoly. This leads to excessive user fees and hinders their potential for developing tourism.

Travel agents in developing countries are at a disadvantage with regard to the use of modern technology compared with their counterparts in developed countries because of poor information network infrastructure and the shortage of professionals to manage, operate and maintain the system. Human resources assume importance in the operation of GDSs and other electronic media, and this calls for staff training in mastering the systems and their application to marketing, through specific training programmes provided by both the public and private sectors.

Emerging Use of the Internet for Marketing and Sales

Deregulation, globalization and radical shifts in leisure and tourism behaviour on the demand side have driven the tourism industry towards information-oriented activities, as seen in the introduction of IT systems in a wide range of spheres in the tourism and leisure sector. The increasing use of the Internet for destination marketing, direct sales and bookings has given rise to electronic tourism markets and at present tourism is among the most important application domains in the World Wide Web.

The development of websites has made possible the direct delivery of comprehensive travel information about tourism suppliers to potential travellers. Text-based websites with photos and graphics linked to websites of tourism suppliers at the destination is another innovative approach to marketing. Developing an effective travel website has now assumed importance for obvious reasons. International tourists are increasingly using the travel websites on the Internet that were launched by most international companies in the late 1990s. However, the real volume of Internet bookings can only be estimated and estimates from market research companies are contradictory. According to one estimate, between 33 and 50 per cent of Internet transactions are tourism based. Available evidence show that as yet only a tiny percentage of business travellers are booking on-line. On-line sales in Europe, for example, represented only 0. 1 per cent of the European travel market, and in 1999 only 1 per cent of the world's airline tickets, hotel and other bookings were purchased over the Internet, although the proportion of airline and other ticket sales through the Internet is expected to grow sharply over the next three to four years.

The Internet helps to make travel products globally accessible at much lower cost – without transaction costs and the costs of intermediaries – and has comparatively low entrance barriers with regard to financial resources and human know-how. For many suppliers, tourism marketing efforts are increasingly focusing on Internet users.

A new business environment and new ways of doing business have sprung up as a result of the accessibility and relatively low cost of the Internet which is bringing businesses and consumers, buyers and suppliers on-line. Internet and Internet protocol technology is the driving force behind the growth of e-business. The Internet will have repercussions on business in the areas of e-commerce, e-working and e-procurement. A recent global survey of more than 500 business leaders lends support to the idea that e-business will be a key factor in competitive advantage in the future.

In the sphere of air travel, attempts are frequently made to bypass traditional travel agencies by direct booking via the Internet or corporate implant offices. Customer demands are becoming more technology driven, such as the demand for professional travel and billing management in place of mere ticket issuing. Advances in technology in the hotels and tourism industry, as exemplified by readily available information to guests and employees, faster service delivery, shorter cycle times and more dynamic markets, also require prompt action from service suppliers if marketing opportunities are not to be lost. Strategies of growth and concentration through mergers and acquisitions are becoming increasingly important from the mediators' perspective as a response to cost and performance pressures in international business travel. In addition, traditional kickback contracts are increasingly being replaced with new performance-oriented arrangements.

All aspects of business are being reshaped by the Internet and its related technologies, intranets and extranets. Hospitality enterprises will need to focus on providing customers with real-time access to rates and product information. The Internet also provides hotels and restaurants with opportunities to redesign the way in which they interface with employees and suppliers.

The high growth in global commerce accompanied by the emergence of electronic commerce driven mainly by the Internet has raised concerns about the need to regulate cyberspace by setting standards to regulate the use of the Internet for all aspects of travel and other fast-growing categories of electronic commerce. The primacy of the rules of the network economy will significantly lower transaction and communication costs, thus allowing more flexible pricing. The regulation of the Internet through the enactment and implementation of cyberlaws and privacy standards will most probably be perceived as an encouraging initiative which will guarantee safety and security in Internet business transactions, especially in shopping and travel accommodation bookings, where the Internet is most frequently used.

As a way of managing the increasing volume of guest information, the introduction of data warehousing and data mining technologies is becoming increasingly important. Hoteliers and restaurateurs have already expressed marked interest in these technologies as means of exploiting the advantages which can be derived from, for example, increased guest loyalty and market share. By using data warehousing and data mining as well as the Internet, the hotel industry can provide higher levels of personalized services and value. The Internet is turning out to be the most sought after amenity in hotel rooms, providing communications access, information, entertainment and education. It enables more self-service oriented transactions to take place, especially in the area of reservations booking.

Information technology impacts on all aspects of the hotel organization value chain and transcends all departmental and geographical boundaries. Decisions on technology-related issues need to be made at top management levels of companies, and this means that qualified information technology personnel are needed at those levels.

Another key issue is the source of investment capital required to fund information technology initiatives. Lack of capital seriously hinders the implementation of information technology and competition for fund sourcing.

The Internet has brought about some very significant technological changes that enhance its capabilities and viability and its potential to drive electronic commerce. Besides introducing new and innovative business models in both the business-to-business and business-to-consumer markets, the Internet has shortened the value chain and put pressure on all players, especially intermediaries, by giving rise to the so-called "disintermediation" process, that is, the elimination of intermediary organizations such as travel agencies and global distribution systems (GDSs).

Online service and ticketless travel have significantly reduced the need for travel intermediaries, as a result of which travel agents in the United States, for example, have seen a reduction in commissions paid to them by airlines.

The use of information technology in the tourism industry is determined by such factors as the scale and complexity of tourism demand and the degree of expansion and sophistication of new tourism products. Tourism plays an important role in a significant number of developing countries, many of which enjoy a competitive advantage. Current changes in the hotel and tourism industry in the context of globalization, as described in this report, show that there are more opportunities in the field of e-commerce than in any other existing technology which developing countries can exploit to their advantage in order to improve the marketing of their tourism products. However, in the developing countries, tourism development is constrained by a number of factors which have been summarized by UNCTAD.

Computer software represents one of the largest segments of services delivered through the cross-border mode of supply, with a growing number of developing countries using the Internet both to market and to deliver these services. The Indian software industry is a case in point. Electronic commerce facilitates access to new markets, as well as being cost saving and time saving. However, its effectiveness depends to a large extent on the establishment of a sound telecommunications infrastructure; in most low-income countries, that infrastructure is inadequate. A wide range of factors prevent the great majority of developing countries from accessing foreign markets through the Internet. Those factors include monopoly pricing for long-distance telephony, uncertainty about the regulatory environment, lack of human resources, lack of awareness among developing country companies of the relevance of the digital economy, and the high cost of setting up, upgrading and redesigning a significant e-commerce site.

. The status of the developing countries' readiness for e-commerce is an important issue.

Providers of tourism services must also have the capacity to invest in or have access to the physical infrastructure for logistics services and information technologies. The major obstacle to increased use of e-commerce in developing countries is the lack of pervasive low-cost telecommunications, broadcasting, Internet services and associated infrastructures, especially in rural areas. At the same time there is a need to involve more hotel and tourism enterprises from developing countries in the actual use of information technologies and information networks. If African businesses fare better than consumers in terms of accessing e-commerce, they nevertheless face the same infrastructure problems, although progress has been made in the development of e-commerce activities.

The shortage of IT specialists on the market, especially in the developing countries, is a serious impediment, given the rapid growth in Internet use. The demand for IT skills is increasing and the need for retraining of existing employees in both the public and private sectors in hotels, tourism and catering is clearly felt. One solution would be for developing countries to take advantage of forthcoming GATS negotiations to ensure access for their suppliers to the most important generating markets, and they could make use of certain mechanisms provided for in the GATS which might enhance the contribution of trade in services to development. They could also seek commitments with respect to the training of personnel and access to the distribution channels which are essential to tourism exports, as provided for in Articles IV and XIX of the Agreement.

Consolidation Strategies

Since the mid-1990s, multinational hotel companies entering foreign markets have devised a wide range of management strategies or methods in response to competitive challenge such as the rapid development of information technology, sophisticated demands from well-informed and knowledgeable travellers and the rise of electronic business-to-business market-places and to seize the opportunities opened up by the network economy. Within each company, core competencies are being developed and renewed through rapid information technology development, international expansion and market cooperation, relationship management, development of customer-oriented products and services, structural re-engineering (involving, for example, organizational restructuring and continuous training of employees and management), new marketing initiatives and campaigns, and quality control.

Within the context of international expansion and market cooperation, companies have had recourse to a number of competitive methods which merit attention. The growing number of alliances is changing industry structures and the level of competition has shifted from the individual company level to alliance groups level. The last five years have witnessed nine major mergers and acquisition transactions in the international hotel market-place. For example, Hilton and Hilton International have merged their sales forces, integrated their logos and marketing efforts, and shared their reservation systems in a strategic alliance considered to be the largest since 1996. Hilton has also allied with

Patriot American Hospitality for market expansion. Starwood has established a strategic alliance with Discovery Hotel Group in Asia to open Four Points Hotels in China. Choice International has done the same with Flag International in Asia.

There are other goals and objectives which strategic alliances can fulfil in order to assist multinational hotel firms in strengthening their market positions, improving partnership relations and supplying diversified products and quality services to their customers. These goals and objectives include: acquisition of new information and communication technology (Hyatt and Starwood with Microsoft's Expedia, Hyatt with MSN network, Carlson and Bass with WizCom to link to global distribution systems); distribution of products and cross-marketing between food-service providers and hotels (Ramada with Bennigan's Restaurants, Marriott, Hilton, Bass with Pizza Hut); distribution and cross-promotion of bank credit cards and financial services between banks and hotels (Bass Hotels and Resorts with Visa and American Express, Marriot with Visa and Chase Manhattans processing system, Hilton, Starwood, and Accor with American Express); consolidation of transportation and hotel services (Carlson and Bass Hotels and Resorts each with more than 20 airlines, Marriott with United Airlines, Starwood with British Airways and Alitalia, and Shangri-la with Canadian Airlines); copromotion of hotels and films and media (Marriott, Choice Hotels and Cendant with new films, Bass with ESPN and Discovery Channel, and Best Western with Sci-Fi Channel and E-Entertainment Channel).

Management contracts are popular competitive methods that are being used by international companies. A good example is that of Nikko Hotels International which through its expansion into Croatia acquired 21 management contracts in 1998. Some well established international companies provide their expertise by leasing out management teams to run local firms. The contracting company benefits from the knowledge and experience of the international company and from its reputation for quality and good service. Quoting figures from Ankomah (1991), Becherel and Cooper point out that in 1979, 72 per cent of all hotels insub-Saharan Africa operated under a management contract; in Asia the figure was 60 per cent, in Latin America 47 per cent, but only 2 per cent in Europe. It can be assumed that these proportions have increased with globalization.

Franchising – a contractual agreement whereby one company allows another to sell and use its products for a fee – presents a number of advantages upon which many multinational hotel companies rely for their growth and expansion. From a local human resources perspective, franchising offers the advantage of recruiting local management and staff with the added benefit of the expertise of the franchiser and any good international practice. This method of market entry is favoured by some of the international hotel corporations. Their international reputation guarantees licensees a ready-made market. In Europe, for example, franchising accounts for 1.5 million jobs, the majority in France, Germany and the United Kingdom. Many franchise agreements have been signed in the past five years. What is more, companies which have not in the past espoused franchising as an expansion tool have started to use it to the full. This was the case with Hyatt and Marriott in 1995 and 1996.

Many joint ventures or partnerships were set up between 1995 and 1996. Some examples are: Choice International with Friendly Hotels in the United Kingdom; Cendant with Mark's Hotel International's cooperation agreement in India; Accor with NH Hotels in Spain, Starwood with Hotel Pelikan in Germany and Demeure Hotels in Europe; and Sol Melia with European Travel.

The emergence of branding is another new issue in the hotel industry which is linked to merger and acquisition activities. With the evolution of the hotel industry towards a more consumer-oriented service, it is the brand rather than the company which assumes importance. In the United Kingdom hotel industry, for example, branding has become very topical and operators are increasingly recognizing the value of brands in delivering profits. The brand is thus turning out to be a fundamental element in defining the market, so much so that it is the name of the brand under which a hotel trades that carries weight, rather than its ownership and management structure. The emergence of a multiplicity of new brand names worldwide in the last five years – Cendant's Wingate Inn, Accor's Studio 6, Hilton's Garden Inn, and others – bears testimony to its increasing importance. All these developments indicate the extent to which new products and services – including the other new competitive methods and customer-oriented technologies mentioned earlier – that have been launched by multinational hotel companies are being developed in an attempt to sustain their respective competitive advantage.

Vertical integration is another strategy that plays a dominant role in particular segments of the tourism industry. For a long time, tour operators have been establishing backward and forward linkages in the areas of service production. Their backward integration includes hotels and charter airlines. These operators also control all stages of distribution via far-reaching forward integration of retail distributors and travel agencies, marketing and package tours sales. This is also true of airlines which extend their level of integration far into the field of primary tourism and travel-related services via their charter airlines which have interests in tour operators, retailers and travel agencies. By contrast, hotels and hotel chains hardly pursue vertical integration strategies at all.

Tour operators and travel agencies are becoming increasingly involved in the process of horizontal integration, which in the recent past has attracted attention through spectacular takeovers like that of Thomas Cook by the German LTU group in 1993, or through joint ventures. An expansionist strategy of diagonal integration is geared to the provision of the broadest possible array of tourism-related service markets by a company, with a view to cutting costs, making the most of synergies between individual markets and achieving systems gains. This includes, for example, the joint use of computerized reservation systems by carriers and travel agencies under the umbrella of a holding company or cooperation between credit card suppliers and tour operators or travel agencies offering the special insurance services of a holding partner.

In the accommodation industry, an impressive amount of consolidation took place in the 1980s, bringing more and more hotel brands under fewer and larger corporate umbrellas. Consolidation offers certain advantages such as cost reduction in the areas of reservation systems, loyalty programmes and staff training and other fixed costs associated with hotel management. Available figures reinforce the impression that the forces of consolidation are indeed gathering momentum.

In the institutional catering sector, franchising and management contracts are also used as management strategies by institutional food-service companies. Compass, which is among the largest institutional catering companies in the world, employing 125,000 workers in 44 countries, is a case in point. It owns, manages or franchises hotels (Forte, Meridien, Posthouse, Heritage and Travelodge). Its food service brands include Burger King, Sbarro, Upper Crust, Caffe Ritazza, Delimento, Little Chef and Harry Ramsdens. In Canada, the institutional catering sector is dominated by large international groups. Sodexho is the largest institutional catering company, employing 212,000 employees worldwide since it purchased the institutional catering services of Marriott – Marriott Services. Another example is Aramak, an American company which employ 140,000 employees in 11 countries based in North America and Europe. One pertinent issue frequently referred to by the developing countries is the need to reduce the risk of "leakage" of foreign exchange earnings. The developing countries in particular are usually unable to make the most of the economic and development potential of tourism, firstly, because of the high import content of construction materials and equipment and consumable goods needed to cater to the needs of international tourism and, secondly, because of the repatriation of income and profits earned by expatriates. The latter is in fact a major obstacle to tourism development.

Nevertheless, a number of advantages can be derived from international companies in terms of capital investment and know-how and technology, management and marketing expertise, training and consultancy. For example, under the "Build Operate Transfer" model, there may be conditions attached such as the requirement to train local staff or build facilities for the community. This enables countries lacking the skills base and expertise needed at all professional levels to run, develop and operate tourist establishments for an international clientele to benefit from the transfer of expertise and technology.

In a globalized economy, skills become an important determinant in competitiveness. The changing composition of the workforce and work patterns resulting from globalization processes in the industry have brought about new challenges in human resources development. Training policies in the hotel, tourism and catering sector will need to be reviewed in a new climate of empowerment and retention of staff. This is particularly the case in many parts of the world where there is an acute shortage of qualified staff to fill positions created by an expanding industry. An internationally focused human resources policy calls for a change in personnel policies and strategies which implies, among other things, management commitment to transnational strategies, the development of IT skills and procedures to support transnational operations in a number of ways such as knowledge and information transfer, and an awareness of the different national policies on health and safety, occupational standards, dismissal, discrimination and workers' rights.

Impact of Technology on SMEs

Globalization has brought about a range of opportunities and challenges which have put additional pressures on SMEs. In addition to having to cope with the effects of globalization, they need to adapt to new business conditions in terms of product positioning and product development facilitated by information technology, with all its potential benefits in terms of market access for SMEs. The potential of SMEs for achieving economies of scale is very limited and the use of computer reservation systems (CRSs) has not spread significantly, quite apart from the fact that SMEs are already disadvantaged because of their high average unit production costs. SMEs are forced by market conditions to install new systems and train their staff to use tourism-related technologybut find it difficult to invest in training or staff development, mainly because of limited investment resources and the fact that many SMEs in the hotel, tourism and catering sector are managed by a generation of staff have had no formal training in the sector. In a globalized market, SMEs need to pursue new survival strategies. The tourism sector at the destination has to cope with the increasing problem of seasonality encountered by many coastal resorts. Competitive advantage then depends on organizational competencies and capabilities.

Local SMEs have to face a number of conditions imposed by large overseas companies. Large tour operators strongly influence the way in which hotels operate at their featured destinations and the prices that they charge, particularly in mass market beach resorts and in short season resorts (e.g. ski resorts); they may also impose conditions on local suppliers, such as compliance with environmental protection standards.

In developing countries, SMEs play an important role in employment creation but are hampered by low productivity levels, poor product quality and lack of access to credit and training. The impact of capital outflows from developing countries resulting from e-commerce is another issue which needs attention. The need to develop competition policy-related disciplines in this area is also clearly felt, in view of the need to establish safeguards to prevent abuse by dominant suppliers. Such issues arising from e-commerce might be addressed in future GATS negotiations.

The global hotel market encompasses a wide range of types of accommodation – full-service hotels, bed and breakfast inns, suites, self-catering short-term apartments and time-share properties. Distribution and intermediation are increasingly recognized as factors critical to the competitiveness and success of the tourism industry in general and of small and medium-sized tourism enterprises in particular. The latter need to develop effective distribution channels either to meet the needs of their independent clientele or to provide direct booking mechanisms to reduce their dependency on tour operators. Hospitality organizations and hotel chains already rely on customer bookings through the Internet. The challenge for tourism sector SMEs is to be able to compete for their market shares and take advantage of emerging opportunities and associated benefits to enhance their profitability and viability in the global market-place.

SMEs in the tourism sector are constrained by the growing concentration and globalization of tourism supply. In addition, lack of professionalism and inadequate management and marketing skills, the absence of economies of scale and limited access to the necessary capital, human resources, marketing expertise and technology, over-reliance on a limited number of distribution partners and inadequate formal education or business training are among other deficiencies which put them at a competitive disadvantage. Overall, the inability to market their products adequately seriously affects their profitability and ability to survive in the globalized economy. SMEs are highly reliant on existing distribution channels, namely, intermediaries such as tour operators, travel agencies, travel information centres and tourist guides. It can be argued that the gradual reduction of SMEs' reliance on intermediaries will enable them to become more profitable, flexible and adaptable and to produce customized tourism products in order to satisfy niche markets. This will also require a rethink of all strategic and operational practices with regard to SME development, as well as development of entrepreneurs' managerial skills and professionalism, training in marketing and management and on the use of information technology.

SMEs can benefit in a number of ways by applying information technology to develop their product, thereby enhancing their market position and increasing their profit margins. Information technology offers new management and business opportunities and can be applied strategically to gain competitive advantage, improve productivity and performance, facilitate new ways of managing and organizing, and develop new businesses. Although information technology entails risks and costs, its underutilization could increase the vulnerability of SMEs and aggravate any competitive disadvantage as greater use is made of IT systems, including CRSs, GDSs and the Internet, to locate and purchase tourism and accommodation products. With regard to electronic data interchange (EDI), for example, empirical evidence suggests that EDI is perceived by SMEs as too complex and cumbersome and that the initial investment is too high.

Although SMEs play a major role in the international tourism and hotel industry, their vulnerability becomes quite obvious in the highly demanding business environment characterized by competition generated by globalization and the transformation of tourism demand. Globalization of the industry means that SMEs in the tourism sector compete in a multinational environment where only organizations capable of providing exceptional value or cost advantage will survive. The opportunity of achieving economies of scale in distribution channels, reservations, marketing, advertising, administration, personnel management, technology adaptation, new product development, training and bulk purchasing of raw material and equipment, has been instrumental in the creation of major hotel chains, international consortia, management contracts and multinational franchising companies, and has placed the independent operator at a disadvantage. The overall trend in the hotel industry appears to be towards a gradual but steady switch from independently owned and operated hotels to hotel chains. SMEs seem to be the weakest and most vulnerable members of the industry and will need to seek competitive advantages if they are to compete and maintain their market share in an increasingly globalized economy.

India has been traditionally a large tea producing country and coupled with the perceived benefits of tea consumption, it is no surprise that the beverage retains its popularity rankings throughout the years. But that said, tea would continue to suffer the mass-market and commodity tag, which makes moving it into the value-added category difficult.

The Indian Tea Board has initiated efforts to bring about an image makeover for Indian tea. The Board has roped in Ogilvy & Mather (O&M) and Lowe India for bringing in the change. This initiative of promotion by the Tea Board has been prompted by the recent surge in domestic consumption of tea. In 2005, domestic consumption of tea in India has crossed the 700 million kg mark and is expected to grow by another 3 per cent in 2006. The global campaign, being worked out by Lowe India, is expected to be launched in '06-07.

Coffee consumption in India has taken a turn by the emergence of the cafe-drinking culture and has had a positive impact on the imagery and occasion. There has been tremendous expansion in coffee drinking experiences and this has stimulated associated rise in coffee consumption at home. Coffee parlours are increasingly found throughout the country. South India accounts for an overwhelming proportion of home consumption of coffee brewing and drinking.

A vast potential still remains to be tapped in India's rural hinterlands, hot drinks still derive most of their volumes and value from urban India, although a discernible trend towards greater rural involvement is visible. Urban India still remains the core that will adopt value-added hot drinks much faster than rural India. However, increasing competition and a saturation effect is forcing companies to look anew at the rural markets now for increasing per capita consumption on a national level.

The perception that ready-to-drink fruit or non-fruit based drinks are being made up of cheap, low quality drinks targeting children is rapidly being shed with the emergence of high quality premium brands from a plethora of small companies and of course the bigger players. This category has gained from the slowing demand for carbonated soft drinks.

According to a new report from leading beverage industry analysts, Canadean, 2005 saw an impressive 5.5 per cent jump in sales, to take the market to a size of nearly 32 billion litres. Growth has now averaged 5 per cent over the past six years and the market is expected to expand by more than 4 billion litres by the end of 2008.

In contrast, the carbonates category has been more sluggish, averaging just 2 per cent growth between 1999 and 2005, with a compound average growth rate of just one per cent expected by the end of 2008. In size however, the two categories do not compare, with carbonates accounting for a massive 194 billion litres, six times that of the still drinks market-despite the differing growth rates, in actual volume terms the carbonates category will have added more than 7 billion litres by the end of 2008. Each of the world's drinkers, drinks an average of around 30 litres of carbonates and just five litres of still drinks.

Coffee is to grow faster than tea in 2005-2009, according to a market research forecast. Building on a small base and positively impacted by increasing sophistication and product knowledge, coffee sales are expected to outperform all hot drinks over the forecast period. By contrast, tea and other hot drinks will be extremely watered down as consumers seek to explore with other drink alternatives as the total volume Compound Annual Growth Rate (CAGR) of hot drinks in India clock just under 3 per cent.

FABs (flavoured alcoholic beverages) have recorded dramatic growth over a period, emerging as the fastest growing sector within the Indian alcoholic drinks market in both volume and value terms, albeit from a small sales base. FABs effectively meet consumers' desire for lower alcohol content drinks, flavour variations, image and individuality, especially among women. Innovative marketing campaigns by Bacardi-Martini have found favour among women and the younger generation, who look to these alcoholic beverages as new status symbols.

The growing wine culture and the increasing popularity of white spirits also led to sales of alcoholic beverages growing at robust rates. Moving away from the leading cities within each region, manufacturers are increasingly focusing on the second tier cities, with considerable success. Growth has been driven by a combination of a more relaxed attitude towards alcohol consumption, Westernisation and exposure to other foreign cultures, and growing affluence, supported by new product launches, intense advertising and promotional campaigns.

India is a country known for its price sensitivity, but value sales of alcoholic drinks grew more strongly in value terms than volume terms over the review period, due to a combination of price rises and trading up by consumers. More specifically, there were price hikes within spirits-the dominant sector-as a result of the failure of the sugarcane crop in several parts of the country, leading to a shortage of the molasses used to make potable alcohol. Further, the continued strong performance of the higher priced wines imported from Australia and Chile helped drive value growth.

In tandem with the continued progress of the Indian economy, and rising affluence and purchasing power, alcoholic drinks are predicted to record a compound annual growth rate (CAGR) of 5 per cent in constant value terms between 2005 and 2009. The alcoholic drinks market is expected to benefit from increased consumer interest, arising from new launches, shrewd marketing, smaller consumer pack sizes of 180ml, 250ml and 330ml, and a continued review of the tax structure of the domestic alcoholic industry.

According to Danny Brager, ACNielsen's vice-president for beverage alcohol, "flavoured spirits" should continue to be a hot segment in 2006, given the number of new product introductions and marketing support behind them. Anaylsts had suggested that this is the next big trend, and had predicted sales to reach $550 million for 2005. Soya-based drinks and drinkable yogurts are among fastest-growing categories in global food, beverage market- says ACNielsen.

According to Beverage Industry's 2006 Annual R&D Survey, statistic is just plain wrong last year. Beverage processors report that 75 per cent of new drinks released to market in 2005 were successful.

The research shows that beverage processors have become extremely savvy in new product development methods. This change includes streamlining new product development teams and giving them qualified leadership and autonomy. The survey says that processors believe that consumers are most likely to choose strawberry and tropical fruit-flavoured beverages in 2006. Last year, flavours were all about orange and citrus. This demonstrates how carefully processors are following consumer tastes. It's like a mantra: follow consumer whims or expect drinks to gather dust on store shelves.

With the exception of the tiny Australasian region, Asia is the fastest growing and the largest volume region; growing at 8 per cent in 2005, and being responsible for more than 40 per cent of the world's ready-to-drink fruit or non-fruit based drink sales. Average consumption is limited to a little over three litres per head, about half that of carbonates. The region is being helped along by the huge Chinese market, which is registering annual growth well in excess of 10 per cent and has been recently buoyed by the success of vitamin drinks. In Asia, in general, these drinks are competitively priced and in a price sensitive market they should go on and make future gains. Say cheers!

3

Training in Hospitality Management

As a housekeeping manager, ever wonder if you reflect the industry norm when it comes to responsibility, pecking order within the organization or job title?

Depending on the organization and facility type and size, cleaning managers hold a variety of titles. Responsibilities, too, vary. Similarly, some managers boast a strong academic background, while others have a more technical or trade background. Some managers are new to the cleaning profession and some have years of experience. Male? Female? Certainly more men today than 20 years ago. More than likely, though, certain facility types are more gender-specific than others.

Housekeeping Solutions asked industry leaders, experts and readers what kind of professional composite they would come up with based on their experiences. First of all, we found that "manager" tends to be an overused tag in housekeeping.

"Define manager," says John Walker, president of Management, Salt Lake City. "It could be anyone from a way-high boss to a head janitor with three workers."

Beth B. Risinger, CEO/executive director for the International Executive Housekeepers Association (IEHA), sees an assortment of cleaning managers among IEHA membership.

"The facility services manager, director of environmental services, or director of housekeeping — or whatever the title —

of today can be seen wearing professional business attire, having excellent management and people skills, maintaining their educational knowledge through seminars, conventions, and testing processes; and, commanding excellent salaries and benefits," she says.

How did they get here?

A variety of paths have led housekeeping professionals to their current positions. For some, this path was a direct line; for others, the route was more circuitous.

"Very few people think of being a custodian or cleaning as a goal in life," says Raymond A. Francis, custodial manager, University of Wisconsin-Eau Claire. "It's not considered a really nice job, so it's not on a high-priority list of careers for most people, but some people end up doing it well and even like it."

Francis has been a custodial manager at UW-Eau Claire for 20 years. He worked as a part-time cleaner for a building service contractor while he was in the U.S. Navy in the 1970s. He left the Navy and got a bachelor's degree in business administration in 1983. After graduation, he worked at Menard's for a short time before applying to UW-Eau Claire for his current position.

Bob Carr began his current job — custodial coordinator, Edmonds School District (Lynnwood, Wash.) — after 22 years in the Navy where he spent time cleaning or supervising sailors in cleaning ships, planes, hangars, barracks and bases.

"I was able to convince the school district that coming up through the ranks in the military to Navy chief petty officer to lieutenant gave me the experience required in a cleaning manager," Carr says. He completed his bachelor's degree in business management during his 5.5 years in the job.

Experience as a law enforcement officer gave Gary Symons, safety and environmental services manager, Kaiser Permanente Hospitals, Orange County, Calif., the skills to manage staff. "I learned 'command presence,' which means present authority and people will listen," he says.

Symons, who has worked in environmental services since 1996, has a bachelor's degree in business administration, a master's degree in business administration (MBA) and a certificate in occupational health and safety.

Janelle Everett, currently a housekeeping supervisor, started a cleaning business in 1990 after her husband left her with three children. "Living in a small town, you have to be service-oriented," she says. "I got the word out at church [about the business], got business cards and a vacuum cleaner, and in two weeks I had nine houses." After 10 years, the physical plant director at Presbyterian College, Clinton, S.C., approached Everett, whose business had grown enough to employ 10 workers, with a job offer. (Everett has a bachelor's degree in Christian education.)

Education vs. Hands-on skills

A person with a combination of a college background and extensive experience in management and cleaning might be an attractive candidate to most employers. But not all housekeeping managers have degrees in management or found management training, let alone in combination with cleaning experience. Whether or not one or the other is more important depends on the organization.

Some organizations require at least some college education, like St. Ann's Mercy Hospital, Toledo, Ohio. Julie Kanthak, an environmental services manager at one of the hospital's campuses, has been cleaning in the healthcare environment for 30 years. "I started when I was 18 years old and got real comfortable in the position," she says. "I got on-the-job training, some college experience, and was promoted through the ranks."

"My degree [in business administration] helped open doors when I applied for supervisor jobs and for manager jobs," says Tom Parrish, custodial manager, Washington State University, Pullman, Wash. "But you can gain an awful lot of knowledge through on-the-job experience. There are people who went through the school of hard knocks who know how to deal with people better than I do."

Someone with a master's degree and no cleaning experience might not be the best person to train workers on how to clean or to give direction to front-line cleaning workers. "The last thing you need is someone who sits behind a desk," says Barry Meyer, manager of housing services, Johns Hopkins University, Baltimore. "You need someone who has been out in the field and has done the work. That's very critical." For example, he used to work at a hotel where he once had to jump in and help one of his housekeepers clean 36 rooms when he was understaffed.

Meyer, who has a bachelor's degree in political science and a MBA, says he "doesn't fall in the mold" because most people who work in housekeeping management for the university do not have college degrees. He says that he thinks degrees often aren't required of housekeeping managers because people, in general, view the job as easy -- but it is much more difficult than many people realize.

In addition to cleaning knowledge, housekeeping managers, like most of their management peers, need to be common-sense grounded. Also, strong communication skills are essential.

"Being a custodial manager is about managing people. About 90 percent of your budget is labour," Parrish says. "The rest — buying products, managing a budget and so on — is just common sense."

Cleaning managers often deal with higher turnover and employee absenteeism than other departments. Written and verbal communication skills are necessary for putting written policies and procedures into place and making sure they are followed. Communication skills are necessary not only for managing employees, but for interacting with customers and bosses. Basic computer skills and knowledge of spreadsheet programs also help in managing department inventory, quality control and other data.

Facility Roles and Perceptions

Whether or not a housekeeping manager has the people skills to interact with building occupants, superiors and organization executives determine how the housekeeping manager and his or her employees are perceived. It doesn't hurt to also be conversant in a broad range of facilities management topics.

"We believe that [cleaning managers] are receiving much more respect for the position today than they were 10 years ago," Risinger says. "They are involved with construction projects and many are on strategic planning committees within their facilities. Many work closely with infection-control nurses. Others are involved in the landscaping, laundry-linen, dietary, engineering, and waste-management areas."

Although cleaning managers are becoming a more influential part of the facilities management team, they still usually have many bosses above them. A housekeeping manager might work under an assistant director of facilities, a director of facilities, a physical plant director, and a vice president of operations.

Pecking order and perception still tend to haunt many in the cleaning industry, however. "They are living below a glass ceiling they will never penetrate," Walker says, adding that cleaning managers often feel disconnected to their organizations. They are dealing with physical plant directors and facilities managers who know how to do business – they understand projects and construction, renovations, security, transportation and grounds, he says.

"Custodial managers try very hard and they are frustrated because they don't know how to play the game," Walker says. "They retire tired and frustrated because they don't know how to change things in their organizations."

There are endless theories regarding what fuels housekeeping stereotypes, or impedes upward mobility among cleaning professionals.

"Everyone knows how to clean," says Bruce Boggan, director of engineering, Valley Regional Medical Centre, Brownsville, Texas. "It's not like engineering. No one can come down here and tell me how to repair a chiller. No one is going to tell the materials manager how to run the warehouse, but you can ask for your area to be cleaned better. Housekeeping loses that little bit of aura or mystique."

Others contend that most cleaning managers fail to articulate the critical nature of the cleaning mission. Many observers feel that if building occupants and other departments understood the housekeeping mission better, they might respect it more. In other words, housekeeping managers could use a little public-relations mentoring.

"You need to let people know what it is, how challenging it is, the importance of the position and what's involved," Meyer says. "You need to raise the image as a job, a discipline, as a career— so people don't think it's beneath them."

It's what's inside that counts; "If you get beat up all the time, pretty soon it hurts your self-esteem," Boggan says. "Soon you develop a shell, throw up barriers and become callous to people's complaints."

Housekeeping managers receive criticism from all areas of organizations. Regardless, they still take a lot of pride in their work.

"[Housekeeping managers] generally have warm and caring personalities, and care deeply about the cleaning industry," Risinger says. "They believe in what they do."

Similarly, the growing importance of housekeeping within the facilities management scheme of things has helped elevate it as a profession in recent years. Today, housekeeping boasts a greater diversity of professional backgrounds, represents — on average — a better-trained and educated practitioner, and the mission itself is more critical to facilities and parent organizations.

Cleaning managers continue to work hard and strive to elevate the housekeeping profession. "There is a hunger out there to do something to change the profession," Walker says. "There is a desire to match the custodial department up with other departments."

Housekeeping Management

Organizing a Housekeeping Department

The Housekeeping Department serves all areas and departments of a hospital. Hence the Housekeeping Department needs to be centrally located and close to the vertical transport system to facilitate easy movement of housekeeping materials and equipment.

Facilities and space requirement:

- Office for the housekeeping manager
- Clerical work area
- Chief housekeeper's desk and bulletin board to put up daily duty charts and other housekeeping information
- Store room for the housekeeping equipment and materials
- Housekeeping closets on all floors of the hospital with space and shelves for housekeeping equipment and materials, and trolleys. As a matter of routine, supplies for daily use should be delivered to their respective closets directly.

Housekeeping Control Desk

The housekeeping desk is the nerve centre of the entire department and its efficiency determines the smooth operation and effectiveness of housekeeping. It is the focal point for the dissemination of information and communication to various points in the Housekeeping Department as well as to other departments for coordination. The area of the control desk must have:

Information Board

- Duty chart for housekeepers and sweepers
- Cleaning schedules
- Hospital staff room accommodation details
- Other general information and important announcements.

Key Board

- Patients' room keys
- Office room keys
- Entrance key
- Others.

Registers, Files, Forms

- Housekeeping equipment and supplies list
- Attendance register for sweepers

- Request form for supplies and equipments from stores
- Request form for repairs to be carried out in other departments
- Inventories of supplies and equipment
- Checklist for patients' rooms
- Year planning calendar
- Inventories of furniture and furnishings
- Inventory of linen.

Organization Chart

The Housekeeping Department has multiple functions to perform. Housekeeping services may be requested any time of the day or night, hence the staff structure must be so arranged as to provide the necessary services. Personalized services remains very much an important part of "quality" health care and this too is largely provided by the housekeeping department. The Housekeeping Manager, as Head of the Department, must coordinate the performance of these functions for the most efficient operation possible. Since the housekeeper cannot single-handedly discharge all the functions of supervision, requisition, scheduling, budgeting and so forth, the Department must be organized in such a way that each of these jobs is capably done. Delegation of authority through a clear chain of command will accomplish this objective. It must however be remembered that although authority is delegated, the Manager retains full responsibility for the department.

Job Descriptions

This is an important position in a hospital as it carries the responsibilities for the cleanliness, maintenance and aesthetic appeal of the hospital. An efficient housekeeping manager must possess a high degree of tact as well as good organizing ability, because of the need to work with other departments and with so many different people.

Work Performed

- Collaborate with other departments to ensure delivery of quality services

- Interview, select, train, evaluate and counsel staff in the hospital Housekeeping Department
- Instruct and advise staff on changes in policies, procedures or working standards
- Listen to the problems if any, of the housekeepers and sweepers and try to resolve them
- Conduct meetings with the housekeepers and sweepers separately to exchange ideas and solve problems
- Attend to the complaints and queries, if any, from other departments, or patients regarding the housekeeping functions and take necessary action.
- Go on rounds every morning to inspect the floors of the hospital and to correct any mistakes on the part of the housekeepers
- Prepare a report as required by the management
- Train all staff to efficiently perform the standard procedures as applicable to their job positions
- Work closely with the administrator on day to day housekeeping requirements
- Monitor departmental activities to ensure that maximum efficiency is maintained in the services being provided
- Assist in developing, delegating and monitoring departmental goals, objectives and programs to ensure timely completion
- Monitor the use of supplies and equipment and prepare a monthly request list including purchase of cleaning supplies.

Job Title: Housekeeper.

Reports to: Housekeeping Manager.

Work Performed

- Co-operate with the staff of other departments
- Deployment, supervision, control and training of staff
- Check the standard of cleanliness of all areas of the hospital

- Keep inventories and records of equipment and supplies
- Supervise and instruct the sweepers on the day to day activities
- Enhance the decor of different areas of the hospital with floral arrangements
- Control and supervision of the work in the linen room
- Train new recruits
- Check all the safety items on allotted floors
- Record all "lost and found" items on as per laid down norms
- Report to the Housekeeping Manager on sweepers' performance.

Job Title: Sweeper.

Reports to: Housekeeper.

Work {erformed

- Receive the allocation of floor and area of cleaning
- Clean the rooms twice a day
- Clean the common toilets and bathrooms twice a day
- Follow instructions and cleaning procedures given by housekeepers
- Take care of cleaning materials and ensure economical use of supplies given from the department
- Remove and dispose off refuse and rubbish at the assigned area
- Report missing or broken hospital property to the housekeeper
- Maintain a polite, dignified and helpful attitude toward the patient
- Hand over the lost and found articles to the supervisor
- Attend over daily briefings and give attendance.

Job Title: Gardener.

Reports to: Housekceper.

Work Performed

- Clean and maintain the garden
- Take good care of newly cultivated plants
- Take an interest in adopting new technology in the development of the garden
- Water and prune the plants
- Be creative in arranging the plants in a garden
- Attend work regularly.

Responsibilities of the Housekeeping Department

Direct Responsibilities

- Daily cleaning
- Periodic cleaning
- Trash and garbage removal including proper hospital waste disposal
- Exterminating bugs and pests
- Preventing spread of infection
- Ensuring clean linen
- Safety and security of the hospital
- Creating an aesthetically pleasing environment
- Gardening
- Making the necessary arrangements for meetings, workshops and conferences.

Indirect Responsibilities

- Saving electricity by switching off lights and fans when not in use
- Ensuring an economical use of supplies
- Developing goodwill by a courteous, helpful and caring attitude towards patients and visitors
- Promoting safety rules and measures by observing them and reporting dangerous conditions

- Maintaining a harmonious working relationship with the staff of other departments
- Arranging accommodation facilities for visitors and providing food during their stay at the hospital.

Qualities Required in a Housekeeper

- Basic knowledge of health care and sanitation, including principles of bacteriology, chemistry and related sciences, applicable to the prevention and control of infections and communicable diseases. The housekeeper should also have the ability to convey this knowledge in a nontechnical way to subordinate supervisors and workers so that it can be applied in their daily work.
- Ability to plan, administer and develop all phases of a comprehensive housekeeping program that will provide a suitable environment for the hospital's medical and administrative activities
- General working knowledge of sanitation, laundry operations, linen service and interior decoration
- Ability to assign, supervise and evaluate the work of subordinate supervisors and their personnel
- An interest in people and tact in handling them
- A pleasant personality and the ability to converse with all types of people
- An ability to hide personal likes and dislikes and to be conscientious, fair and just
- Be strict with respect to punctuality and observance of rules and regulations of the hospital
- Loyalty to the hospital and to her staff
- A sense of humour
- A cool head to deal with emergencies
- Adaptability and willingness to experiment with new ideas
- Powers of critical observation.

Recruitment, Selection and Training of Manpower

Having decided on the layout and facilities in the

Housekeeping Department, the next task is to decide how many people are needed for the department.

The number of people would depend on the structure of the hospital (block construction or cluster of rooms), number of floors and rooms per floor, number of public areas, size of landscape, the flow of patients and the time required for each task.

Recruitment and Selection

The Administrator of the hospital and Housekeeping Manager make the final decision regarding the selection of housekeepers. The process involved in recruitment and selection is:

Planning the Selection Schedule

- Print application form
- Inform public and staff through bulletin boards, advertisements and by word of mouth
- Issue application forms
- Collect application forms
- Shortlist and file applications
- Arrange interviews
- Conduct written exam and interview
- Shortlist the selected candidates
- Send employment letters
- Conduct an orientation program for the selected candidates
- Conduct a basic training program
- Give an on-the-job training.

Selection Criteria for Housekeeping Staff

Educational Qualifications

12th(HSC) passed with 500-700marks.

Age: 18-20 years.

Experience: Fresh candidate with no prior experience in hospitals.

Skills : Ability to talk clearly and politely. Ability to listen well. Ability to influence others. Knowledge of knitting, drawing, stitching.

Understand and speak the local language.

Personality : Independent, responsible, open, bold, bright and pleasant disposition.

Background : A low/middle income family.

Health and appearance: Smart, clean, tidy, simple in dress. Good health – should pass the medical test criteria.

Basic Training Program for Housekeepers

The basic training schedule for the recruited housekeepers should be planned for a specific period and should cover all aspects of housekeeping. The Housekeeping Manager should appoint appropriate well-trained staff from the Housekeeping Department and other resource persons to conduct the training in the related field. The students can then be put on an on-the-job training.

The training schedule can cover the following areas:

- Introduction to housekeeping
- General rules and regulations
- Hospital work culture and values
- Housekeeping and patient relationship – interaction with patients to ensure patient satisfaction
- Housekeeping and other departments
- Microbiology
- Ward management
- Bed making
- General cleaning procedures
- Dusting
- Cleaning of picture-frames and windows
- Sweeping
- Mopping
- Cleaning the surroundings

- Cleaning the room
- Cleaning toilets and bathrooms
- Stain removal and polishing
- Cleaning walls
- Cleaning brass items
- Cleaning the lift
- Cleaning the water filter and cooler
- Maintenance and cleaning of drinking water tank. Chlorination
- Importance of checklists
- Indenting
- Maintenance and use of various equipment
- Other housekeeping activities like making articles for interior decoration
- Linen management and supply
- Waste Management
- Furniture care and maintenance
- Arrangement of meeting and conference hall
- Flower arrangement
- Problem solving
- Manpower planning and management
- Sweeper's job description
- Effective communication.

Welfare of the Staff

To keep up the morale of the staff and to motivate them, it is important to provide a good working atmosphere at the hospital. This can be done by providing:

- Good working conditions
- Good working relationship and accessibility
- Incentive bonus
- Best employee award

- Statutory wages (provident fund, gratuity etc.)
- Medical facilities
- Sick leave and maternity leave
- Meals when on duty
- Proper work methods.

Good employees are hard to come by and once they are found, it is important to consider their welfare. Discipline should be maintained. Rules that are made should always be followed. Managerial policies should be consistent and every member of the staff should participate in the efficient and economic running of the department.

Supervision:

Supervising the workers and getting quality work done is an important role of the housekeeping supervisor.

The functions of the supervisor are:

- Organize the work assigned to him
- Plan the task to be performed
- Direct the work of those responsible to him
- Co-ordinate the resources under his direction
- Control workers and resources
- Evaluate the total job performance and the individual

Guidelines for effective supervision:

- Workers should understand clearly what is expected of them
- Workers should get guidance in performing work
- Good work should always be recognized
- Poor work should be corrected by adopting remedial methods
- Unwanted action and behaviour towards workers should be avoided.

Routine inspection work is required to

- Ensure that correct procedures and methods are being followed, and to make any improvements

- Ensure that standards are met and maintained
- Allow action to be taken to correct defective work
- Identify responsibility for defective work
- Enable complaints to be dealt with effectively.

The supervisor should check each employee's work on each area at least twice during a work period. The first check should be at the beginning of the work to ensure that it has been started on time, and that it is being carried out satisfactorily.

The second check should be made before the work in each area is completed to ensure that the work is satisfactory and to inform the worker to correct any faults, if necessary. It is also important to check that the work is being achieved in the stipulated time.

Checks should not be carried out at the same time each day, as the staff would be alert and responsive. Spot checks in the course of the work period are useful. More frequent checks are necessary for new recruits who are under training.

Handling the difficult worker:

- Find out the reasons for the problem – health, personal problem, or problem with the work procedures
- Arrange refresher training if required
- Frequently monitor and supervise the work
- Ask them to repeat the work if found unsatisfactory
- Motivate him to adopt new procedures and techniques adopted by the department (inculcate positive thinking)
- Encourage the worker through incentives, and bonus for festivals.

Evaluation of Workers

In order to ensure continuing efficiency, it is important that the staff is evaluated from time to time. This exercise will be effective, if the following points are kept in mind

- Pay individual attention to each worker and supervise his work
- Observe if he completes his work in the stipulated time

- Help him if he has a problem related to his work
- Plan additional training for the worker, if you think he requires it.
- Observe his attitude to other workers in the department.

Organization of Work

A well managed housekeeping department relies on the ability of its housekeepers to organize work efficiently and manage the use of equipment, space and human labour with minimum effort. It is also important that she concerns herself with the staffing requirements and modern cleaning equipments, agents, and methods. She should study their advantages and disadvantages and bring into use those that make cleaning easier for her staff, spare time and ultimately cut down costs.

Work organization involves the preparation of:

1. Work specification
2. Work schedule
3. Job procedure
4. Work study
5. Work simplification.

Work Specification: This is a detailed description of the work to be carried out in a specific area. There should be work specifications for every area covered by the Housekeeping Department.

Eg. Work specification for cleaning corridors:

a. Collect the required equipment and materials
b. Store the equipment and materials neatly in the corridor to be cleaned.
c. Empty the waste bins and collect any other waste that may be on the ground
d. Remove the dust from the walls, windows, curtains and picture frames
e. Spot clean areas such as door handles, window sills and shaft

f. Frequency of corridor cleaning – to be decided based on the patient flow.

Work schedule: This is a list of actual work to be carried out by an individual staff member during a particular period of the day. It would also include meal breaks and allow time for cleaning and tidying up of equipments. The number of schedules necessary indicates the number of staff required to clean an area once a day.

Job procedure: This specifies the way a job is done and is to be prepared for each job individually.

E.g.. Procedure for cleaning a telephone:

Materials: Damp Cloth, Dusters, Disinfectant

Method: Dust the telephone completely with the damp cloth. Wipe down with a disinfectant solution paying attention to the dial, mouthpiece, phone. Wash, rinse and dry the dusters, and put them back in their place.

Work study: A work study involves work measurements that are required to determine the work involved in a particular job, the time taken to carry out a job under normal; circumstances by an average worker. This helps in determining the number of staff required and in standardizing labour costs.

E.g.. A work study on bed making showed that the distance covered by the staff during bed-making can be reduced if she were to strip the bed more systematically and did not tuck in the sheets and the covers till the end of bed-making.

A work study must be carried out whenever there is a waste of time, labour or material. When there is a delay in carrying out the work, or when the complaints made by patients increase, it is a sure indication that one worker is overburdened with work, and another is not fully occupied. This is an indication that a work study needs to be carried out.

A work study involves the following procedure:

a. Select the job procedure and identify the problem

b. Observe and record the present work method

c. Develop an improved method

d. Conduct periodic checks to ensure that the improved method is working satisfactorily.

A work study cannot be carried out unless it gets the full cooperation of the staff involved throughout the investigation. It is possible to get a clear picture of the old working method, and implement the new method only with the full support of the staff.

Work simplification: While a worker is busy and on the job, the muscles of his body need moments of rest between motions. Tensed muscles produce neither high quality nor great quantity of work. The worker finds the work easy or difficult depending on the way he uses his body. New methods need to be developed to make the work easier and to reduce the stress factor for the worker.

A few methods of work are listed below:

- o Movement of the worker should be limited to the minimum necessary.
- o The work should be in a pattern of curved line motion
- o Both hands should begin and complete a motion at the same time
- o Arms should move in opposite and symmetrical directions to give the worker proper balance
- o Daily activity should be restricted to normal reach level. Objects out of reach can be cleaned periodically
- o Use of different parts of the body should be restricted to a minimum
- o Before starting work the equipment and materials should be arranged conveniently to avoid unnecessary movement
- o Wherever possible, adjust work heights to make the work easier.

Planning the cleaning procedure in a hospital:

Cleaning requires a systematic and planned approach, both, towards the individual tasks involved and towards the hospital's cleaning operations as a whole. This involves two areas:

- The cleaning process
- The work schedule.

The Cleaning Process

The objective of the process of cleaning is to remove as much dirt as possible without damaging the surface, and to prevent dirt from resettling. To do this effectively and safely, we need to identify the different types of dust and stains involved, along with ways in which they are introduced into the building. This information helps to decide which cleaning method, equipment and materials are most appropriate. The Housekeeping Department should establish methods of cleaning and work schedules.

The Work Schedule

Before any cleaning program can be carried out, a suitable work plan must be drawn up. The work schedule gives the actual work to be undertaken by a particular staff member during a particular period of the day. This should take into account several factors, which affect the way in which the work is carried out. These factors include:

Standard of cleanliness: Cleaning standards vary in different parts of the hospital. In every hospital, the area of work can be classified as high risk and low risk areas. The standard of housekeeping services depends on the level of risk.

Housekeeping cleaning standard has been defined as:

Housekeeping Cleaning Standard = Method x Frequency

When cleaning methods are correctly selected, correct equipment and agents are used for each surface and cleaning tasks are carried out methodically, the housekeeping standards are said to be efficiently met. The following table shows the standard of cleanliness required in different areas of the hospital:

- Area
- Standard
- Requirement
- High risk areas (operation theatres, special units)
- Prestige standard
- Highest possible standard of cleaning, dust and infection control

- Medium risk areas Kitchen, toilets
- Special standard
- High standard of cleaning, and infection control
- Low risk areas
- Corridors, offices, waiting areas, patient rooms
- Normal standard
- Good standard of cleaning, absence of soil, dust and stains.

The activity in the area and the time of day: Consideration should be given to the level of activity and amount of traffic in the areas to be cleaned. Where possible, cleaning will be undertaken when these levels are at their lowest. Each part of the hospital has a primary function which should be disrupted as little as possible. Cleaning should fit in as modestly as possible with the main activity of that area. Administration areas and most departments have a standard working day. Hence cleaning in these areas can be programmed to take place either before or after working hours.

The planning schedule: The Housekeeping Department should plan and apply a systematic cleaning procedure. This includes:

- o Daily and weekly cleaning schedule
- o Periodic cleaning schedule.

Daily and weekly schedule: This includes all tasks that are to be carried out regularly in a specific functional area on a predetermined basis set by management according to area usage and the need for cleanliness. (dusting, sweeping, mopping)

Periodic schedule: This includes tasks, those additional to, but in combination with routine tasks, which have a frequency of once every 15 days or once every month. (changing curtains, removing stains, polishing, cleaning water tanks, cleaning septic tanks) records should be maintained to show when and where a particular task is started and completed.

Frequency of cleaning: Frequencies are to be based on sound quality cleaning, especially as they relate to "routine" cleaning. A set time schedule is not considered appropriate for routine cleaning. If an area requires cleaning, it should be cleaned, if it does not require cleaning, it should not be cleaned. Cleaning on the basis of "it has to be cleaned everyday even when it does not need it" is not applicable.

Even though waiting area, patient examination area, refraction area and pathways are considered low risk areas in the hospital, frequency of routine cleaning is to be followed to keep the area clean all the time. The area supervisor should check now and then and instruct the sweepers to go for special cleaning.

The following table may be used to plan the frequency of cleaning:

- Area
- Frequency of cleaning
- Special attention
- Special care.

OPD

- Registration
- Waiting area
- Corridors
- Continuous
- Patient flow is high; rainy season
- Provide doormats at the entrances and clean them frequently
- Common toilets
- 4-6 times a day
- Patient flow is high.

WARDS

- Patient room
- Twice a day
- Emergency, spillage, vomiting
- Take immediate action to clean
- Corridors

- 4 times a day
- Emergency; spillage
- Take action immediately
- Room toilets
- Twice a day
- More usage
- Common toilets
- Four times a day
- More usage.

Office Area

- Camp office
- Finance Department
- Personnel Department
- Once a day.

Laboratory

- Biochemistry lab
- Twice a day
- Lab. toilet
- 4-6 times a day
- Patient flow is high
- Use odonil, a good disinfectant.

Outside Area

- Twice a day
- Sprinkle water to settle dust.

Use of appropriate cleaning agents;

Usage Area

- Cleaning agent
- Dilution
- Time for cleaning agent to act

- Frequency of use
- Floor, tiles, wash basin, outside of w/c closet, flush tank
- LOC, Vim or any other good detergent
- 20ml: 5litre, 8gm/washbasin/toilet
- Direct
- Twice a day
- Floor, glass mirror
- LOC, seespray/colin
- 20ml:5Llitre 18ml/litre
- Direct
- Weekly
- Toilet closet and all stain removal
- Harpic
- No dilution
- Direct
- Once a day
- Mopping the floor. Cleaning the toilet
- Pursue
- 18ml/litre
- Direct
- Twice a day
- Septic tank-1kg/wash Water tank-500gms/wash
- Bleaching powder
- No dilution
- 2 mins
- Septic tank-weekly Water tank-monthly
- Brass items
- Brasso
- Direct
- Special cleaning

- Drawers, wardrobes, sinks
- Naphthalene balls
- Direct
- Weekly
- Toilet odour control
- Odonil
- Direct
- Weekly
- Disinfections
- Dettol
- 100ml/5litres
- Direct
- Daily.

Communication

Effective communication between housekeepers and workers is very important. Generally the cleaners are illiterate and recruited from the rural areas. Hence they understand only very simple language.

Thus, it is necessary for the housekeeper to use very simple language when explaining the work procedures, so that the workers are not mislead into using incorrect procedures. This will lead to poor quality work.

Factors to be considered:

- Workers should understand clearly what is expected of them
- Unwanted actions should be avoided
- Use simple and clear language
- Adopt demonstration methods to explain the work procedures
- Proper job specification
- Two-way communication is essential to avoid misunderstanding the work procedure

- Guidelines given to the workers should neither be over commanding, nor easy. They should be moderate.
- New policies and procedures should immediately be communicated to the workers and their queries clarified.

Poor communication results in:

- Following incorrect cleaning methods
- Improper use of cleaning materials and equipment, which results in increased costs
- Taking more time to finish the given task
- Arguments with the housekeeper
- Frequent absence from work
- Discontinue from service.

Inter Departmental Relationships

Maintenance: One of the most important functions of housekeeping is the maintenance of keeping furniture, fixtures and facilities in working order. Housekeepers need to constantly check on various things throughout the hospital on a daily or a weekly basis and inform the maintenance department through a requisition form about any repairs that need to be done. The maintenance work could cover a number of aspects such as plumbing, carpentry, electricity and civil works. Hence a close coordination with the maintenance department is absolutely necessary.

Stores: Hospitals stock all housekeeping equipment, materials and supplies, except linen, in the general stores. Coordination with the stores ensures availability of day-today requirements of housekeeping. Housekeepers can indent materials from the stores on a daily or a weekly basis. These indented materials can be issued directly to the staff or can be stored inside the department or under the staircase with proper safety measures. The stores consult with the Housekeeping Department regarding purchase of materials.

Laundry: Most small hospitals prefer to outsource laundry on account of limited space and manpower. Larger hospitals usually handle the laundry in-house to issue clean and quality linen to the operation theatres and other departments. Whether in-house or out-sourced, coordination between hospital and laundry is very important.

The housekeepers should check the need and use of materials with the ward staff. The senior housekeeper should maintain registers for checking stock and transaction of materials, planning the laundry process, and salary of in-house dhobi.

Nursing: The Nursing Department works closely with the Housekeeping Department. It is this department that is involved in bed-making in the patients' rooms, and informs the Housekeeping Department about any requirements by the patients. The Nursing Department also contacts the Housekeeping Department if there is any need for emergency cleaning in a specific area, in case of spillage, breakage, or if the patient has vomited. The nurses maintain the admission and discharge details of the patients. When the patient is discharged, it is the nurses who check the room, lock the door and handover the key to the housekeeper. The housekeeper then sends a sweeper to clean the room thoroughly and get it ready for the next patient.

Catering: If a hospital has catering facilities, then the kitchen and dining room needs to be cleaned at least twice a day. This comes under the purview of the Housekeeping Department. The Housekeeping Department also needs to co-ordinate with the Catering Department when making arrangements for guests and special occasions.

Personnel: The Housekeeping Department deals with the Personnel Department for the recruitment of the housekeeping staff, salary administration, indiscipline and grievance, identity cards for the staff, promotions and exit facilities.

Other

Departments: Since every department in the hospital needs to be kept clean, the Housekeeping Department interacts with every department. When electrical equipment is not working or a door does not close properly, it is the Housekeeping Department that takes down the complaint and makes sure that the problem is rectified. Thus, the Housekeeping Department is an important and indispensable department in the smooth functioning of a hospital.

Budget: Anatomy of a Housekeeping Budget

Regardless of your tenure as a cleaning professional, budgeting is difficult to master. Many facility managers often don't know where to begin. What are your priorities? Labour, training, purchasing equipment, or the cleaning needs within the facility? What about cleaning frequency or those non-cleaning tasks the department is responsible for?

Carl Costanza, director of facilities at Oakton Community College in Des Plaines, Ill. says, "all of the above." "It took a lot of time to gather all this information," he says, "but in the end, it was well worth it."

As a result, Costanza has a better understanding of his facility and found a way to save time and money in the long run.

Assessing Your Facility

Every facility manager knows that the best way to clean is "faster, cheaper, easier, healthier, and safer," all while achieving the desired result. But none of this is possible without a good understanding of your facility.

"Knowledge is key when budgeting," says Steve Spencer, facility specialist at State Farm Insurance in Bloomington, Ill. "Know your facility." This means familiarizing yourself with the ins and outs of each building. Many industry experts recommend that facility managers put together a good business case analysis of their facility. Know the quality levels and square footage of each building – the number or rooms, light fixtures, types of flooring, etc. Once this information is collected, compare it to the history of the facility. What advancements have been made to the facility since the last budget was developed?

A change in the facility can drastically alter a budget. For instance, have traditional light fixtures been replaced by lights with sensors? Has tile replaced what was once carpeting? Has your facility expanded, increasing square footage that workers need to clean? "When you have a good grasp on your facilities needs, you can put a price tag on it," says John Watson, director of facility services at North Lake Còmmunity College in Irving, Texas.

Evaluating Cleaning Specifications

Developing a "needs analysis" will help facility managers determine the building's desired level of clean, as well as the frequency of cleaning and manpower necessary to reach the desired goal. A proper needs analysis will also take into account both the data on the building, as well as high traffic areas and impression areas, such as restrooms and entryways.

"Look for the cleaning tasks that will effect the life-cycle of the building," says Watson. "Also be aware of the impact that the cleaning schedule has on the building and look for those jobs that require more time and attention for little quality improvements."

Evaluating "frequency of tasks" can save budget dollars in the long run. Gary Brezinski, director of buildings and grounds at the West Ottawa School District in Holland, Mich. recommends "moving outside the box and changing what you are currently doing" in an effort to become more efficient. "Sit down and figure out what absolutely needs to be done," says Brezinski.

Evaluate what tasks can be reduced in frequency, while continuing to maintain quality. "I visited an office where they scrubbed the tile every day," says Spencer. "It could just be swept, saving time and money, while cutting labour in half and reducing expenses such as chemicals and water."

Spencer also recommends taking a look at trash collection, which can add up to around 25 percent of the labour budget. Most garbage is paper and reducing the amount of times this trash is taken out can save significantly.

When evaluating work it is also important to include those activities that don't involve cleaning. Omitting this when putting together a comprehensive budget will skew the numbers drastically.

"Managers can get into trouble if these activities are not calculated when putting together a budget," says Dave Frank of the American Institute for Cleaning Sciences. "Activities such as room setup and breakdowns can take as many as 10 hours a week."

Sitting down and developing a time study for every task required to maintain a building will help facility managers determine where to cut time and save money. Coming up with this calculation will outline the annual hours spent on each task.

"With this information, facility managers can manage the building and cleaning activities more accurately," says Frank. "Don't clean areas that aren't dirty. You can save a lot of money over time by cutting back and still not impact standards for the appearance."

Taking a Look at Labour

"In addition to an exhaustive knowledge and database of your facility, take a hard look at labour costs when working on a budget," says Jack Van Reeth, manager of environmental services at Geisinger Health System in Danville, Pa. "Almost 90 percent of your budget is going to be related to labour."

When factoring labour into the budget, facility managers should consider both productive and nonproductive time because both will impact budget dollars. Does your facility provide vacation, family medical and sick time? Those are all days where employees are being paid, but work is not getting done. Analyzing this may determine that of the total paid hours, maybe only 70 percent are actually work hours. This needs to be factored in.

Many industry experts realize that dealing with the high cost of labour is difficult, but if managers can figure out better ways to do the job and become more efficient, they will save valuable budget dollars.

"Eliminate duplication of services," says Spencer. "Our facility had day maids and porters, as well as a cleaning crew at night. We realized that they all do the same thing so we moved everything to daytime so that the work is only done once a day."

Training is also an important piece of the budget pie. Without proper training on policies and procedures, employees may take longer on tasks, or worse, do them incorrectly, causing others to pick up the slack and sometimes duplicate tasks.

Costanza has worked training into his bid specifications so that once a month, the distributor comes in for an hour or so to educate workers on both products and proper cleaning procedures.

Van Reeth chooses to use the free services from both the distributors and manufacturers he works with, but wished the help was available more often.

"This industry has high turn-over and although the training is helpful to the employees, when we have someone new, we don't always have time to get the distributors in here again," he says. "It would be so helpful to have those training courses on DVD or VHS so we could reference them more often."

Brezinski found a way around this problem by conducting his own training. "I use our vendors to get information and start up programs. I then educate myself and use what I have learned to train my employees," he says. "The information out there is so valuable that it is well worth the time."

Testing the Equipment

Purchasing is obviously a large part of any housekeeping budget, but this is also one area that facility managers can control. Often times, implementing specific cleaning programs may cost money up front, but will cut dollars overall. This includes automatic appliances in the restroom, which will save on water, electric, soap, paper towels, etc.; installing improved floor finishes that require less frequent cleaning and saves on labour; or implementing programs such as microfiber technology that can save on chemical purchases, as well as labour costs.

In addition to these programs, the initial purchase of large cleaning equipment can eat up a lot of the purchasing budget. If new equipment is necessary, Costanza recommends using his bidding process.

"In the past, we would call a couple different suppliers and just go with the lowest price," he says. "We probably weren't getting the best price because we didn't create loyalty to any one supplier. Not to mention we were spending a lot of time with the process. Now we are loyal to one supplier and we have seen more savings than ever before." Preventative maintenance will also save on the budget. Listening to workers is a great practice in preventative maintenance. Because they use these machines often, workers will know when maintenance is necessary.

"Value the opinion of your staff when considering budgets and purchasing decisions," says Watson. "They will tell you what needs to be done and what improvements are necessary."

Approaching Management

When industry experts were asked what was most important when approaching top management with a budget concern, the answer was overwhelmingly unanimous: Be prepared.

"Don't go into a meeting with the boss without a defined scope of work," says Frank. "The more data you provide them, the more pull you will have with the budget. Communicate, realistically, what can and can't be done."

Spencer adds that it is also important to know where the dollars are currently being spent, the time that goes into the tasks, and how employees are working. "Bring these statistics into the meeting, present them with the plan and explain who will be hurt by cuts, who can help get the work done and how to allocate the money. Then let them decide where to cut the budget."

Watson agrees, and adds that feedback from your employees may also prove to be valuable when arguing budget dollars. "Go in with the data behind you," he says. "Put together different options that all work and let them choose the best plan."

"Provide management with the facts," says Brezinski. "Show them the need as well as the savings. Also be prepared to provide answers to their questions immediately."

Van Reeth recommends being prepared at the very first meeting with superiors and emphasizes the importance of staying calm.

"Maintain your composure and don't become emotional when they challenge your decision," he says. "Calmly and logically respond with prepared stats rather than emotional appeal."

Finally Costanza suggests that facility managers be proactive with their budget dollars. "Look for areas where you can save throughout the year," he says. "If you can't find a place to save, you aren't looking hard enough." If managers are constantly looking at the overall operation, they will be better prepared to defend the department during budget negotiations.

Managing the Monthly Household Housekeeping Budget

One of the upsides of being hugely pregnant and on maternity leave while the kids are at school & a completely clear diary free of rushing around doing things is the amount of time available to do things one usually never gets round to. While the rain is lashing down and the wind is howling I'm staying warm and dry in our home office.

Last week we were the delighted recipients of a beautiful (if you like shabby chic) cream two-drawer filing cabinet from a generous Freecycler. It was perfect timing for us as we'd just reached the point where our trusty one-drawer cabinet would not accept a single extra piece of paper yet we needed to create some new files. This week I've been merrily drinking tea by the gallon while I take each file and review its contents, its label, its position, discard outdated papers and noting anything needing actioning.

We've taken the opportunity to make a comprehensive list of all the bank accounts, pensions, insurance schemes in a password protected spreadsheet along with their policy/account numbers, login details and the like. Very reassuring. I've added a lockable/ fire & flood proof safe or document store to my birthday wish list so I can print the information and have a hard copy stashed away in case of emergency along with our birth certificates, passports etc.

As mentioned in my recent post I am really enjoying being right on top of what we are spending against what we are earning and aiming to save a contingency fund as well as making any excess we save work for us.

A new way of my managing the household housekeeping budget is to draw 50% of it out as ACTUAL CASH at the beginning of the month (50% is left in the bank account so I can pay for online grocery shopping electronically) and keep in kitchen storage jar. Every time cash is removed from the jar it is replaced with a receipt for household things bought. We're hoping that at the end of each month the receipts will add up to the amount spent from the jar. We have agreed that all food, medicine, children's shoes/ clothes, household items are to be bought from the monthly housekeeping budget of £400.

So far this seems to be a very effective deterrent for overspending and also seems to be easier to keep track of what is being spent on what. Already I can see that the bank account is very low on funds despite it only being the 8th day of the month probably due to an enormous supermarket delivery where I ordered two of each essential non-perishable item to cover my absence when I am in hospital sometime during the coming few weeks.

With this in mind I am finding myself looking through the food cupboards, freezer and fridge and actively thinking about meals we will be able to enjoy given what we have to hand and will try to run down the supplies by the end of the month so that we no longer have overflowing cupboards with no real clue as to what is lurking in the back.

I'm looking at the ongoing list of things we 'need' and deciding which ones can wait until next month (my daughter having new party shoes can and so can a new chest of drawers for the guest/ baby room).

Issues and Constrains of Manpower Supply in Indian

Hospitality Industry

Tourism has been the fastest growing industry in the world for the past 50 years, and today it is the world's largest industry relating to employment, foreign exchange earning and overall economic development of several countries. It is India's third largest export industry after Readymade Garments and Gems & Jewelry (Min. of Tourism, GOI). Tourism provides opportunity for economic growth, employment generation and poverty alleviation. Tourism holds the key for creation of rural wealth, opportunity for the hitherto neglected segments of society, artisans and service providers in the backward areas. As per WTTC this sector employs

212 million people world wide, generates $3.4 trillion in gross output and contributes $655 billion towards government tax revenues. Travel and Tourism is the world's largest industry. By 2008, the industry is grown to $9 trillion. The industry accounts for 10.7% of the global work force and provides 1 in every 9 jobs. Between the years 1995 and 2000, the industry is adding a new job every 2.5 seconds. It will contribute up to 10.3% of the global GDP. According to the same estimate, the global travel and tourism activity is expected to increase by 4.7% between 2007 and 2016.

Tourism sector holds immense potential for Indian economy. It can provide impetus to other industries through backward and forward linkages and can generate huge revenue earnings for the country. In the recent 2007-08 budget, the provision for building tourist infrastructure has been increased from US$ 95.6 million in 2006-07 to US$ 117.5 million in 2007-08 (Min. of Tourism). Tourism is no longer looking at it as a leisure activity, but as a major source of employment. The labour capital ratio per million rupee of investment at 1985-86 prices in the tourism sector is 47.5 jobs as against 44.7 jobs in agriculture and 12.6 jobs in case of manufacturing industries.

Human Resources in Hospitality Industry

The success of any industry depends to a great extend up on the quality of human resource and tourism is not an exception. Tourism is labour intensive industry, which provides employment to skilled, semi-skilled and unskilled workers directly and indirectly. The progressive labour force with dynamic management and responsive government and responsible society are the pillars of the tourism industry. Traditionally, the employment has been seen as an area that is reactive to changes in the wide business environment. There is a widely accepted assumption that the role of people within organizations is required to change and develop in response to developments in markets, products and technology. Most of the large tourism companies recognized this assumption and has been started organizing work and support human resource functions such as training and development. This is possible only when the external labour market permits employers to adapt these changing dimensions.

Human Resource in Hospitality Industry – Supply Side

Some of the services required in the tourism and hotel industries are highly personalized, and no amount of automation can substitute for personal service providers. Human resource development in the tourism industry normally includes manpower training in two main areas: (1) the hospitality and catering sector and (2) the travel trade and tourism sector. The hotel and catering sector is now highly personalized. Customer satisfaction is the prerequisite for a smooth and successful operation in the hotel industry, requiring professionally trained and highly skilled personnel. According to estimates of requirements for additional hotel rooms, the number of personnel who will need formal training in the hospitality and catering sector would increase by about 400 a year, from 16,000 to 20,000 people a year by 2010. The existing training facilities currently produce only about 5,000 to 6,000 trained personnel a year. Different types of jobs available in hospitality industry in different levels and are in annexure-I.

The central government and the state governments have collaborated to provide resources in order to train people in the hospitality sector as part of overall development efforts. There are now 20 institutes of hotel management throughout the country which are sponsored by the government and directly affiliated with the National Council for Hotel Management and Catering Technology (NCHMCT). These institutes of NCHMCT are located in Ahmedabad, Bangalore, Bhopal, Bhubaneshwar, Calcutta, Chandigarh, Gurdapur, Guwahati, Gwalior, Hyderabad, Jaipur, Lucknow, Madras, Mumbai, New Delhi (Pusa), Panjai (Goa), Patna, Shimla, Srinagar and Thiruvananthapuram.

These institutes offering several types of courses in hotel management, craftsmanship and food and beverage services, including three year diploma courses, 14-month postgraduate diploma course, one-year post-graduate diploma courses, one and a half year post-graduate diploma courses, six-month courses and certificate courses. There were 1,605 students trained in 1995, 2,250 students in 1996, 2,500 students in 1997, 2,900 students in 1998 and 3,600 students would graduate in 1999 and 4,000 would graduate in 2000, according to data provided by Economic and

Social Commission for the Asia and the Pacific (ESCAP). In addition to these 20 institutes, there are also 15 food crafts institutes around the country. The food crafts institutes are located at Ajmer, Aligarh, Alwaye (Kerala), Chandigarh, Darjeeling, Gangtok, Faridabad, Jodhpur, New Delhi, Patna, Pondicherry, Pune, Tiruchirapali, Udaipur and Vishakhapatnam. These institutes offer training courses from six months to one year, training students in food production, bakery, confectionery, front office operations, bookkeeping, restaurant and housekeeping. The institutes of hotel management and food crafts institutes have been set up with assistance from the Ministry of Tourism in collaboration with the state governments. The two agencies of government share financial responsibilities for these institutes. Some states have raised tuition fees so that the institutes can be self-sufficient.

All of the institutes in hotel management and food crafts are managed by autonomous societies registered under the Societies Registration Act, 1860, and have Boards of Governors consisting of representatives from the central government, state government and the hotel and trade industries. Each Board of Governors is chaired by the state's secretary of tourism.

The National Council for Hotel Management and Catering Technology (NCHMCT) is also registered under the Societies Registration Act, 1860, and is managed by a Board of Governors which includes representatives from the central government and the private sector. The NCHMCT regulates all academic activities of the institutes of hotel management. It also oversees all admissions, course design, examinations and certificates. The faculty development programme, research, cooperation and coordination and affiliation with professional organizations at the national and international level also come under NCHMCT. In addition to the central governments support for training tourism industry personnel; there are other training courses and programmes carried out by various agencies, including universities, state governments and private organizations. The Department of Labour has set up a Central Apprenticeship Council (under the Central Apprentice Act) to conduct training courses and short courses lasting three months to one year in cooking, bakery, confectionery, housekeeping and other services. The Central

Apprenticeship Council trained about 1,600 people every year at Delhi, Fairdabad and Meerut centers ever in 1998. State governments trained about 250 people at craft institutes. The major hotel chains trained about 250 people, universities trained about 500 people and private institutes trained about 750 people. The total number of trained personnel from these agencies was 3,350 people.

Comparing this total with the need for 20,000 additional personnel each year, it is clear that further analysis is required. A survey being conducted to identify the requirements for trained manpower at each level of employment would focus on general management trainees, trainees in kitchen management, housekeeping management, operational trainees, front office and accounting management, chefs, butlers, captains, bakery, confectionery and other specialized cooking.

Middle management positions would be filled by people holding three-year diplomas, while other jobs could be filled by craft trainees. Craft institutes could be targeted for expansion in order to meet the needs for lower-level skill areas.

Human Resources in Hospitality Industry – Demand Side

In India there is a tremendous shortage of trained manpower in the hospitality sector. Tourism sector on an average requires manpower about 20,000 per year. Against such a requirement the actual trained output from Govt.. institution is only 5000 per year. When we consider all other private institutions, the total available trained manpower does not exceed 10,000 in a year. Thus there need to develop required human resource in various segment .of the tourism industry, as a consequence of the rapid growth in tourism, changing technology and markets both national and international level.

By the very nature of tourism as a service industry, its efficient administration and successful operation depend largely on the quality of manpower. In the Asian and Pacific region, the shortage of skilled manpower poses a major threat to the overall development of tourism. International tourism is a relatively new phenomenon and therefore the lack of managerial capability exists at all levels of the industry.

In particular, the rapid expansion of hotels of an international standard in the region is creating a high level of demand for skilled and experienced staff. The nature of the decisions facing hotel management is continually expanding. For their business to remain competitive, managers must be skilful in many diverse areas. For instance, they must possess a good understanding of how current events and the economy affect the market and develop skill in marketing their products. They must also strive to keep up with the technological innovations in the operational side of the industry. As part of the service industry, tourism is labour-intensive and generally requires well-developed social and language skills in a cross-cultural working environment. These demands have placed considerable strain on small, independent operators, who cannot rely on the broad management expertise available to their multinational hotel chain competitors.

The availability of skilled and trained manpower is a crucial element in the successful long-term development and sustainability of a tourist destination. In the ultimate analysis, skilled and trained human resources will ensure the delivery of efficient, high-quality service to visitors, which is a direct and visible element of a successful tourism product. High standards of service are particularly important in sustaining long-term growth, since success as a tourist destination is determined not only by price competitiveness or the range of attractions available, but also by the quality of the services provided. Repeat visits, a vital factor in maintaining growth, will be deterred if standards of service do not meet expectations. Issues and Constrains facing Human Resources in Tourism Sector as:

The major problems and constraints facing human resources development in the tourism sector can be summarized as follows:

(a) Shortage of qualified manpower, particularly at the managerial level, which poses a major obstacle to the overall development of the tourism sector,

(b) Shortage of qualified and experienced teaching staff in hospitality training institutes

(c) Shortage of training materials and facilities according to the present day industry need

(d) Lack of strategies and policies for human resources development in the hospitality sector

(e) Difficulty in keeping pace with rapidly changing technological innovations and dynamic changes in the global market place;

(f) Complexity of the multidisciplinary nature of tourism studies;

(g) Huge Gap between the training capacity of training educational institutes and the actual need of the industry;

(h) Shortage of higher-level programmes for management development in this sector.

The South Asia Integrated Human Resource Development Project, funded by the European Commission, has done much work in developing human resources, such as setting standards, securing industry acceptance of standards, preparing manuals for important trades, training of the trainers, setting up a system for testing standards and certification of trainers and trainees. However, follow up is needed because further funding from the European Commission is not now available. The National Commission set up to oversee the project must be activated and the industry must implement the system so that quality can be ensured to make Indian tourism competitive internationally.

The apprentice scheme being implemented by the Ministry of Labour is another activity that should be reviewed. The scheme started operating many years ago, and in view of development in the hospitality sector since then, the syllabus requires revision and the infrastructure for training in the council institutes at New Delhi, Faridabad and Meerut requires major upgrading.

Trainers also need to upgrade their skills. Currently, they are providing training in cookery, bakery, confectionery, stewardship and housekeeping, with 1,600 trainees graduating annually. If the administration of this scheme and the institutions are handed over to the National Council for Hotel Management and Catering Technology under the Ministry of Tourism, there should be considerable synergy generated among the institutions for training in the hospitality sector.

The Universities of Madras and Bangalore have also affiliated several catering institutes and award the Bachelor's Degree in Hotel Management. However, the industry has been reluctant to accept the students, because they lack practical experience. There is need to upgrade the curriculum of these university courses to meet the expectations of industry. Another 35 private institutes affiliated to the All India Council of Technical Training (AICTT) provide training in hospitality and catering to about 500 students. However, they have not been able to meet the expectations of the industry and there have been numerous complaints about the quality of training. As a result, students find it difficult to get good job opportunities. An exception to the teaching shops is some private institutes run by reputable hotel groups like Oberoi, ITDC, Taj and the ITC Mayura Group. Other hotels are also setting up similar training institutes. These institutes award their own degrees and diplomas and some have ties with the American Hotel and Motel Association or the Swiss Hotel School. Some universities in Australia and in the United Kingdom have started offering split campus training in India. A proper system of admissions is required, because there are often allegations that the management of these institutes charge exorbitant entry fees.

Recommendations to the Government

The Government could constitute a steering committee to review the demand and supply of the human resources in the hospitality industry and prepare plans for developing qualitative human resources which are require for the present day global industry. The committee should constitute with the members from all concerned areas like.

- State and central tourism development commissioners
- Representatives form all areas of hospitality industry
- Member's/president/secretary of the hotel management associations
- Member's/president/secretary of the Travel and tourism associations
- Representative from hotel employees associations
- One member representative from international hotel chain.

The committee should review the present situation and suggest the steps to be taken to reduce the gap between the demand and supply of human resources in the industry.

The committee should concentrate on the following issues mainly:

- Create a policy on Industry institute interaction
- Establish an apex body to coordinate all the hospitality management institutes in the country
- For conducting Common entrance test for all Govt.

University/AICTE/Private Institutes in the Country

- Curriculum development from time to time as per industry requirement
- Fees structure for different courses in different institutes
- Appoint a committee to identify the requirements of qualified manpower for International Hotels and also identify the ways to develop.

Recommendations to Hospitality Industry

- *Tie-ups with Institutes:* It is the duty of the Industry to make necessary tie-up/arrangement for their required human resources with one or two hospitality institutes in the country.
- *Continuous Training:* There is a need of continuous training to all categories of employees in the organization. When they have a tie-up with the institutes, the institutes will offer in –house training to different category of employees from time to time to update their skills.
- *Sponsoring:* It is the duty of the industry to sponsor some amount/equipment to the institute for their betterment. If possible they sponsor a chair for continuous funding and research for that institute.
- *Research:* Every institute should spend some amount for the research which is essential for further development and understand the present situation. The industry should involve in the researchers by providing timely information and data which is ultimately useful for them only.

Recommendations to Hospitality Institutes (Academic)

- Industry institute interface/interaction: Every institute must make necessary tie-ups with hotel/tourism industry for providing employment to their students.
- Arranging guest lectures from industry: The management of the institutes must arrange guest lectures/visiting faculty from the industry to give complete industry information to the students about the industry and its developments.
- Visits to hotels (students): The institutes should arrange field visits and training in star hotels for their final year students.
- Nominating the industry people: Every institute must nominate one or two people from industry in their advisory body for the betterment of students.
- Revise the curriculum: It is the duty of the institute to revise the curriculum as per the industry needs from time to time.
- Pay good salaries to trained staff: Several educational institutions are offering very low salaries to their teaching staff, this influence the quality of teaching and there by it produces inferior quality managers which indirectly created unemployment though there is a demand in the industry.

The need to develop the required human resources in various segments of the tourism industry has become imperative as a consequence of the rapid growth in tourism, technology and dynamic changes in the international tourism market. The shortage of quality human resources can be solved when the government and private go together with a standard education & training system and better working conditions.

Quality Management for Laundry Services

The changes impacting the health care industry have opened up significant opportunities for the suppliers/reprocessors of reusable textiles. These include products that play an active role in patient care/healing, protective apparel for patients and staff, reusable products that can reduce costs over disposables and products that are environmentally friendly. In order to compete with other laundry operations or expand these products and services, it is essential that a formalized quality system be in place.

Why do we need a Quality Assurance Program for the Laundry?

To begin with, if anyone believes that quality systems will offer immediate benefits, more than likely they will be disappointed. Quality systems do not usually offer immediate paybacks, but rather benefits for the longer term. The benefits of a good quality system for reusable textiles include:

1. Ensuring the best possible patient care.
2. Ensuring a safe working environment.
3. Ensuring a cost-effective reusable textile program.

More than 100 million Americans are covered by managed care, and these numbers are growing by 10% a year. Ineffective products, procedures and even health care professionals are being purged from these systems. This change, by itself, requires that managers of laundry services become actively involved with outcome assessments for the products and services they offer. The cost of a reusable textile program is no longer limited to acquisition and processing. For certain products, cost assessment will include their role in patient care. Products that can deliver an outcome that prevents such health ailments as decubiti or that help speed up recovery times will be favorably evaluated and purchased.

In order to benefit from the opportunities presented by managed care and the focus on the outcomes of patient care, reusable textile programs must be able to quantify product performance and durability. Quality systems can offer facilities the means to monitor, track and ultimately communicate these issues to administration.

There are many components to a total quality system, but they generally include knowledge of current laundry practices, defining users' needs, performance reporting and end-user feedback. Each situation will be different and what one facility does is not necessarily appropriate for another. Below, I will outline some of the more common laundry quality practices and subsequently discuss how to decide what is appropriate and how to implement it.

We are all familiar with the terminology "garbage-in, garbage-out," and this concept is certainly applicable to laundry operations. Performance and durability of the textile inventory requires that the textiles, laundry chemicals and equipment are all designed and appropriate for the facility's needs. Programs for control of raw materials include:

Product Specifications

All products purchased (textiles, chemicals and equipment) should have written specifications so that there is no confusion about what is expected from your suppliers. This is critical, especially when there is a perceived problem and you are working with the suppliers to resolve your concerns.

Product Certification

For critical products, such as attire that protects against infection, it may be appropriate to have the vendor certify that the product has been tested and meets its predetermined specification. Usually product certification allows certain products to be put directly into service without internal verification. This usually necessitates a good history with that supplier as you are relying on their information as being accurate.

Vendor Certification

Larger operations may have a vendor certification program. In general, these programs outline a tiered approach for handling vendors. New vendors with no history or vendors with a less than desirable history have most, if not all, of their new products checked or evaluated prior to putting them into service. Vendors that have some history or only minor concerns may be put into the second tier with their products randomly checked. Finally, there is usually a class of vendors that has a good quality history and their products are checked only if a problem exists.

Product Testing

A means to check a product against its stated specifications should therefore be in place. For some textile products, this may be as easy as checking a size with a tape measure, but for others it may require the use of an outside laboratory to check strength, absorbency or barrier performance. For laundry chemicals, checking pH and colour is usually enough to verify that the product is what it should be.

Soiled Linen

Most facilities overlook soiled linen as a raw material that they have some ability to control. By handling soiled linen as soon as possible after use, every facility can benefit in reduced rewash rates and can usually use less aggressive laundry formulas, thereby extending the life of their textile inventory.

Microprocessor Program Verification

It is critical that the laundry cycle is actually doing what you expect it to be doing. Because these electronics can be affected by power surges or human error, these programs should be periodically checked.

Chemical Titrations

Usually the chemical supplier performs and reports the activity of the laundry chemicals within the cycle. It is important that staff be trained and periodically perform titrations to not only double-check the chemical supplier's results, but also to generate this information on a more frequent basis.

Chemical Delivery Rates

Checking to ensure that all chemical pumps are operating correctly is important and can be done in conjunction with chemical titrations to verify that, over time, chemicals are being used appropriately.

Equipment PM/Repair Program

This helps ensure that the equipment is operating at peak efficiency and reduces down-times.

Calibration

Most laundry operations rely on temperature monitors for washers/dryers and scales for load size. Because of the critical nature of these items, they should be periodically calibrated to ensure their accuracy.

Performance Test Swatches

Several companies offer performance test swatches that are able to quantify the level of soil removal, degree of whiteness, tensile strength loss, pH and residual chlorine. Some laundries run them on a periodic basis, but swatches also find use in comparing the performance of different chemical companies or formulas.

End-Product Testing

Some end-product testing may be done on a fairly regular basis or if a perceived problem exists. Usually pH and residual chlorine indicators can be used on textiles to check on and prevent durability problems from chemical damage. These can also be used to ensure compatibility of these products with human skin.

Production Records

Weekly production reports should indicate the type and amount of products that have been processed through the system. Weekly reports should be trended periodically-monthly, quarterly and/or yearly. Usually these reports are related back to laundry costs and patient days so that cost per pound or total cost per patient day can be assessed over time.

Shortage Reports

Tracking the delivery of products against what is expected is important. If there is one area that the staff and end-users will notice and be critical about, it is not receiving products when they're expected.

Rewash Rates

Rewash rates are a very good barometer of the system. Consistent rewash rates over time generally indicate that handling of the soiled linen and operation of the wash cycle are all under control.

Discard Report

Periodically, a review of the discards should be done to classify what product has been removed from the system and why. This can help identify problem areas that prevent a facility from getting the expected use-life from a product.

Complaint Records

A formal complaint procedure can ensure that complaints are controlled and resolved in a timely manner. It can also give an indication of problems in the system. However, it is important to emphasize that the goal of a quality system should be to prevent problems from being experienced by end-users in the first place.

Linen Replacements

Tracking linen replacements can give you an indication of the relative durability and textile costs per category.

The type and frequency of quality control programs will vary, depending on the user needs, production volume, product mix and history of the laundry's performance.

Over the years, numerous quality management programs have been described pertaining to laundry management. The one common denominator seems to be empowering the staff to take an active role in not only the day-to-day operations but also the design and direction of the reusable textile program. This makes sense from the standpoint that the individuals who work with the program on a daily basis, whether as soil sorters, equipment operators, delivery personnel and/or end-users, are probably the most knowledgeable individuals regarding their specific function. In addition, employees who are involved with making decisions are much more likely to "take ownership" and follow through on what is needed. A linen task force/committee charged with the quality, performance and cost is the best place to start. A good initial step for the group is to survey the end-users of the products and services to determine whether they meet/exceed their expectations and where there are areas for improvement. This group should have a clear mission statement and develop specific goals.

Initially, these goals could be as simple as development of a policy and procedure manual, but eventually this committee would take a more proactive stance and interface directly with nursing and patient care needs. They would be charged with answering such questions as:

1) Are there other opportunities to replace disposable items with reusables?
2) Are there new technologies or products that can improve patient care and rehabilitation time? and
3) Is there a better way to utilize textiles in patient care areas?

It will be the ability of laundry operations to quantify their value through such formalized quality systems that will enable them to be successful and grow. This is what is being expected by managed care. Laundry professionals serving these customers must realize how their products and services ultimately affect the outcome of patient care, and how cost-effectively they do so.

Finding Savings in Laundry Operations

As the reimbursement noose tightens, many healthcare financial managers are faced with the need to cut costs within their organizations. Often the most immediately apparent way to cut costs is through service cutbacks and/or staff reductions. Many times the potential savings to be found in routine facility operations such as linen service are totally overlooked. Although expenditures for such operations may not comprise a large percentage of the total budget, the dollar amounts can be significant.

The Elements of Total Cost

The total cost of linen service is the sum of four cost elements: processing cost, replacement cost, level of consumption, and cost of delivery and collection. The processing cost and the replacement cost (usually measured on a cost-per-pound basis) often receive the most attention. Examining only these two cost elements, however, will not provide an accurate picture of real costs. The actual cost of service should be measured on a total dollar-cost or cost-per-patient-day basis, since it is materially influenced by the level of consumption, as well as the cost of delivery and collection. The level of consumption factor of operation can be misleading. A higher level of consumption will result in a lower cost-per-pound if poundage and cost-per-pound have become the only measurement of a facility's linen service operation. The astute financial manager will look beyond cost-per-pound to cost-per-patient-day.

The cost of delivery and collection also can be a misleading indicator if not considered in relation to the other costs. In some on-premise laundries, the responsibility for delivery and collection of linen is assigned to the housekeeping or materials management departments; associated expense does not appear as part of the cost of linen service. Some hospitals contract to have their linen washed on a "wash-job" basis and are quite satisfied with the low processing cost they have negotiated. In these instances, they must add to that low cost of service the costs associated with mending, marking, replacing, purchasing, preparing user area deliveries, distributing, collecting, and warehousing linen.

Laundry Management: The Soft Water Advantage

Whether you're operating a nursing home, a restaurant or other commercial establishment, equipment costs represent a sizable part of overall expenses. In the case of nursing home laundry operations, equipment purchases and maintenance, as well as the cost of the chemicals used, can have a tremendous impact on overall profitability. One of the key factors affecting these costs is the quality of the water being supplied to the nursing home.

Hard water, defined as water containing calcium and magnesium, is found in most water supplies, whether the water originates from a private source or municipality. Hardness levels can vary dramatically and have varying effects on laundry equipment. Hard water, if left untreated, will cause scale damage to laundry equipment by forming lime curd buildup on moving parts. All parts that operate in hard water are subject to corrosion or calcium fouling that will shorten the life of the equipment and increase overall operating costs.

To avoid these problems, many commercial establishments condition their water with an ion-exchange water softener. Even leading manufacturers of laundry equipment often recommend the use of soft water vs. hard water for optimum performance of their equipment. Softened water not only increases the efficiency of laundry equipment, but also enhances the cleaning action of detergents, decreases the amount of detergent needed and might eliminate the need for fabric softeners. Industry experts estimate that chemical costs can be reduced by 20 to 35% when soft water is used, adding up to a tremendous savings over just a two-year period.

In addition, laundry will actually look better and last longer if not subjected to repeated hard water washings. Clothes and linens cannot be thoroughly cleaned because hard water minerals interfere with the cleaning action. In fact, they can actually cause whites to yellow or gray over time. The combination of calcium carbonate and detergent that is deposited on laundry causes scale buildup and colour deterioration. It can also shorten the life of the laundered product by breaking down the material's fibres, causing a premature replacement of linens, bedspreads, towels, washcloths, nightgowns and lab coats. A study conducted at Purdue University concluded that the life of clothing and household textiles was prolonged up to 15% when washed in conditioned water.

So, what are the facility's options in accomplishing this?

Most nursing homes have two separate water sources plumbed into the laundry, one for hot water and one for cold water. Ideally, all water supplied throughout the nursing home should be conditioned in order to deliver noticeable benefits in the kitchen, individual bathrooms, the laundry room and the plumbing that runs throughout the units. If the current water supply has a very high hardness level and also contains manganese and iron, the benefits of conditioning all the water are especially noticeable.

For budget reasons, however, nursing homes that don't experience this kind of problem water could choose to just soften the hot water supply. There are several good reasons for this. Both hot water tanks and boilers are subject to scale buildup. When water is heated, it accelerates the precipitation of calcium carbonate, which is colourless in water.

When heated, however, calcium carbonate becomes a white or crystalline compound, CaC[O.sup.3]. This, in turn, will scale all hot water distribution lines, as well as equipment, eventually affecting water flow and overall operating efficiency. In addition, calcium carbonate acts as an insulator that interferes with heat transfer, resulting in poor heat distribution and higher heating bills.

Table: Water Quality Association Hardness Classification Chart

Term	Grains/Gallon
Soft Water	Less than 1.0
Moderately Hard Water	1.0-3.5
Hard Water	3.5-7.0
Very Hard Water	7.0-10.5
Extremely Hard Water	Over 10.5

Considering all the problems caused by hard water, it is easy to see why soft water is essential for all hot water supplies. However, even if tighter budgets do not allow for soft water to be supplied throughout the nursing home, a return on investment (ROI) analysis will usually indicate that in addition to softening the hot water, at least the dedicated cold water line to the laundry should also be conditioned.

Before choosing a water conditioner, however, be certain to have your water tested by a water-quality professional to determine its level of hardness and whether or not other minerals (e.g., iron, manganese, etc.) are present. Only in this way can you ensure that the system you select is perfectly matched to your specific water-quality conditions.

Second, ask about third-party certification. Many systems on the market today are certified by outside companies, such as NSF International. This unbiased certification ensures that the system will perform according to the manufacturer's claims.

Third, investigate the reliability of the system. Only twin-tank conditioners can guarantee the delivery of soft water 24 hours a day, since one tank continues service while the other regenerates (cleans itself). Also, according to leading consumer-rating publications, water conditioners with timers and electrical components are less reliable, since they're subject to power outages and electrical part repairs.

Finally, take the time to investigate the history and reputation of the manufacturer. The bottom line is that it should produce a quality water conditioner that lasts as long (if not longer) than your laundry equipment.

Operational Efficiency: Possibilities in an Institutional Laundry

Brijesh Rathore takes a look at the various parameters involved in the operational efficiency of an institutional laundry, their impact on the overall cost and how to keep the same under control

Brijesh Rathore

Operational efficiency means optimal results at minimum overall cost. Let us understand, what constitutes the total cost in a laundry. The total cost in laundry operations is a combination of utility cost (steam/water/electricity), labour (time), chemical, linen replacement/textile, depreciation, maintenance and transportation (applicable in case of a commercial laundry).

Energy

Impact of energy on the overall cost is approximately eight per cent.

How to control energy cost: Optimise wash times. Main wash after reaching the desired temperature should not exceed beyond 12 minutes. Energy (heat) used in the washing machine is 1/3rd of the energy (heat) used in the dryer/calendar. Optimise tumble-drying time and temperature. Also to achieve energy efficiency, optimise vacuum and speed of the calendar. Clean lint from the dryer at regular intervals to provide clear airflow. Excess lint deposition is also a fire hazard.

Labour; Impact of labour (Time) on the overall cost is approximately 37 per cent.

How to control labour (time) cost: *Check* the wash process of the different linen categories in the laundry. One process for all is waste of time, energy, chemicals, and leads to high maintenance cost of the machine.

How much time is required to fill the machine with water and heat up to required temperature. A narrow fill line and poor water/steam pressure can lead to unnecessary waste of time.

Check if the mixed/hot water fill line is used when high temperature is required. This will cut down the time required to raise the temperature of the water to the desired level.

Check if the optimum time/temperature combination is used in the dryer and the calendar.

Do we load the machine optimally? Underloading of the machine will lead to excess mechanical action and overloading will lead to poor soil removal and mechanical damage.

How the people in the various shifts are used? How are they trained to do various jobs? Are they trained to handle different jobs at the work place? How are they being monitored?

Textile

Impact of Textile on the overall cost is approximately 32 per cent.

How to control textile cost: Is the laundry buying right type of textile?

Does laundry analyse textile before purchase? Does laundry have COA (certificate of analysis) of tensile strength/lifetime of textile? Get specification of the linen being purchased.

Is the right wash process being used, especially the bleaching process? Ensure that bleach is being used at the right pH, temperature, concentration and for the right time. Any of the above parameters going wrong will lead to irreversible fabric damage. Is the water and steam being used is free from iron? High iron content (> 0.1ppm) will cause yellowing of linen and iron particle deposition (from the steam lines) in the presence of chlorine bleach will lead to pin holes.

***Linen replacement cost*:** Maintain current accurate records and conduct physical inventory of the linen at least twice a year. Management knows exactly what linen is needed to maintain service par, when the new linen should be inserted into service, and above all where critical losses are being incurred. Accurate linen replacement cost is calculated in following manner: Linen at last inventory + New linen inserted into service = Total linen. Total linen-present inventory = Linen replacement cost.

Depreciation

Impact of depreciation on the overall laundry cost is approximately 13 per cent.

***How to improve machine life*:** Maintain the machine in the top running condition at all times. Machine should not have any leaking problems or soil deposition.

Keep stock of critical machine spares to prevent high downtime.

Maintain the proper preventive maintenance schedule of the machine. Staff should be trained to report any machine failure.

Chemical

Impact of chemical on the overall laundry cost is approximately six per cent.

How to control chemical cost; *Always* use formulated detergents in the laundry. Good quality formulated detergents along with right wash program play the most important role in reducing the overall laundry operational cost.

Good formulated detergent should consist of the following:

Alkali: It helps in maintaining the pH of the wash bath, neutralises the acidic soil, helps in faster removal of the soil (swelling of the fibre).

Surfactants: Surfactants acts as wetting agents and also help in the removal of fatty soil.

Sequestrants: Builders or sequestrants help in binding heavy metal and hard water ions in the wash bath and do not allow their precipitation onto the fabric.

Optical brighteners: Make the linen appear brighter than it "actually" is. It absorbs the UV rays and re transmits it into the visible spectrum.

Anti redepositing agents: They give overall negative charge to the fibre and thus prevents deposition of the negatively charged soil onto the fabric. Use of a good neutraliser will help in saving water and will give the desired 5.5 to 6.5 pH. It will also control minerals in the final rinse preventing encrustation and controlling iron.

So, we have seen how following the correct procedures at each step of the linen flow can control various cost parameters in laundry operations. This not only ensures a long linen lifetime but also optimum utilisation of resources at disposal.

Women Development Programme

Against the background of the patriarchal system of society, the women need special attention to ensure their development and participation in the decision making process at home, in the community and governance.

With the objective of bringing about economic and social development of women and improving their status in the community the programme for Women Development was being implemented by CSR in and around Tiruchendur of Tuticorin district and Thovalai blocks of Kanyakumari District.

The various activities planned and carried out are:

- Formation and Training of Self Help Groups
- Group Development
- Capacity Building
- Income Generation Activities
- Credit and Savings Mobilisation
- Establishment of linkages.

These activities had made impressive impacts in empowering women and improving their economic and social status in their families and communities.

Education and Empowerment of Rural Women

Assistance : The project is implemented with the financial assistance of PWDS, EED.

Objective : To strengthen the socioeconomic and educational status of the weaker sections and to empower women and pave way for the wholistic development of rural people in a sustained manner.

Target area : Tiruchendur, Udankudi and Alwarthirunegari blocks of Tuticorin District.

Focus on : Rural artisans, marginalised women and palmyra tapers

Activities

The various activities implemented were:

- Formation of Self Help Groups
- Income Generation Activities
- Credit And Savings Mobilization
- Establishment of Credit Linkages
- Entrepreneur Development Programme Trainings
- Establishment of Manufacturing Units
- Promotion of Kitchen Herbal Garden
- Promotion of Federation.

The thrust of the programme is organising women and federating them at different level to enhance their social status. Due to the entrepreneur development skills promoted, the women took up various income generating activities as individuals and as a group such as mat weaving, dairy farms, palm crystal candy making, flour rice, fancy shops, petty shops, soap manufacturing, textile business and paper cup. So far 58 groups are involved in income generating activities and 3173 individuals have taken up income generating programmes.

The federation of women SHGs called 'Sangamam' was formed by the members themselves based on their own experience and the exposure they received. It decided to start a supermarket and a building was constructed. As a share of Rs.10,000 was collected from each SHGs by the federation. All the SHG members buy the provisionary items from their own Sangamam store and steps are taken to distribute the items at their door steps through vans. The federation has assumed maximum responsibilities and there is ample scope that soon it will become fully self sustaining entity.

Tips on Accommodations

One of the best developments in the past decade has been the increase in luxury boutique-type options offering international standards of service and comfort and flavored with Indian accents — like beautiful craftsmanship and ancient traditions (we're talking Ayurvedic masseurs on tap) — which means that the subcontinent is now a very desirable destination for the visitor wanting relaxation and pampering. To find the most unusual independent hotels, guesthouses, and homestays, an excellent resource for those who don't want the classic resort or chain hotel experience is Alastair Sawday's *Special Places to Stay: India*. Though the properties listed pay to be reviewed, they are all, almost without exception, special in some way; the best are included in this guide (plus many more that cannot afford or choose not to pay for publicity).

Of course we all knew India had "arrived" when the ultraluxe Amanresorts entered the fray with Amanbagh, arguably the finest resort-style property in India, but the pace was first set by the Vilas properties, owned by India's very own, very fabulous Oberoi chain.

Besides the Vilas properties (the best of which is Amarvilas in Agra, though some rate Udaivilas in Udaipur as their top choice), Oberoi runs some of the very best city hotels, as well as several spa resorts in key tourist destinations and a luxury backwater cruiser in Kerala. You will pay top dollar, but you can generally count on superb service and attention to detail. Best of all, you can often get great discounts on room rates by reserving in advance over the Internet. Note that Oberoi also operates a tier of smaller, less opulent hotels under the Trident Hilton banner, aimed principally at business or family travellers.

India's other famous hotel chain is the Taj Group, with an enormous inventory of properties, particularly in South India, where Oberoi is largely absent. Quality varies somewhat (and service does not match that of the Oberoi group), but comfort is generally guaranteed, particularly in big cities and resort destinations — the best properties are the Taj Mahal in Mumbai, Rambagh Palace in Jaipur, Lake Palace Hotel in Udaipur, and Umaid Bhawan Palace in Jodhpur.

Safari experiences are also set to change forever since the Taj group launched Taj Safaris, teaming up with acclaimed South African conservation group CC Africa. Their first luxury safari lodge, Mahua Kothi, at the Bandavgarh tiger reserve in Madhya Pradesh, is a sublime, sexy property with some of the country's best guides. They already have two more lodges in Madhya Pradech— at Kanha and Pench — and are planning dozens more in the next few years. Meanwhile, Amanresorts' tented lodge at Ranthambhore, Aman-i-Khas, is superlative.

Homestays

All over Kerala (and a few other places), people are converting rooms of their homes into guest rooms for tourists to rent, at incredibly reasonable prices. Guests share the public spaces with the family, which lives in the home, and often dine with them. Many of these homestays are gorgeous heritage homes and their owners extremely hospitable. It's a good way to interact with an Indian family and get a taste of local culture and cuisine. But don't expect room service and the kinds of amenities you get at a full-service hotel.

Heritage Hotels

Staying in a medieval palace or fort is a unique and wonderful option among India's accommodations (particularly in Rajasthan), especially when your host is the aristocrat whose forebears built the palace or fort in which you're overnighting; the best are discussed in detail in relevant sections throughout this guide. Many were built centuries ago, so it's not surprising that heritage hotels are seldom the most luxurious option, with the possibilities of many stairs, dodgy plumbing, low ceilings, strange room layouts, and other eccentricities. Acting principally as marketing agencies for privately owned palaces, forts, and *havelis* (Indian mansions).

Tip: Be aware that any hovel will attach "palace" to its name in the hopes of attracting more customers. This is often amusing if you're walking past, but can be disastrous if you're checking in.

City Hotels

The biggest problem in big cities and popular tourist areas is that the good hotels are often priced way out of reach, while moderate options are thin on the ground. Mid-range hotels are substandard by Western standards, though considerably cheaper. Wherever possible, we've provided budget options that are scrupulously clean and moderately comfortable. A new chain of budget hotels is called Ginger (tel. 800/22-0022 or 022/66014-634. Launched by Indian Hotels (owners of the Taj group) and catering specially to the middling business market, these 101-room "Smart Basics" hotels offer accommodations priced at under Rs. 1,500 ($22/£19) for a double. They won't have any of the opulence of the Taj hotels; in fact, rooms are small and rather plain in design, albeit comfortable and with all the amenities, including an ATM in the hotel. Eight Ginger hotels have already opened (Bangalore, Bhubaneswar, Durgapur, Haridwar, Mysore, Nashik, Pune, and Thiruvananthapuram), and another 17 are promised by the end of 2008.

Most of the top-of-the-range city hotels are operated by major international chains, including many of the usual suspects: Sheraton, Hyatt, Radisson, Le Meridien, Shangri-La, and Marriott.

The Rating System

India's hotel rating system refers to size and facilities on offer, not the potential quality of your stay. Often the best hotels have no rating because they are heritage properties and — despite their overwhelming loveliness — don't conform to the norms laid down by India's tourism department.

Tip: One hotel chain to avoid is the so-called "five-star deluxe" government-operated Ashok group. Most of its properties have "five-star facilities" and an inventory of hundreds of rooms, but they are often decaying concrete blocks with disinterested staff. In fact, as a general rule of thumb, government-run properties are best avoided throughout the country.

Bargaining

In India, even hotel rates are up for a bit of hard-core bargaining. If you're thin-skinned, bargain online (many hotels offer Internet-only discounts); alternatively, show up and stay tough — when you hear the rate quoted, brazenly pretend to walk out; there's no shame in India in turning back and accepting the rate. You'll also be surprised to find that luxury hotels in cities can often be had at mid-range prices, simply because room occupancy is low. Always ask about daily specials, and call and check prices at hotels that may appear out of your reach because of high rack rates — you may actually get a room there for a song. In remote areas, small towns and villages, and many places in Goa and the Himalayan foothills, you can find good (basic but clean) budget accommodations at unbelievable prices. The same cannot generally be said of the major cities, where a cheap, dingy hotel may expose you to bedbugs and despair; stick to the budget recommendations in this guide.

Note: Prices in a number of the hotel listings are stated in U.S. dollars or, increasingly, in euros — this is, in fact, the way hotels targeting foreign markets quote their rates.

Tip: All over India, floors are marked and understood differently from many in the U.S. First floor is the floor above the ground level, second floor is the floor above that, and so on. The ground floor or lobby level is just that.

Of Hotels & Taxes

Almost every hotel in India will quote a rate to which an additional luxury tax is added; this varies from state to state. This tax applies to all luxury hotels, or the moment the room price goes above a certain level (which depends on the state, and sometimes the city). Restaurant and hotel bills get a different tax, and alcohol and other luxuries get a different set of taxes all together. Some states such as Tamil Nadu add an astronomical 73.5% tax to imported liquor; as a rule, locally produced alcohol is taxed less than foreign imports. *Always* check whether the tax has been included in the rate you've been quoted and, if it hasn't, exactly how much it is.

Surfing for Hotels

In addition to the online travel booking sites Travelocity, Expedia, Orbitz, Priceline, and Hotwire, you can book hotels through Hotels.com; Quikbook; and Travelaxe.

Most of the budget or moderate hotel recommendations do not have websites, and many hotel websites are poorly maintained, which means you may come across tariffs and information dating as far back as the previous decade. Smaller hotels change e-mail service providers almost as often as they change sheets. For basic information on about 3,000 listed hotels in India, the website for the Federation of Hotel and Restaurant Associations of India can be a useful if undiscriminating resource. You'll also come up against a plethora of accommodations booking services that presume to be direct representatives of the hotel you're searching for, but that actually hike up the lowest available tariff considerably, which may leave you feeling ripped off before you even bed down. Always compare the website rate with the cheapest rate offered directly by the hotel before making a reservation. On the upside, several hotel networks offer unbelievable Internet discounts that simply can't be ignored.

For Kerala and Goa, *Hip Hotels in Kerala/Goa* gives detailed reviews of Kerala's stylish small hotels and retreats and some interesting rooms to book in Goa.

Landing the Best Room

Somebody has to get the best room in the house; it might as well be you. First, make sure your room has air-conditioning. Ask for a room with split air-conditioning (an air-conditioner with a separate indoor and outdoor unit); it's far less noisy — and ugly — than a window air-conditioner. If it doesn't, ask whether there is a ceiling fan or a water-cooling system. Be sure to request your choice of twin, queen-or king-size beds. Ask for rooms with views (many hotel staff don't understand this concept in India, so it's best to look around on arrival), showers or tubs (tubs in medium or budget category are usually old and stained, so don't shy away from shower-only options), and bed size. Ask for one of the most recently renovated or redecorated rooms — bathrooms in particular seem to suffer heavy wear and tear in India.

Tip: Indians often use the term "hotel" to refer to a restaurant or eating place, so don't be surprised if someone suggests you eat at a hotel down the road, and you arrive there to find a five-table shack.

4

Human Resources in Tourism Sector

Overview and Objectives

Tourism sector industries generate a large number of highly diversified jobs in different branches of activities such as hotels, restaurants, travel agencies, tour operators, leisure activities and passenger transport. Human resources are a key element in ensuring the quality and content of tourism products. There is a growing need for skilled manpower able to meet the needs of a changing environment and to maintain the competitiveness of tourism enterprises. In a competitive labour market, the tourism sector suffers from a relatively poor image and finds it difficult to retain employees on a longterm basis. In the light of these changes and challenges, strategies for managing and promoting human resources have a central role to play in a sustainable development approach to tourism. The understanding of labour markets in the tourism sector remains inadequate.

The effects of the new practices introduced by certain governments and the industry to improve skills and enhance the competitiveness of the sector in the labour market have not been widely shared and assessed. The pursuit of strategies to promote the skills needed in a globalizing tourism industry must be continued. Lastly, in a context of liberalisation and globalization of tourism services, the possibility of harmonising the differing regulatory approaches to the labour market in the tourism sector should be discussed in depth with all actors on national and international labour markets. The conference on "Partnership in Vietnam's tourism human resources development" was the second annual conference held by the Vietnam Human Resources Development in Tourism Project at the Furama Resort, Danang.

The conference on "Partnership in Vietnam's tourism human resources development" was the second annual conference held by the Vietnam Human Resources Development in Tourism Project at the Furama Resort, Danang. It took place on 30th November 2006 and followed the conference on "Vietnam tourism human resources development and regional integration", held in Hanoi during December 2005.

Among the 150 participants (international and local) were representatives from Vietnam National Administration of Tourism, the National Steering Committee for Tourism, representatives from ministries, the Delegation of the European Commission to Vietnam, the Secretariat and National Tourism Organisations of ASEAN, provincial tourism departments, representatives from hotel and travel enterprises, tourism training institutions, etc. By attending the conference, regional tourism representatives viewed the activities of Vietnam's tourism human resources development at first hand, and Vietnam's tourism administrators and experts gained further insights into regional practice.

After the introduction by Mr. Jozef W.M. van Doorn, the Co-Director of the Project, presenting the Project's outputs to date, Mr. Jaap Funnekotter, Chairman of the conference, reviewed outcomes from last year's conference. Conference 2006 followed the same format as last year's edition in order to create continuity, so speakers from both public and private sectors presented their experience of partnership in tourism human resources development.

After the presentations, there was a panel discussion on the topic: "Has any synergy between the educational institutes and the hotel and tourism enterprises taken place in the last year?" along with some further discussion of best practices.

Attending the Gala Dinner, participants were introduced to a training DVD on housekeeping according to the Vietnam Tourism Occupational Skill standards (VTOS). This is one of 14 videos that will be developed by the Project as support for training. It is designed to be used in conjunction with the Project's Trainer Development Programme training manuals, or for entry-level staff training within enterprises.

The second day of the conference was spent on a field trip to My Son and Hoi An, two of the World Cultural Heritage sites.

UNWTO Summit Discusses New Reforms for Human Resources in Tourism

According to the January 2009 issue of the UNWTO World Tourism Barometer, in 2008, international tourist arrivals worldwide increased by 2%. The Middle East registered the best performance among all world regions with 11% growth in international tourist arrivals in 2008 over the previous year. Based on passenger traffic data from worldwide airports for the first two months of 2009, it appears that of all the world regions, the Middle East is the least affected the global crisis thus far. It was the only region with a positive traffic growth of 3.1%.

The Summit has demonstrated the complexity of labour markets in the region and constantly returned to the fact that the rapid growth of tourism in the region brings with it issues of labour supply gaps and skills shortage. The Qatar Summit identified a range of human resource challenges for tourism.

Tourism employment comes in the shape of a broad spectrum of roles and varied tasks, across all sectors benefiting in particular women, the young and the unemployed. Tourism is well known as a generator of employment, so a well-trained tourism labour force will both anticipate and remedy such economic crisis.

Longer-term challenges include the poor image and lack of understanding of tourism jobs, and the fact that availability of labour and skills is highly variable across the region.

The Summit addressed these issues into four key pillars of reform:

The first one is the need to change the mindset of both governments and communities towards employment in tourism, as well as the need for the industry to change its view of human resources to one that values peoples, their skills and knowledge, develops them and treats them as valued resources.

The second pillar means the necessary understanding of labour markets. With the Tourism Satellite Account (TSA) methodology, it is now easier to understand and measure labour markets, diagnose the problems and act. Governments will be able to plan for future labour and training needs.

Re-engineering education and training, the third pillar of reform, will demand national standard setting in partnership with industry and the development of articulated and legible pathways to allow students to gain qualifications, and ensuring that programmes are creatively packaged, innovative and utilize edge technology for lifelong learning.

The final pillar of reform relates to the work and leadership of both the UNWTO and Qatar in addressing these challenges and engaging stakeholders to craft new strategies. The solutions demand the forging of effective partnerships and working together to implement the recommendations of the Summit, as well as the findings of the Bali conference and the ILO's Decent Work Agenda.

> Professor Chris Cooper, summit moderator, commented: *"The message of this summit is clear-tourism is a people-centred industry, the sector must invest in the education, training and development of the labour force to secure the future." Alongside the Qatar Summit, the 32nd meeting of the United Nations World Tourism Organisation commission for the Middle East took place on April 22nd and 23rd.*

Dr. Taleb Rifai, Secretary General of the UNWTO, presented to the members of the Commission a snapshot analysis of the current economic downturn's impact on tourism in the Middle East and North Africa. Country briefs and response measures were also discussed in a regional perspective. The Secretary General presented the research programme: "Tourism towards 2030", as well as regional training programmes and possible adjustments in the light of the global economic downturn. This meeting of the UNWTO commission for the Middle East reviewed the preparations for the eighteenth session of the General Assembly of UNWTO, that will take place in October 2009.

On the occasion of the conclusive press conference, Mr. Ahmed Al Nuaimi, Chairman of Qatar Tourism and Exhibitions Authority, declared, "I am really pleased Qatar Tourism and Exhibitions Authority hosted this UNWTO conference. With 250 participants, we shared different experiences and had very fruitful discussions that enabled us to create a roadmap with four pillars of reform. Tourism is a key economic pillar and we need to ensure the future of the region."

Tourism Human Resources in Shortage, Weak

Weakness in Foreign Languages

According to statistics of the Vietnam National Administration of Tourism (VNAT), the total number of workers in the tourism sector is around 850,000 at present, including 250,000 workers who directly serve tourists. However, only around 50% of them are trained.

The tourism sector needs an additional around 35,000 trained workers each year but training centres can provide only about one-third of the volume.

Besides weakness in terms of professional knowledge and skills, the largest disadvantage of Vietnamese tourism workers is foreign languages. Besides English, the major foreign language, Vietnamese tourism workers are also weak in other languages like Japanese, Chinese and Korean.

Specifically, the number of Korean travellers coming to Vietnam is increasing fast (ranking second after Chinese) but Vietnam currently has only 50 tour guides who can speak Korean. For the Japanese market, the third potential market of Vietnam, just 8% of tour guides speaking Japanese can fluently speak this language.

English: Below Standards

As part of a programme to raise the quality of the tourism human resources of Vietnam, the Test of English for International Communication (TOEIC) Vietnam has currently made a survey to test the English ability of some occupations in the tourism sector.

Based on the need of using English in each position, TOEIC Vietnam performed nearly 400 surveys of the need for English skills of nearly 200 hotels of three-to five-star standard and travel agents throughout the country. The major subjects of those surveys are directors, human resource managers and direct managers like team leaders who clearly understand the need for English of their staffs.

Random surveys of 1,000 workers at tourism companies reveal that the English skills of most of them are low and below the standards required by their employers. The survey also points out that hotels of higher standard have high percentages of staffs that don't meet standards in English.

According to Doan Hong Nam, director of the TOEIC Vietnam, the standards that we apply to evaluate the English skills of tourism workers is to ensure the minimum quality of service so the survey results show that the English skills of surveyed tourism workers is even lower than the low standards.

This is not only a hindrance for the development of the tourism sector but others as more and more foreign tourists are coming to Vietnam to seek business opportunities. Mr. Nam said that Vietnam needed to quickly improve the quality of the current tourism services by issuing common standards for foreign languages for each position in the tourism sector. This is a necessary foundation for the training tasks of training centres and tourism firms.

Philippines: DoT holds 1st Tourism Human Resources Congress Today

In line with the Department of Tourism's (DoT) "Gandang Pilipinas, Galingng Pilipino" GP2 campaign which aims to further develop tourism services, DoT Secretary Roberto "Obet" M. Pagdanganan will lead the launch of the 1st Tourism Human Resources Congress today at The Peninsula Manila Hotel.

Pagdanganan said the activity, which will be held until tomorrow (June 18), will further enhance the industry's manpower resources enabling them to meet the international standard of tourism service.

"In order to cope with the global challenges in the tourism industry, we must arm ourselves with the changes in the international market. Quality services and products are fast becoming a norm in the new global economy. We must make precedence by introducing speed, innovation and customization," he added. The Tourism Industry Board Foundation, Inc. (TIBFI) organizer of the event, is a non-stock, nonprofit institution composed of representatives from the government (which include the DoT as founding member), private and labour sectors.

The foundation aims to provide manpower development, ensuring an adequate supply of trained workers who will match the skills of the labour force with the manpower requirements of the tourism industry. TIBFI invited distinguished guest speakers including World Tourism Organization (WTO) representative Professor Chris Cooper to talk about the TedQual Programs, which focuses on quality service assurance and the WTO products and services standard.

Human resources directors and heads of various tourism subsectors, associations, industries and government agencies (TESDA, CHED, Government Training Institutions), tour guides and the academe including state colleges and universities are invited to participate in the two-day assembly. Registration fee is R1,500.

Tourism Human Resources

The Tourism Industry

* Tourism is the largest earner of foreign exchange in Antigua & Barbuda.
* It is estimated to be the largest employer when all enterprises providing direct and indirect services to the sector are combined.

Tourism and The Labour Force

* Though there are no definitive statistics on the labour force involved in tourism in Antigua & Barbuda, a recently produced Antigua & Barbuda Tourism Strategic Plan (2005-2009) stated that surveys suggest that approximately 8,000 workers or 26% of the total labour force could be employed in the accommodation sector: hotels, guests houses, apts., villas, with other sectors of the industry creating a further 3,000 jobs.

* Therefore, the total number of workers employed in the tourism sector is 11,000 representing 40% of the total labour force.
* When compared to statistics which indicate that globally tourism accounts for 8.3% of the total work force, Antigua & Barbuda can clearly be considered one of the, if not the most tourism dependent countries in the world.

Tourism Human Resource Audit

- A tourism human resource audit should be conducted to give true and reliable data relating to the tourism work force.
- Such data must of necessity address the issues of:
  * male/female ratio.
  * age-group.
  * percentages employed in various sectors, for e.g. accommodation, F&B, yachting, adventure, etc.
  * education.
- It is important to note that the paucity of reliable data is a regional problem and unfortunately the experience of many economic sector areas, the tourist industry being no exception.
  * As recently as February 2006, CTO in recognition of this situation include the improvement of data collection as one of its Key Focus Areas.

Assessing Training and Education Needs

* In a 1998 study conducted by the CTO within its member countries, the focus was on assessing training and education needs for the tourist industry in the new millennium.
* The study was designed to provide data about the nature and level of skills deficiencies in the industry so as to inform Caribbean Governments and regional training agencies where their training priorities should lie and how their training $$ should be spent.

* It was intended that the study would provide a launching pad for tourism training in this millennium as well as to represent a benchmark for future studies.

* The information provided on HRD in the Caribbean region as a whole (through this study), is quite applicable to the Antigua & Barbuda situation.

Highlights of the Study

- Industry Profile:
  * Majority of the responding organizations were from the Accommodation sector, with F&B and Transportation sectors running a far second and third behind, respectively.
  * Events and Conferences and Attractions provided least number of respondents. Reflection of the level of development of these two sectors in the Region.
  * ¼ less than 5 yrs. Old/¼ over 20 yrs. Old
  * Majority of the work force permanent full-time staff with more males than females (56% to 44%). Over 70% under 40 yrs.
- Recruitment and Retention of Staff:
  * Local and regional tourism training institutions are not a preferred source of employees.
  * Most organizations recruit their staff from secondary/ primary schools and from university, depending on the level of staff.
  * Many also hire from their competitors or from among relatives and friends.
  * Generally, managerial and professional vacancies are difficult to fill.
  * Also difficult to recruit skilled/semiskilled persons in the accommodation, F&B and adventure sectors.
  * Unskilled positions generally easier to fill.
- Industry Training and Development.
  * Only 1/3 of the establishments in the survey had a full-time trainer on staff.

* Training done primarily in customer relations and technical skills.
* Of 1/3 of the respondents providing information on training budget, 2/3 spent less than US$5,000 for a year.
* On the job-training is the preferred training strategy for all levels of staff.
* External trainers and local tourism training institutions used but to a much lesser extent.
* Local and regional tourism training institutions are not perceived by the industry as important or effective in satisfying its training needs.

Training Needs Identified

- General and technical training deficiencies identified at different staff levels.
- General training needs:
  * Interpersonal skills deficiencies found at all staff level.
  * Marketing and management deficiencies at managerial level.
  * Computer literacy and foreign language deficiencies (also found).
- Technical training needs: these were linked to deficiencies within the various tourism sectors; accommodation, food & beverage, transportation, travel trade, adventure and tourism services.

Accommodation

Technical Skills:

* Culinary.
* Maintenance.
* Housekeeping.
* F & B Service e.g. Bartending, Waiting.
* Front Desk.
* Tour Guiding.

* Customer Service.
* Other, e.g. Safety & Security, Tourism Awareness, Computer.

Food & Beverage

Technical Skills:

* Culinary.
* Food & Beverage Services e.g. Bartending, Waiting.
* Customer Service.
* Other e.g. Inventory Control, Maintenance, Cashing, Sanitation.

Transportation

Technical Skills:

* Ticketing.
* Customer Service.
* Tour Guiding.
* Maintenance.
* Other e.g. Customer Procedures.

Travel Trade

Technical Skills.

* Ticketing.
* Tour Guiding.
* Other e.g. Customer Service, Maintenance, Computer, Marketing.

Adventure

Technical Skills.

* Tour Guiding.
* Watersports e.g. Boating, Sailing, Scuba Diving, Fishing.
* Maintenance.
* Culinary.
* Other e.g. Customer Service, Golf, Housekeeping, First Aid, Piloting, Food & Beverage Service.

Tourism Services

Technical Skills:

* Statistical Analysis.
* Property Management.
* Environmental Protection and Conservation.
* Public Relations.

Attractions

Technical Skills:

* Tour Guiding.
* Customer Service.
* Other e.g. Ticketing, Heritage Conservation/Preservation, Museum Management, wildlife Management, Environmental Protection, Marine Biology, Heritage Studies.

Meeting Technical Training Needs

The Antigua and Barbuda Hospitality Training Institute.

Antigua & Barbuda Hospitality Training Institute.

* Mission To provide training and education with a commitment to excellence; to equip persons to work in the Tourism and Hospitality Industry with a high degree of professionalism.

One Year Certificate Programme

* Food and Beverage Service.
* Training at Skills level.
* Basic Cookery.
* Knowledge & Skill in basic Cookery techniques.
* Housekeeping.
* Training at skills level.

2 Year Diploma Programme

- Culinary Arts.
  * In depth practical and supervisory level training.

- Reception and Sales.
  * Broad base training in Front Office Operations.
- Hospitality Management.
  * Knowledge and skill to embark on supervisory or junior management level.

Accreditation

- 2 Year Diploma Programmes.
  * Hospitality Management.
  * Culinary Arts.
- University of the West Indies.
- Monroe College.

In-House Training Courses

* Butchery Techniques.
* Caribbean Cuisine.
* Art and Science of Service.

Collaboration with Tourist Operators

- Federation of Tour Operators.
  * Food Hygiene & Safety Seminar.
- Antigua Hotels and Tourist Association.
  * Internship for students.
  * Membership on Board & Sub committees.
  * Partnership with Trans Caribbean Marketing & US meat Export Federation.

Regional Collaboration through Caribbean Tourism Organization

* Core Curriculum.
* Certified Hospitality Educator.
* Dynamic Supervisory Management Programme.
* Quality Assurance and Articulation.
* Human Resources Conference.
* Promotional material on careers in Tourism.

Sources of Funding

* Consolidated funds of Antigua & Barbuda Government.
* European Commission.
* Organization of American States.
* First Caribbean International Bank.

Annual Government Funding Allocation

* ABHTI Estimates 2006 $1.8 Mil 21%.
* ASC (Antigua State College) $5.7 Mil 65%.
* ABICE $1.2 Mil 14%.
* ABIIT unknown-
* Total $8.7 Mil 100% Revenue (2005) ABHTI $122,000 ASC $60,000.

Conclusion

* Tourism is a high-touch, high-tech, high-involvement industry where it is the people who make the difference.
* The ability for the industry to succeed and the future performance of the industry and related activities will depend largely on the skills, qualities and knowledge of its employees. Indeed the challenges facing the industry can only be met successfully by a welleducated, well-trained, bright, energetic, multilingual and entrepreneurial work force.
* A high-quality tourism work force can only be achieved through high standards of tourism education and training which in turn will impact our destination's ability (the ability of our twin-island state) to compete successfully in this global competitive industry.

Special Symposium on APU's Tourism Human Resource Development Project

A Special Symposium on APU's Tourism Human Resource Development Project titled, "Creating the Future of Regional Tourism-Fostering Talent for the Next Generation" was held at Beppu B-con Plaza on Friday, March 10. The Special Symposium was held for people who will have major roles in the future of the tourism and service industry including the accommodation sector.

APU's "Tourism Human Resource Development Project" was commissioned by the Ministry of Economy, Trade and Industry as part of its "AY2005 Power Supply Regional Service Human Resource Development Business." Mr. TOYODA Masakazu, Director-General of the Commerce and Information Policy Bureau of the Ministry of Economy, Trade and Industry Mr. TOYOTA Masakazu commenced the first-half of the Symposium with a keynote address on "Promoting the Hospitality Industry." Afterwards, the President of the All Japan Ryokan Association, Mr. Kohara Kenji gave a presentation on "Creating a Tourism-Orientation Nation."

A panel discussion on the theme of "Creating the Future of Tourism in Kyushu-Regions and Business/Developing Human Resources" took place in the second-half of the Symposium. The participants listened attentively to the animated exchange of ideas.

Human Resources in Tourism: Still Waiting for Change

People, we are frequently told, are a critical dimension within the successful delivery of tourism services. "The story of successful tourism enterprises is one that is largely about people—how they are recruited, how they are managed, how they are trained and educated, how they are valued and rewarded, and how they are supported through a process of continuous learning and career development" points to recognition of this philosophy in the mission statements of hotel companies within which a far higher proportion of respondents include reference to human resources than is the case within manufacturing companies.

This contemporary manta or reflection of the "'soft' rhetoric of people as an organisations's greatest asset" (Bolton & Houlihan, 2007) may have had equal veracity at various points during the development of tourism over the past century, but the practical implications of the claim, in terms of the role that people play, will have been interpreted in different ways at varying points over this timeframe.

In particular, there is an apparent paradox in the dramatic evolution of the global tourism sector over the past half century and, within it, the manner and conditions in which people deliver tourism services which have remained timeless in many respects but also subject to significant change.

During this time, debate about labour intensity, the number and cost of people required to work in many areas of tourism, has sat alongside discussion of the skills necessary to deliver quality tourism services, remuneration and working conditions and the role that technology plays in both supporting and changing this delivery.

Inevitably, the nature of such analysis has shifted over time. In particular, the profile of many workers, but by no means all of those in tourism's work force, and the role that they play in the labour markets of developed countries, has been subject to change. At the same time, tourism work must be set alongside major economic and labour market restructuring in post-industrial societies so that direct comparison between tourism and traditional heavy manufacturing work in shipyards, mines and steel works, which formed an important element of the early industrial sociology in the emerging service sectors, is less relevant.

Rather, tourism work now sits alongside and is compared to other activities within the dominant service economy of developed countries, and the analytical paradigm for such comparison should consider employment opportunities in the sector in a rather different light. Whether such comparison leads to a positive assessment of work in tourism is a matter that we shall consider in this paper.

In the light of external change, in developed countries, certain aspects of human resource management in tourism demonstrate evolution over time, by responding across the breadth of the contextual environment within which tourism is located, notably in sociocultural, marketrelated and technological terms. Such change is clearly evident within some of the large tourism companies in transport, entertainment and accommodation.

At the same time, the headlines of change do not reflect reality across the totality of the tourism sector. There is a real contrast between major multinational tourism companies and smaller operators within some subsectors of tourism (particularly accommodation and restaurants) which contain areas of work where many things have not changed over the past 20 years—productivity remains stubbornly low, working conditions are poor and remuneration levels are well below national averages in many countries.

In some areas of tourism, businesses have been unable to cope with the pressures of external change-induced competition so that, for example, work opportunities in traditional travel agents have declined in many countries.

By contrast to the developed world, in poorer countries, the picture is rather more homogeneous whereby much work in low labour cost economies, including that of the tourism sector, has an appearance of timelessness so that change, if any, has been at the margins of the overall employment experience.

This paper seeks to make a partial assessment of the impact of external change on the human resource environment within tourism over the past 20 years, with particular focus on work and employment themes within the sector. In addressing a topic as broad as this, there is a real danger of uncritical generalisation within a highly heterogeneous sector such as tourism.

There is real and ongoing debate with regard to definitional issues in the tourism sector and this has presented some challenges in the context of this paper. Discussion here seeks to embrace an inclusive interpretation of tourism with illustrations of human resource practices across various subsectors. This challenge is illustrated by highlighting features such as the diversity within tourism with its various subsectors (accommodation, food service, transport, facilitation, heritage); the size of operations; the location of these operations; business arrangements that are in place to deliver services within tourism; and the economic context within which operations do their business.

Published empirical and conceptual analysis of human resource issues in tourism has focused disproportionately on the hospitality subsector and, inevitably, evidence here is substantially drawn from hotels and restaurants to the possible neglect of major areas of employment such as transport. This is a challenge faced by others in considering human resource themes in tourism in this way. Our assessment is further complicated as a result of ambiguity in understandings of what the term, human resources and its management, encompasses. This ambiguity includes the consequences of changes that have taken place at a functional level as the traditionally accepted concept of personnel management has given way to a broader functional application in human resource management, operating as part of a company's wider business and strategic environment.

Human resource themes are also applicable at both the levels of the firm and in a macronational or regional context. This paper adopts conscious selectivity in focusing on human resources in the specific context of the work place and considers whether and how the employment environment has altered over the past 20 years.

Attempting a retrospect, with regards to a theme such as human resources in tourism, presents a challenge in determining an appropriate benchmark against which to measure possible change. Notionally, a 20-year yardstick is used, taking us back to the mid-1980s. At the same time, it is important not to ignore the insights from earlier times and to consider these in a contemporary context. Conceptually, the most useful and comprehensive framework against which to judge change is that provided by Wood's (1992, 1997) consideration of work in the hotels and catering subsector of tourism.

While Wood's discussion purposefully does not address the breadth of what is taken to be tourism here, it provides a valuable insight into research and analysis across the largest of tourism's subsectors, but one that is both the best studied and most problematic. Wood's assessment of the evidence discussed in his book, much of it drawn from the 1970s, 1980s and early 1990s, is that Hospitality work is largely exploitative, degrading, poorly paid, unpleasant, insecure and taken as a last resort or because it can be tolerated in the light of wider social and economic commitments and constraints.

Our concern here is to consider whether the context of and practice in contemporary tourism is such as to allow work in the sector to have moved significantly beyond the bleakness of this assessment and, if it has, to consider the extent to which wider contextual change has imposed itself on the management of human resource within tourism.

Therefore, this paper is concerned with assessing the nature and extent of contextual change on the management of human resources across the international tourism sector. This is a very broad aspiration, given the scope and scale of tourism as an economic activity, consisting of widely differing subsectors and located across virtually all communities, countries and cultures. The themes and contexts addressed here, therefore, must necessarily be selective, and include dimensions that appear to have broad salience across major tourism destinations, both established and more recently emerging.

The paper commences with a brief look back to the nature of work in tourism as depicted in early research into the sector, substantially the sources which led Wood to his bleak assessment. The paper then focuses on a number of themes which allow us to evaluate the extent of change and its impact—undertaking an assessment of the practice of the management of human resources in contemporary tourism; followed by consideration of the consequences of global and social forces on perceptions of work and careers; the impact of ICT on work and employment in tourism; changing interpretations of skills within tourism; and, finally, the increasingly diverse nature of the tourism work force in developed countries.

The paper concludes with an assessment of whether change, within these selected areas, outweighs the dead hand of the status quo that may appear to pervade tourism employment in other respects.

Where we have Come From

Recorded and formal accounts of what was and is involved with work in tourism, beyond passing fragmentary evidence, are relatively recent. One of the first in-depth pictures of aspects of tourism work comes from the 1930s and the writing of George Orwell (1933). His description of the work of the plongeur within the working hierarchy of Paris hotels is as perceptive as it is moving and, in many ways, provides a benchmark against which much subsequent sociological discussion of working conditions in the tourism and, particularly, the hospitality industry can be assessed.

Orwell's approach is to describe his own experiences of working in Paris hotels and his relationship with colleagues and superiors from the perspective of the foreigner and the 'down and out'. Orwell's objective is to expose the extremes of social deprivation during the depression of the 1930s and, as such, is one of extreme pessimism. He considers the work of the plongeur in its social context.

When one comes to think of it, is strange that thousands of people in a great, modern city should spend their waking hours swabbing dishes in hot dens underground.

The question I am raising is why this life goes on—what purpose it serves, and who wants it to continue, and why I am not taking a more rebellious attitude. I am trying to consider the social significance of the plongeur's life. I think I should start by saying that the plongeur is one of the slaves of the modern worldy he is no freer than if he were bought and sold. His work is servile and without art; he is paid just enough to keep him alive; his only holiday is the sack.

Orwell was looking at society through eyes that would have sat comfortably alongside that of other social commentators of the time, such as Seebohm Rowntree, a major contributor to understanding of poverty in Britain during the first half of the twentieth century. Rowntree prepared three assessments of social conditions in York and these progressively analysed the causes of poverty at the respective times, gathering increasing optimism as greater levels of state engagement with work, health and related social matters impacted upon British society and the work place.

Rowntree and Orwell shared a faith in the capacity of the state to improve the lives of the poor and were part of a movement that spawned detailed analysis of social conditions through initiatives such as the Mass Observation project. This included the domain of work.

Political change since the early 1980s has, perhaps, weakened the basis of such faith, notably through the impact of "Thatcherism" in the UK and elsewhere.

Therefore, contemporary commentators question the basis for optimism in assessing the conditions of work to which may service workers, including those in tourism, are exposed. For example, Orwell's disenfranchised and marginalised world of the plongeur has resonance in more contemporary studies.

Toynbee (2003), walking in the footsteps of Orwell, describes life in low-wage Britain, including her experiences in sectors of hospitality, and this world is not dramatically different from that of 1930s Paris within which Orwell talks about work as a "sort of delirium" within which "we were going as though we had only five minutes to lively. It was now that the tempo of the shift moved from hard and fast work to a controlled frenzy of washing up. Conversation came to an end. We were, I suppose, cheaper than industrial dishwashing machines but we imitated them quite well.

The tough reality that is presented in early descriptions, building from the influence of Orwell's analysis and, subsequently, reflected in Toynbee, can also be seen in other more recent studies of the industry (primarily but not exclusively, hospitality), many of which focus on problematic aspects of tourism work in a comparative social context. There is, therefore, little evidence, notwithstanding exceptional best practice examples by some organisations from across the industry, that working conditions in tourism have improved significantly from the time of Wood's pessimistic assessment.

Returning to Orwell, however, also brings us to his depiction of the craft and professionalism of hospitality work, set so starkly alongside the grim "below stairs" experience out of which the waiter seamlessly moves.

It is an instructive sight to see a waiter going into a hotel dining-roomy. As he passes through the door a sudden change comes over him. The set of his shoulders alters; all the dirt and hurry and irritation have dropped in an instant. He glides across the carpet with a solemn priestlike air. And you cannot help thinking, as you see him bow and smile, with the benign smile of the trained waiter, that the customer (is) put to shame by having such an aristocrat serve him.

There is another side of the coin which perhaps depicts tourism work in a rather more positive light and one which highlights what Riley et al. describe as "the obvious contrast of glamour on the one hand and low menial status on the other". One example of the glamour, that is equally precise and from the same period as Orwell, is represented by the accounts written, between 1937 and 1942, in five books by Ludwig Bemelmans.

However, in contrast to Orwell, Bemelmans is the supreme optimist and describes hotel work from the point of view of someone climbing to a senior position in a luxury New York hotel.

In a similar vein, Le Sueur's (1998) account of managing a hotel in Tibet presents an upbeat and very positive perspective on work at this level within the industry. The airline sector was also, historically, held up as the glamorous side of work in tourism, particularly in the 1950s and 1960s, and was widely depicted as one of the "blue ribbon" sectors for employment within personal services. During the 30-year period up to airline deregulation in the United States (1979) and Europe (early 1990s), it is fair to say that employment in the airline sector, especially with major national flag carriers, had many of the security of tenure attributes of public sector work and its attendant benefits combined with high levels of trade union participation while, at the same time, offering perceived glamour and a "fun" image. Calder describes this in terms of "A job in aviation—glamorous, secure, well-paid employment".

This perspective of airline work has been critically assessed by, among others, Bolton and Boyd (2003), Tyler and Taylor (1998) and Williams (2003) and further debunked as a result of high profile disclosures relating to work in some new model lowcost airlines as well as post-2001 changes within the aviation industry.

However, vestiges of status and glamour remain current in the airlines of many developing countries. Other areas of tourism work, while not well covered in the research literature, also point to clear ambiguities with respect to the working environment of tour guides and tour operator representatives.

Riley's application of internal labour market models to tourism provides a useful analytical framework in seeking to understand and explain the lack of significant change with respect to working conditions and remuneration in many areas of tourism work.

Riley and Szivas describe tourism as a sector "where easily acquired, transferable skills coexist and engender weak internal labour markets in organisations that economically are bound to a rate of throughput." Riley (1996) points to the features of employment in these conditions in terms of recruitment, training and professional status and, unsurprisingly, notes that many areas of tourism work typify weak internal labour market characteristics.

Alongside this assessment sits trends within most developed countries and within economic regions such as the European Union which point to erosion of elements of labour market strength and a general weakening of work place conditions. This has been driven by both economic and labour relations changes, notably in countries such as Spain and the United Kingdom but also, to a lesser extent, in bastions of strong labour markets such as France and Germany. As we shall see, access to low cost sources of migrant labour in many European countries has further acted to weaken labour market conditions within businesses in the tourism sector, despite the introduction of national minimum wage levels in countries such as Ireland and the UK.

An assessment of progress or otherwise, with respect to the overall working conditions and remuneration levels of tourism employees, does not provide clearcut answers.

There has been progress in some countries and within many, particularly, larger, organisations where case examples of high quality working lives and opportunity can be found to match that within most other sectors of the economy. However, much tourism work remains menial and undervalued and the plethora of smaller organisations also point to working environments where practices remain Dickensian and show little change from Wood's let alone Orwell's depiction.

Reflections on the Role of Human Resources in Tourism

The underlying premise of Failte Ireland's ground breaking

strategic plan for human resource development in Irish tourism is predicated upon the argument that "good HRM practices will be adopted because they deliver bottom line profitability". This primarily economic justification for investment in HRD has underpinned much of the history of this field, whether in the guise of personnel management, strategic human resource management, high commitment management or the management of human capital, among other iterations.

This, in turn, is manifested in a range of good practices, adopted by companies recognised for their leadership in the management of people within the tourism sector. Failte Ireland (2005a, 2005b) identify a number of good practice themes, based on a study of excellence in the tourism sector in Ireland and other countries.

Bolton and Houlihan (2007), in their powerful plea to reintroduce a human dimension to our consideration of HRM, note that these dimensions are uni-dimensional in their focus on employer benefits so that they ignore any notion of reciprocity. They effectively encapsulate this oneway street in their assessment of the HRM contract in terms of its humanity.

Bolton and Houlihan's case is, on the face of it, simple. Arguments in favour of work place flexibility among other forms of accommodation and change in the work place are generally, business and employer driven. Notwithstanding blandishments that advocate recognition of employee lifestyle requirements and work-life balance, some of which is enshrined in legislation addressing matters such as paternity leave, the overwhelming evidence is that reciprocity with regard to flexibility and accommodation in the work place is relatively rare, both for remunerated employees and among volunteer workers in tourism and heritage organisations.

Bolton and Houlihan point to imbalance in the expectations of contemporary industrial relations within tourism. As a weak labcur market sector, tourism in most developed countries has never been highly unionised and what strength trade unions may have offered in seeking greater reciprocity in the human resource contract has been eroded further in recent years. High profile disputes in international tourism companies have taken place in recent years, primarily in larger organisations located in transport related subsectors. Examples of these include disputes in Irish Ferries, Gate Gourmet.

Unions have succeeded in achieving partial amelioration of employer plans, but in no sense can these be taken as indicative of change in a general labour market process which is designed to weaken the position of employees within the sector.

Indeed, in the wider context of services, especially in smaller businesses, Korczynski argues that if trade unions "are to have meaning for frontline workers, their strategies must be informed by the daily work experiences of these workers" and that strategies that are derived from such experiences are likely to appear contrary to traditional union practice.

He notes the failure of trade unions to adapt to the needs of the contemporary service economy but, in the context of most businesses in tourism, this does not really represent change from past experience within which trade unions were of but marginal relevance within the sector. There are specific contexts within which trade unions can operate effectively in tourism.

"Traditional" airlines are one example as are hotels in Dublin, Ireland where Piso (2003) reports structural factors in the local labour market as being supportive of union participation. Perhaps the main barrier to unionisation in tourism's private sector is the attitude of management. Royle (2000), in considering work in the McDonalds fast food chain across a number of European countries, identifies the strategies employed by the company to ensure that unions cannot operate effectively.

Within tourism businesses, a process of organisational delayering and the reduction in specialist human resource staff means that many human resource responsibilities have substantially been devolved to front line managers.

Brewster and Larsen (1992) suggest that there are a number of reasons why many human resource activities have been devolved to line managers, and these are cost reduction, to provide a more comprehensive approach to HR Management, and to place the responsibility with the people who are most responsible for it.

Renwick's (2003) study established that line managers are now responsible for a larger number of employees than ever before, which in turn means that there are more issues in this area for them to manage. Storey (1992, 1995, 2001) suggests that if the work force is so critical to organisational success, the responsibility for human resource activities rests with all line managers and should not be left to HR specialists.

While larger organisations have undoubtedly invested in providing frontline managers with the new HR skills necessary for the responsibilities identified, there is little evidence that the majority of smaller tourism businesses have done much to meet this need. As a result, it is arguable that the quality of human resource management has deteriorated.

Approaches to human resource management that are suitable for a complex sector such as tourism remain contentious. The evidence is that larger organisations have become more professional in their application of key HR principles within the work place, but that such professionalism frequently remains absent in smaller businesses. The notion of reciprocity, which we introduced with regard to work place flexibility, can also be largely absent when organisations implement wider HR policies and practices.

People management may be recognised as a concern for all those in positions of responsibility in organisations, but there is little evidence that those charged with this responsibility have a full comprehension of what this strategic role means in practice.

This failure or neglect is not just one that is of concern at the level of the tourism firm but reflects a charge that can equally be directed at tourism development policies and practices at a community, regional or national level.

Liu and Wall are rightly critical of this neglect when they state that "tourism's human resource issues are poorly conceptualised and the many studies of tourism development approaches, both theoretical and practical, provide no consolidation of useful recommendations to situate the human dimension as an integral part of a comprehensive planning framework for tourism".

There is little evidence that this recent criticism has any less validity today than it might have done in the mid-1980s, and this is a real indictment of the large number of master plans and similar documents for tourism that have been funded by international agencies during this time.

A Global Industry, A Global Work Force

The tourism sector offers many and varied opportunities for working lives across its diverse subsectors and at different levels throughout the world. The industry's heterogeneity, geographical spread and stochastic demand cycle provides both opportunity and challenge in terms of mapping these against the aspirations and expectations of those attracted into the tourism industry, either as new entrants to the labour force or in the context of change opportunities within their working lives.

In most developed countries, traditional models of one sector working lives, built on the notion of a logical and progressive career "ladder" represents a reality which will face fewer and fewer entrants to the jobs market in the future. For some people, this is not a concern or a fear but provides the basis for challenge and opportunity, the ability to take control of aspects of their lives and to respond to changes within the external environment in a positive manner. Unlike their grandparents, today's school leavers and college graduates are more likely to think of their working lives in terms of finite segments rather than sustained and permanent careers, viewing the future in terms of what have been called "boundaryless careers" or "fragmented futures". Sennett, in recognising this phenomenon from a somewhat different perspective, notes that "flexible capitalism has blocked the straight roadway of career, inverting employees suddenly from one kind of work into another".

The trend data in many countries also point clearly to people being more mobile in their working lives and spending less time in the same job. For example, with respect to the UK, Macauley highlights evidence that "in 1996, half of all employees had been working for the same firm for 5 years or less. This had fallen to 4 years by 2001". The same source, points to the decreasing proportion of both full-and part-time employees who had been in their current job for at least 12 months during the same timeframe.

Similarly, the same UK labour market has seen a significant increase in the proportion of people in nonpermanent jobs. McOrmond (2004) reports on changes between 1993 and 2003 which point to increasing temporary engagement by, in particular, those aged below 24 years and those aged over 50 years.

Notably, the intermediate group, both male and female, saw a decrease in temporary employment over the same time period. Given the importance of younger workers to the tourism sector, this trend is evidence of this process of fragmentation and its likely impact within the industry and has stimulated response through, for example, recruitment from new labour markets.

Notwithstanding the trend indicated here, temporary employment in the UK, by wider European standards, remains quite low at about 7% of the total work force compared to a figure of 32% in Spain, 20% in Portugal and almost 18% in Finland. The temporary employment of female workers is consistently higher than then of males throughout the European Union. The structure of tourism is particularly conducive to supporting vocational mobility, particularly because of stochastic demand within the sector. However, the working environment in many sectors of tourism is such that labour turnover is higher than in other sectors of the economy.

Weir (2003) reports labour turnover in the UK and notes that the hotel and restaurant industries display the highest job separation rates of major sectors. High labour turnover is a reflection of the work environment within tourism and also of economic prosperity and opportunity combined with changing demographic structures and increased educational opportunity in developed countries. In the Irish Republic, for example, a centralised recruitment service for craft-level courses in tourism has seen demand move from a situation of very significant under-supply of training places in the late 1980s to one today where many courses are significantly under subscribed and some have been withdrawn.

Bauman's (2005, 2006) concept of liquidity is equally effective in explaining movement from one dimension of life to another and between relationships, whether in personal or working terms. Liquidity also points to blurring in the distinctions between working and nonworking lives, or as Hochschild puts it "family life had become like 'work' and work had become more like 'home'".

Adler (2004) reinforces this notion in his discussion of how the initiation of new work place practices, based on interdependence, can spread over into the home and change domestic behaviour in terms of a weakening of traditional gender roles. Fluid movement between working life segments allow individuals frequent mobility between different sectors of the economy, periods of study within models of lifelong learning and episodes that consist of travel or volunteering sabbaticals.

Vocational mobility is greatly facilitated by recognition of the underpinning "generic" skills set which much education and working experience provides today and which permits ease of both formal (qualifications driven) and informal (experience driven) transition, particularly within the tourism sector's weak labour market conditions.

Fragmentation or fluidity may be a relatively new phenomenon in the context of many sectors of the economy, but the reality of such employment models, generally employer rather than employee driven, is well established in many areas of tourism. Writing more than a decade ago, Riley infers that, in moving towards a future of "rising insecurity of job tenure, more unsocial hours working, more uneven workflow, a greater sense of immediacy in tasks", production industries are, essentially, playing what might be called "catch down" with a range of low skills service industries, including tourism.

Fragmentation or fluidity have long been features of work in these sectors, as noted by Orwell (1933) and are driven by, among other things, employer management of stochastic demand and growing responsiveness to customer demand or whims. What is new, however, is that work place mobility and job change are increasingly employee driven, with workers unwilling to make longterm commitments to one organization or work place. Unlike the disapproval that fragmentation or liquidity in working lives may have attracted in the past, today such mobility is less likely to be seen in terms of a lack of commitment or disloyalty to an employer nor does it necessarily create a sense of fear and insecurity for those moving between various working phases.

Perceptions of working lives held by younger people today are focused more on short-term wealth accumulation or debt reduction and much less on job status, security or permanence of employment than was the case with previous generations. Therefore, within the timescale allotted to work in a particular company or sector, commitment may be strong despite the transitory nature of the employment relationship.

Alongside the flexibility which characterises working relationships within the contemporary global work force, vestiges of the past remain within the labour market.

Major cities undergoing post-industrial transformation can face the paradox of high residual, longterm unemployment, mainly within the former work force of heavy industries such as automobile manufacturing alongside a large number of unfilled vacancies in contemporary tourism businesses, most of which can only be filled from student or migrant worker labour pools.

Sennett (2006) talks about the "spectre of uselessness" which haunts post-industrial society, in his terms the result of automation and technology substitution in the industrial work place but equally relevant where communities have witnessed growth in service, notably tourism, work and parts of the work force have not been enabled to buy into this new model of employment. At the heart of the causes of this uselessness is Bauman's notion that "the impetuous growth of new knowledge and no less rapid ageing of the old combine to produce human ignorance on a massive scale, and continuously replenish, perhaps even beef up, its supplies".

At its simplest, leading businesses have already recognised the changing nature of the employment relationship and have responded by a reconfiguration of operations and service delivery at certain levels within the traditional quality spectrum. As a leader within this process, McDonalds early on accepted that they would offer, at best, transitory job opportunities for many school and college students as well as others in the work force.

Therefore, they ensured that processes can be learnt very quickly by able people who are productive within a short period of time. Both parties know very well that there will not be a longterm commitment to the working relationship but that, while it lasts, both sides seek to maximise respective benefits.

For McDonalds and similar operators, this involves streamlining and simplifying processes and relying on the energy and enthusiasm of their workers for the delivery of their services. McDonalds have recently taken acknowledgement of the transitory nature of employer–worker relationships a step further with their announcement of the McPassport, providing opportunity for their employees working anywhere within the European Union to transfer to positions in McDonalds' shops across boundaries elsewhere in the EU, for short or longer periods of time, thus facilitating lifestyle and educational opportunity.

Other tourism businesses have recognised the value of this approach. In major cities in the UK and elsewhere perhaps half of all tourism workers are notionally full-time students. As a result, the tourism industry is configured to depend upon this source of labour and education providers have also had to adjust their delivery models accordingly. For businesses, there has been some modification of both product and technical skills demands with a greater focus on "generic skills" of communication, personality (aesthetic and emotional labour) as well as greater use of technology. Traditional training, as offered through tourism colleges in the form of formal courses and qualifications, plays a lesser role in meeting industry needs within this new model of tourism employment.

The decline in relevance of and demand for technical courses in tourism also increases the marginalisation of those with low qualifications in contemporary society (the traditional recruitment pool for such courses) who, as a result, may be further economically and socially excluded. In their place, the flexible student labour market offers employers many perceived advantages which traditional training routes do not.

Likewise, many tourism businesses in rural areas have turned to short-term labour pools of students and others from abroad, in

Ireland/UK to learn English (from countries such as Spain or Germany) or for their year out (from New Zealand or Australia) as ready made, articulate and, in some cases, lower cost alternatives to local labour.

"Lifestyle"—attractive employment in Donegal, West Cork or Kerry in Ireland can be offered seasonally to workers from elsewhere in Europe at lower cost and difficulty than would be involved in drawing on local labour markets. Training required and offered is minimal and there is hassle-free disengagement at the end of the tourist season. An extension of this employment culture is reflected in the increasing use of other flexible labour strategies within tourism. Shackleton (1998) points to the contribution of targeted part-time labour in the development of 'superservice' in food retailing.

Likewise, agency staff, in some areas of tourism employment, are of increasing importance, particularly in urban locations. Hotel housekeeping and banqueting are the main work areas where agencies provide a "just in time" model for businesses which allows for rapid response to variable demand and eliminates surplus staffing on an employer's books. This also creates an environment where longer-term employment relationships and structured longitudinal training models have little relevance. These expedient models of employment are most prevalent within the systematised, middle quality rankings and "fast" delivery sectors of the tourism sector. The concept of a career within this sector for all but a minority in positions of managerial responsibility is of limited and decreasing value.

The role of education and training in the context of transitory working lives, both within the external college environment and in industry itself, is to support mobility, mid-life entry and re-entry to the sector and development in relation to new technologies and products. This represents a fast-moving, ever-changing and challenging model of lifelong learning which, in the future, will play an important role in support of the "popular" sector of the tourism industry.

"Fragmented" and transitory employment relationships and practices may still leave problems for those "high end" businesses which remain locked within traditional skills paradigms and which employ craft personnel in the conventional mode. For them, the concept of the traditional, longitudinal career within a chosen craft area has relevance and career management in this sense requires active participation by employees themselves, their employers but also by those responsible for maintaining, managing and enhancing quality within tourism. At the same time, paying for and marketing the outcomes of such skills necessitates premium pricing and careful management of the price–value relationship.

The working lives projected for today's young people bear little relationship to the linear career models aspired by their grandparents and will be characterised by change, short-term goals and ongoing renewal.

Those planning for human resource development in tourism may need to more responsive to the challenges and opportunities presented by fragmented learning and working lives and recognise, as Adler and Adler (2004) do, the diversity of motivations and interests that workers typically bring into their employment relationships with tourism sector employers. Change, with regard to this theme, has moved employee aspirations for reciprocity in the utilisation of flexibility up the agenda so that notions of work place flexibility, as introduced by Atkinson (1984) and others, can no longer be seen solely in terms of approaches that are designed to benefit organisational needs.

The response to global trends in tourism, by educational and training providers, has been mixed. Baum (2000) points to the institutional and cultural barriers to change within most educational systems, factors that mitigate against the adoption of common tourism programmes and qualifications across national boundaries, notwithstanding the intentions of initiatives such as the Bologna agreement in Europe. The range of national case studies that address educational and training themes in tourism and the wider economy also points to the intransigence of diversity.

At the same time, there has been a growth in programmes in tourism education offered to a worldwide audience online and demand for education in this field through overseas study in Australia, Hong Kong, the UK, the USA and elsewhere remains high. However, such provision is largely structured upon demand from students from developing countries seeking to acquire skills and knowledge as imparted by academic and professional experts in the developed world.

This is a questionable model of knowledge transfer and one that Botterill and Baum (2006) describe as neo-colonial in impact. It is similar to the underpinning assumptions behind the growth of tourism education in many developing countries over the past 20 years, assumptions that see European and North American models delivery put uncritically in place in the colleges and universities of recipient countries.

The Impact of ICT on Work and Employment in Tourism

There is little questioning of the impact of technological development on all aspects of working and living in developed countries and, to an increasing extent, within the developing world as well. The impact of such change on the work place and beyond is well documented.

These assessments highlight the importance of changes in the work place linked to a wide range of issues, including perceptions of time and work intensity within the work place; organisational fragmentation; flexibility and enabling the recognition of work-life balance issues in the work place; the polarisation of skills and the decline in demand for less skilled workers; disparities in remuneration linked to use/non-use of ICT in the work place; outsourced working; home and teleworking; social inclusion, ICT and the work place; ICT and knowledge management; and technology substitution among a much wider range of concerns. These changes in the work place mirror wider adoption and use of technology within society and, in many respects, feed off familiarity with and expectations of technology that stem from everyday life. A comprehensive assessment of the impact of ICT and wider technology on the work place and working lives in tourism and beyond has the potential to be a subject for separate analysis in its own right. Here, we touch on a number of key themes and issues drawn from this discussion.

What is true, with regard to ICT in a general sense, is equally valid as an assessment of change within services and tourism and, in particular, within the context of work and employment and the changing role that people play as a result of such change. It is not an understatement to argue that ICT and wider technological change have revolutionised aspects of tourism operations (particularly distribution) while leaving others virtually untouched (food preparation and service in many smaller operations).

In terms of employment in tourism and the past 20 years, technology has had a direct effect on both the elimination of work areas and on the creation of others. Some destinations, dependent on airline and other transport stopovers for their tourism business, have been bypassed by advances in transport technology so that the work associated with this industry may no longer exist. For example, Gander in Newfoundland, Canada, a major refuelling stop for trans-Atlantic flights until the early 1980s now no longer serves this purpose and work associated with the sector has ceased to exist.

Similarly, changes in technology mean that the work of hotel telephonists has faded and, in many cases, disappeared with the advent of automated telephones in bedrooms and guest mobile phones. The technology challenge, particularly the consumer option to purchase and manage the booking of tourism products direct with suppliers such as airlines and hotels via the Internet, has reduced the need for and changed the role of travel agents, check-in staff and others involved in work in the sector in developed countries.

Such change is dependent on the availability and quality of the technology and, in many developing countries, the role of the travel intermediary remains important in the absence of Internet or, at least, Broadband connectivity. A final example of changing or diminishing role is that of the tour guide whose work can, in part, be superseded by flexible, electronic alternatives at tourism sites, allowing choice of language and giving visitors a selection of perspectives on events and the site environment.

However, ICT in particular has also created new forms of work in tourism, notably through the application of ICT and its use in distribution and management of key functions such as yield. The advent of specialist Internet travel companies such as

Expedia is clear evidence of this change, but the growth of specialist electronic distribution is complemented by website communications, marketing and booking options within virtually all "traditional" tourism companies so that the boundaries between them and e-companies has narrowed greatly. These developments have created demand for technology specialists in the tourism sector and also for new marketing and management skills in a more general sense, allowing companies to maximise the benefits they derive from ebusiness.

ICT has also changed the role of management information within the sector, allowing far greater depth and access to key information about guests and their behaviour. At the same time, it has revolutionised the management of pricing and yield so that human intervention is far less frequent than it would have been in the past.

Technology has also changed the nature of work and skills required for many employees, not least in tourism. Many areas of work have been moved from relatively skilled levels to the routine or lesser skilled. A good example of such change is in the area of hotel front office where enhanced reservations and guest management systems have reduced the training and technical skills requirements of such work by up to 90% in terms of the time required to acquire full competency. As we shall see, the technical demands of such work have been more than compensated for by the wider bundling of skills requirements within such work.

Moving Beyond Technical Skills

Tourism work has, historically, been calibrated in terms of its technical skills demands. This is most evident in the approach adopted by the International Labour Organization (1979) in their Taylorian breakdown of hospitality work into individual, measurable micro-tasks that, in turn, can be rebuilt into a training curriculum and assessment instrument.

On the basis of this, tourism and related service work has traditionally and widely been characterised as low skills although this stereotype is challenged in the context of hospitality by a number of authors on the basis that this represents both a technical and western-centric perception of work and skills.

In developed countries, the merging of family and working life has particular pertinence here in that many of the technical and interpersonal skills demanded of employees in tourism have close parallels with those learnt during socialisation in the home. Baum's (2006a) notion of social distance between the experience and behaviour of the tourist and employee is also of relevance here in that, in developed countries, there is considerable role crossover between the two in terms of transfer of experiences between the contexts. In less developed countries, such crossover is less likely.

Grugulis, Warhurst, and Keep (2006) talk about the evolution of what we understand to be a skill over time. In terms of tourism work, perhaps the first manifestation of change from a dominantly technical focus can be found in Hochschild's (1983) seminal study, which was one of the first to take our understanding of such work beyond the technical and professional domain, focusing on "the relational rather than the task-based aspect of work".

Hochschild's work inspired recognition of what Westwood (2004) notes are commonly referred to as 'soft skills' and, in doing so, highlights less tangible dimensions in the bundling of skills and work in tourism. Hochschild argues that service employees are required to manage their emotions for the benefit of customers and are, in part, paid to do this. Likewise, Seymour (2000) considers the contribution that this notion of emotional labour makes to work in fast food and traditional areas of service work and concludes that both areas demand considerable emotional elements in addition to overt technical skills.

Bryman defines emotional labour as relating to Employment situations in which workers as part of their work roles need to convey emotions and preferably to appear as though those emotions are deeply heldy (emotions) that are supposed to make the recipient of the emotional labour feel good about the worker and the organization for which he or she works.

Sandiford and Seymour (2002) take this definition a step further in talking about the management of emotions for financial reward. This link between human emotion and commercialisation has not been without detractors such as Wouters (1989) and Newton,

Handy, and Fineman (1995). The expectations of emotional labour add significantly to the skills demands of work in tourism.

There are few areas of frontline or boundary spanning work in tourism that do not have a very evident and, in some cases, all important emotional dimension.

In many respects, as Bryman notes with respect to Disney, employees are expected to give the appearance of enjoying their work as much as visitors are enjoying their time in the theme park. Maintaining this emotional facade in working conditions that are, often, anything but conducive to such behaviour takes its toll and requires skills and the outcome of extensive training in order to be maintained.

Blythman (2005) discusses the problems that such demands present in the context of supermarket work. After several hours at a time, any urge to be cheery or pleasant was overtaken by an all pervasive, mindnumbing blankness.

I began to feel spaced out, as though dulled by drugs. Any energy I might feel at the start of a shift soon ebbed away. Even if you wanted to try to be pleasant with people, after only so long it was impossible to keep it up.

The demands that emotional engagement in the work place entails have not traditionally been recognised within skills hierarchies and have either been neglected or put to one side as of lower value and status than "real" productive activities.

Bolton (2004) argues a strong case for the recognition of the skills dimensions within emotion work. She argues that emotional inputs are inherently skilled elements within the work routines, control processes and socially constructed demands that typify much service work. On this basis, Bolton argues that "emotion work is indeed skilled work which contains recognisable elements of discretionary content, task variety and employee control". Ritzer (2005) extends this notion of emotional involvement in his discussion of "simulated people". Obvious examples are Ronald McDonald and the characters to be found in Disney theme parks but Ritzer notes that "Far more important, however, is the fact that most of the people we encounter in the new means of consumption are simulations, even if they are not wearing costumes". Ritzer argues that employers prescribe how workers look, what they say and how they behave in a more general sense with the result that "these positions can be filled by a wide range of individuals. There is little or no room for creativity or individuality".

Work with a strong emotional labour component is, however, not exclusively about theatre. Williams (2003) highlights the safety and regulatory context which trumps any considerations of service and emotional engagement with passengers in the work of airline attendants.

Safetyrelated skills may be considered to be technical in nature and this illustrates that, while some areas of tourism work may focus almost exclusively on soft or ephemeral skills, the roles of government regulation and passenger concern are such that emotional engagement must always take second place to the hard skills demands of safety in the work place.

To the requirements of emotional labour in tourism can be added the skills demands of what Warhurst, Nickson, Witz, and Cullen (2000) describe as aesthetic labour, the skills required to look, sound and behave in a manner that is compatible with the requirements of the job and with the expectations of your customers.

In many cases, aesthetic labour involves staff demonstrating the ability to respond to fashion and trend imperatives in the consumer marketplace in a way that can be socially exclusive of many groups and cultures within society. Aesthetic labour is about appearance but can also be underpinned by cultural cache, the ability of frontline staff to understand and engage culturally with their customers on terms dictated by the latter.

Thus, service staff in some tourism contexts (luxury hotels, premium airline cabins, fitness centres, oneto-one personal training or other sports tuition) need to be able to make informed conversation with their guests or clients about politics, music, sport and almost any other imaginable topic, often from an international perspective. This requirement presupposes a certain level of prior education and cultural exposure as well as a commitment to remain up-to-date in these areas, what Nickson and Warhurst describe as the "gentrification of skill demand".

This implies a very significant change in the profiling of tourism skills in that work which has traditionally provided opportunity for those at the economic margins of developed country societies is, in part, now demanding a skills set that lies within the competencies of those with good general education and a more "middle class" cultural profile. This skills set is, therefore, beyond the reach of traditional recruitment pools for many tourism jobs.

Warhurst etal's interpretation of the commodified aesthetics of labour clearly builds upon Tyler and Taylor's discussion of aesthetics and gender in the work place (in the context of flight attendants), which looks specifically at "those particular aspects of women's work which takes place outside formal, contractual relations of exchange, yet upon which formal, contractual relations of commodity exchange depend". Tyler and Taylor's interpretation of aesthetics in the work place draws on "women's attributed nature, femininity and sexuality the commodification of women's Otherness". Thus, aesthetic skills can be seen as both an innate dimension of gender and as an area of skill which processes socialisation, education and training can develop and hone.

Westwood (2004) notes that in ascribing a 'soft skills' descriptor to labour with an emotional and/or aesthetic dimension, there is an implicit assumption that such skills are somehow less important than their 'hard' counterparts.

This is a view disputed in Bolton's (2004) argument that emotional work has a clear high skills dimension. Of importance in wider human resource terms is Westwood's comment that such skills, whatever their level of demand, "are a very long way from the kinds of skills that the UK's education system is used to supplying" which persists in a focus on "the processing and supply of more academic skills".

This indictment is applicable to many other countries and has particular bite in the context of tourism, pointing to a significant mismatch between education and training and the requirements of the contemporary industry.

Managing Diversity in the Work Place

Diversity in the tourism work place is not a new phenomenon, but full recognition of its impact and managerial implications in developed countries is relatively recent, driven by demographic, labour market and legislative change. Wood adopts an encompassing definition of diversity management when he talks of "a set of evolving philosophies and practices concerned with the utilisation of a variety of human characteristics, orientations and dispositions in satisfaction of ethical precepts and the pursuit of business goals".

In the context of this paper, our main concern is with the consequences of diversity in the tourism work place that have arisen through mobility in the form of labour migration, but we will also acknowledge the significance of other forms of diversity to contemporary HRM within the sector.

Indeed, as Adib and Guerrier (2003) rightly point out, it is rarely possible to consider the impact of any dimension within the diversity agenda in isolation in that, for example, ethnicity and disability are frequently closely associated with social class and economic status including labour market participation.

Governments in the developed world increasingly recognise the apparent benefits of labour migration to a country's economy. Home Office research shows that in the UK over a single year, migrants (including asylum seeks and refugees) contributed £2.5 billion to the UK economy.

Migrant workers can be beneficial to the economy in a multitude of ways: in particular, they are able to fill gaps in the domestic labour market and alleviate skills shortages as well as increasing the levels of employment which, in turn, helps to raise gross domestic product. Their age profile is such that they use less in the way of services but contribute to tax and national insurance payments which, in turn, help to finance future pensions.

The importance of labour migration to the work force of the contemporary tourism industry is well documented. Tourism businesses have long relied on a culturally diverse work force. Baum (2006a) traces examples of vocational mobility in the sector in Europe back to the 13th century and discusses the important role that, primarily, southern Europeans played in developing the culture and character of tourism operations in industrialised Europe in the 19th and much of the 20th centuries. However, contemporary labour migration, within tourism in Europe, has received limited attention from researchers. Widespread labour shortages and other labour market changes resulting from the impacts of a combination of, among others, demographic, globalization and economic factors in Europe are leading tourism companies to hire new employees from a wide range of less developed and transition economy countries.

Traditionally concentrated in core, urban centres, multiculturalism within the tourism labour market is now a phenomenon that has reached geographically peripheral areas and has implications for the marketing of destinations such as Ireland which have depended significantly on images of people and place in their destination branding. The numerical impact of migrant labour on the delivery of tourism services in these locations is particularly noticeable.

As an example, it is estimated that there are over 250,000 non-Irish nationals employed in the economy of the Irish Republic or some 13% of the entire work force.

This figure reaches 17% in the Irish tourism industry and is up to 25% of the work force in key areas of hospitality work. This growth was stimulated further in 2004 following the accession of 10 new Member States to the European Union. It is estimated that new arrivals to Ireland from within the Union reached 50,000 in 2004, primarily from Poland. In addition, some 9000 work permits were issued to non-European Economic Area nationals.

The changing nature of labour markets in the tourism sectors of developed countries, as a result of increasing migration, raises issues that have been subject to analysis across a range of the social sciences. Conceptually, this discussion can be located within debate about different forms of mobility in contemporary society and their specific impact in the tourism context. The nature of mobility discussed here and its impact are less common in their analysis in that they are a form of migration (labour) that exists solely because of the presence of another form of mobility, that of tourism.

The issue under the microscope here also responds to Rosello's (2001) notion of the immigrant as guest in her consideration of hospitality and immigration in postcolonial France. If migrants are, themselves, guests in the communities in which they work, interpretative representations of the destination in that context may be provided for guests (visitors) by guests (workers). This context has the potential to place strain on understanding of working roles within the tourism sector and the nature of hospitality provided by those employed as frontline staff.

It is arguable that the widespread recruitment and use of migrant labour in the tourism industry of developed countries has acted to the detriment of real change within the sector's work place. The argument that the tourism sector cannot recruit to unfilled vacancies and, therefore, turns to external labour sources is predicated upon the assumption that the labour economics of the industry remain appropriate and need not change.

There are exceptions, as evidenced in good practice examples across the sector, but much of the industry operates on the basis of a labour economics model that depends upon high turnover, low pay, poor conditions and minimal investment in training. Accessing low cost but untrained migrant labour is likely to act as a dead hand with respect to change within the work place economics of the sector. As a consequence, many tourism businesses do not perceive the need to change.

They are not required to consider strategies designed to enhance labour productivity, notably through real investment in training and development, in order to reduce the numbers they need to employ at higher rates of pay because low cost employees remain readily available. This analysis accords with Riley and Szivas' comment that "by not recruiting fully trained workers, employers forego productivity in favour of lower labour costs". It is also consistent with Riley's assertion, based on conceptual rather than empirical evidence, but valuable here nonetheless, that "where unskilled labour is imported to fill a shortage, the effect is to deflate existing pay levels".

Notwithstanding the advent of minimum wage legislation in the buoyant tourism economies of countries such as Ireland and the UK, there is little doubt that the availability of migrant labour does allow tourism businesses to employ more untrained workers at lower cost than might have been the case had this source of employee not been available, thus imposing deflationary pressures on individual but possibly not total remuneration costs.

Our discussion thus far, in the context of diversity, has focused on culturally induced dimensions. The management of people in the contemporary tourism sector in many countries is increasingly either legally or morally bound to recognise diversity in terms of a far wider interpretation.

These manifestations of diversity are not wholly new in tourism and there is evidence of their recognition, to a limited extent, in early analysis of the sector. However, highlighting such diversity in today's tourism work place is both functionally and ethically important. Dimensions that merit acknowledgement in this context include:

- Gender and the evident and continuing institutionalised disparity that exists in the status and pay of men and women in the services work place. Services work in most societies is highly gendered and this universal reality across national boundaries and continental divides is clearly evident in the range of contexts that are addressed by Sinclair (1997) and her contributing colleagues. Women, as Toynbee (2003) clearly illustrates, often undertake the least desirable and lowest status work in hospitality and other evidence from elsewhere in the services sector suggests that gender has an underpinning influence on rewards, achievement and status in the work place. Likewise the culturally induced absence of working women in the services sectors of some countries is tempered by evidence of gradual change in, for example, Iran and Saudi Arabia. Some areas of gendered work in services can be seen to represent exploitation and degradation and, therefore, combating sex services, particularly in relation to children, has become a major concern of governments and NGOs in some countries. Some areas of services work have, historically, been a predominantly male preserve. Mills (1998) notes, with respect to airline pilots that "In the firs two decades of commercial flying the characteristics of heroism and experience came to form a unique type of organisational masculinity—the pilot. Indeed, British Airways' earliest corporate image was that of the experienced, heroic and supremely confident pilot." While gender balance on the flight deck has improved, Mills notes that it was the late 1980s before British Airways appointed their first female pilot. Progress towards gender balance, in this area of high status services work, has been varied across different airlines but female pilots are commonplace today in many countries. Ali Khan (2004) even reports the appointment of the first female airline pilot in Saudi Arabia. However, this area of work remains masculine in its operating culture so that the experiences of female pilots can be challenging and degrading at times.

- Sexual orientation is a theme that has been addressed in services in terms of consumer markets. The experience of gay employees in the sector is not widely recorded except in anecdotal form. This may be because, as Wood notes, "gays and lesbians are not always visible, indeed adopting invisibility as a strategy is one way in which homosexuals cope with organisational life and avoid the disapprobation of those who possess animus against homosexuals".
- Ability and disability is an area of increasing interest in services. The services industry is frequently portrayed as an industry for the young, beautiful and super-fit and this projection is used to create the image of vibrancy, energy and fun. The services sector can be described as one that offers opportunity to members of a society across much of its ability and disability range. It is a sector that can accommodate the expectations and abilities of those with exceptional talent (in culture, entertainment, sports, technology, entrepreneurship as examples) as well as those in most communities who face challenges of a different sort in terms of physical or intellectual ability.
- Age in the sense that services work is frequently perceived to be an area for the young and historic data in developed countries certainly bears this out. However, changing demographics in wealthier countries means that traditional

sources of labour are no longer so readily available, creating the potential of opportunity for more mature workers, returners to work and those retired from first careers. As we have already seen, this solution is, in part, countered by the availability of low cost and young workers from overseas.

- Social inclusion reflects the capacity of services, as a sector for employment, to provide opportunity to potential workers from across a wide social and economic spectrum. This capacity is not always delivered in what is a growing labour market contradiction within the sector, that of widespread employment vacancies in services existing alongside endemic and longterm unemployment within communities in both cities and in rural areas. A partial explanation can be drawn from the aesthetic demands of the industry in that some sectors of services impose implicit or overt entry barriers based on appearance, cultural cache and education upon those seeking work and many of those from socially excluded communities do not meet such criteria.
- Motivation and choice, in terms of why people choose to work and also factors that underpin voluntary, unpaid work in services.

Uncritical claims for the virtue and value of diversity in the work place must be put forward with some degree of caution. The aspiration of effective diversity management in the tourism work place can easily be blinded by what Wood calls "the worthiness of the concept" which belies the rather more pessimistic consensus of the research literature. Furthermore, as we have argued with respect to the employment of migrant labour in the tourism sector's of developed economies, their impact, while making sound short-term business sense, also has the effect of deflating remuneration, permit the continuation of variable working conditions and allowing employers to fudge investment in skills development. If this is true with respect to one form of diversity in the work place, may be necessary to question whether some of the other forms of diversity touched on here are also adopted with similar objectives.

We started this paper with a fairly damning assessment of work and working lives in tourism, arguing that, in many respects, Wood's bleak (1997) assessment of the industry remains substantially unchanged in many countries, both developed and less developed.

We have considered themes wherein wider contextual change can be identified that has a direct impact upon people and their management in the tourism sector and we have considered the consequences of such changes. The evidence points, unsurprisingly, to conclusions in the form of a curate's egg and, indeed, contradictions in terms of practice across the industry. For example, we have evidence of the gentrification of tourism skills from Nickson and Warhurst (2007) while, at the same time, ready access to low cost migrant labour, both legal and illegal, permits many tourism businesses to sidestep this trend and to ignore issues of productivity, skills development and general work place enhancement.

As in other areas of work, it is clear that polarisation is taking place within tourism work, but the criteria of distinction relates to the branding and image of the work rather than to its technical or professional status. "Cool" work is equated with style, fashion and consumer branding (bars, night clubs, boutique hotels, creative venues) while "uncool" includes the work of drudgery in the sector (cleaning, popular service) and also some glamour work from the past, airline cabin crew, particularly with some newer, lowcost airlines.

Another example of contradiction is that vocational and educational opportunities for most young people in developed countries are such that many areas of tourism work are much less obvious and attractive longterm career options than they might have been 20 years ago. At the same time, growth in tourism in developing countries means that the sector has become an important source of employment for those previously dependent on subsistence living so that what is, ostensibly, the same work in a technical sense is constructed in very different ways across social, cultural and economic contexts. It is true that, at an organisational level, human resource practices in tourism have changed in many developed countries and in most larger operations. This change has been driven by a combination of the effects of commercial, legislative, ethical and external environmental pressures.

At the same time, tourism remains a sector within which, worldwide, very poor employment practices persist, incorporating both minimal compliance with the law and transgression beyond legally accepted behaviour.

Some of the changes over the past 20 years that are considered here, notably the mass mobility of economic and political migrants from the world's poorer countries, have allowed tourism work and employment to remain firmly located at the margins of many societies in terms of benefits and status and has acted counter to attempts to reform and modernise the sector with regard to its employment practices.

In the final analysis, the conditions of work in tourism are attributable to the outcomes of market force pressures, temporised in part and in places by government and wider societal interventions.

In parallel to our bleak assessment of the work environment, it is important to recognise that insatiable and growing demand for low cost tourism services, across the globe, means that consumers must also take responsibility for pressurising operators into undesirable, marginal or even illegal employment practices. It is self-evident that downward pressures on the overall cost of tourism (low cost airlines, aggressive tour operators, electronic distribution, deregulation) encourages the use of low cost labour and, to an extent, may also deflate expectations of service and product quality.

Growth projections for tourism, over the next quarter of a century, are such that it appears unlikely that we will see fundamental change in this environment in the foreseeable future.

Human Resource Module of the Tourism Satellite Account, Update to 2006

The aim of the Human Resource Module (HRM) is to provide timely and reliable statistics on the human resource dimension of tourism. It serves as a useful planning and forecasting tool for policy makers in the tourism, employment and training areas. Various tourism-affiliated agencies, academics, and decisionmakers in tourism will also be able to use it for research and analysis, planning and development.

Travel Services accounted for 47 thousand jobs in 2006, up 1.3%, following a 5.9% gain in 2005. This industry group accounted for only 2.6% of all jobs in tourism. The average hourly compensation for jobs in this industry group was above average ($21.56 per hour versus $17.95), as were the hours worked (1,805 hours per year versus 1,559). Travel counsellor was the predominant occupation, accounting for 42% of the industry's employee jobs.

Jobs, Hours and Earnings in Tourism Industries

A total of 2.8 billion hours was worked in tourism industries in 2006, accounting for 9.7% of the 29.1 billion hours worked in the economy overall. This reflected an average 1,559 hours of work per year, somewhat less than the economy-wide average of 1,738 hours. The lower hours of work reflected the higher proportion of part-time jobs found in tourism. It is interesting to note that the average annual hours worked increased slightly in 2006 in tourism industries, but were unchanged for the economy overall. In Retail Trade, a sector characterized by a high proportion of part-time jobs, like tourism, the average annual hours of work per job fell from 1,584 hours in 2005 to 1,566 hours in 2006.

Profile of Employees in Tourism Industries

The HRM includes details on three characteristics of employees namely, gender, age group and immigrant status. The following highlights some of the HRM results according to these demographics.

Women held 920 thousand employee jobs in tourism industries in 2006, an increase of 22,000 from 2005. These gains were mostly full-time and accounted for nearly half the job gains in the sector. Among women, the number of employee jobs held by those aged 45 and over increased the most in 2006 (+3.5%). Among men, on the other hand, jobs held by those aged 25-34 increased the most (+3.9%). The number of jobs held by women and men aged 35 to 44 hardly changed. Women were notably under-represented in

Other Transportation, holding only 26% of the employee jobs. Conversely, 68% of jobs in Travel Services were held by women. Women were more likely to be working part-time than men. They also earned less. Women working in tourism industries earned $19,100 in 2006, compared to $30,500 for men.

There was significant variation in women's wages and salaries, with jobs in Air Transportation paying the most ($42,269) on average, and jobs in Food and Beverage Services paying the least ($14,632).

Youth aged 15 to 24 years held 658 thousand employee jobs in the tourism industries in 2006. These young workers were more likely to be working in part-time jobs than other tourism workers, accounting for two-thirds of all the part-time work in the sector. Their wages were also considerably lower.

For example, the average hourly wage among workers aged 15-24 was $8.82 in 2006, just over half the average across tourism industries. Over 1997 to 2006, the number of jobs held by younger (15 to 24 years of age) and older (45 + years of age) employees in tourism has grown significantly, averaging 2.8% and 4.8% per year, respectively. Over the same period the number of jobs held by 25 to 44 year olds has declined.

Immigrants (persons born outside Canada) held 344 thousand jobs in tourism industries in 2006, or 20% of employee jobs. They were more likely to be employed in Travel Services and less likely to be employed in Recreation and Entertainment compared to non-immigrants. Immigrants were also more likely to be older: 18% were between 15 to 24 years old, compared to 44% for non-immigrants. Over 40% of immigrant workers belong in the 45+ age group.

Immigrants working in tourism industries were more likely to be men (53% versus 43%) and more likely to be in full-time jobs (72% versus 58%) than their non-immigrant counterparts. These results have been quite stable over 1997 to 2006. On average, immigrants worked longer hours than their non-immigrant counterparts, 1,755 hours per year versus 1,485 in 2006. This was the case for both men and women and for full-time and part-time jobs, across the period covered by the HRM.

Immigrants also earned higher annual wages and salaries on average ($28,769 versus $23,112 in 2006), although this reflects the fact that the immigrant labour force in tourism industries is older and that older workers earn more than younger workers 6: Human resources for travel and tourism Learning outcomes.

By completing this unit candidates will develop knowledge and understanding of human resources procedures and issues relevant to travel and tourism organisations. They will also develop an understanding of the recruitment process and the skills required in an interview situation. Candidates will produce evidence to meet the unit assessment objectives in order to show that they understand:

- the responsibilities of the human resources department in a travel and tourism organisation.
- how travel and tourism organisations manage their human resources.
- the recruitment process.

Candidates will also demonstrate their practical skills in interview techniques.

Assessment Objectives Knowledge, Understanding and Skills

Describe the responsibilities of the human resources department in a travel and tourism organisation Human resources department responsibilities:

- human resources planning.
- recruitment and selection.
- training and development, e.g. induction, mentoring and coaching.
- internal and external training.
- dismissal, redundancy, promotion, demotion, transfer.
- support and advice, e.g staff and line managers.
- policies and procedures, e.g grievance, disciplinary, equal opportunities, maternity, paternity, sickness.
- contracts, terms and conditions, holidays and hours of work.

- adherence to legislation, e.g race, religion, gender, gender identity, sexual orientation, disability or age (equality and diversity).
- staff welfare.
- ethical issues.

Explain how travel and tourism organisations manage their human resources Organisational structures:

- flat, tall Management styles.
- formal, informal Motivation of staff.
- motivation theories.
- job enlargement, enrichment, rotation.
- pay, bonuses, benefits.
- appraisals.

Leadership:

- styles (democratic, autocratic, laissez-faire).
- importance of clear targets.
- communication channels.

Explain how travel and tourism organisations manage their human resources;

- line management Teamwork.
- team roles.
- targets.
- importance of effective communication.

Chart the Recruitment Process

The need for staff:

- staff turnover.
- organisational growth.
- internal change.

Examples of recruitment:

- internal.
- external.

- use of agency.
- headhunting.
- advertising.

Stages of the recruitment process:

- job analysis (production of job description and person specification).
- attracting candidates (timing, different methods and their benefits).
- short listing (from CVs and application forms).
- selection interview (planning, the panel, good techniques).
- testing (psychometric and aptitude).
- appointing (contracts, terms and conditions).
- evaluation of process.
- equal opportunities issues.
- induction.

Costs:

- of poor recruitment.
- poor performance.
- impacts on team.
- advertising, staff time.

Demonstrate interviewer and interviewee techniques Interviewer:

- planning.
- questioning techniques.
- format and style of interview.
- use of interview record sheets.
- awareness of legislation regarding equality and diversity.

Interviewee:

- production of curriculum vitae.
- planning and preparation for interview.
- knowledge of organisation and job role.

- awareness of dress code.
- nonverbal communication.
- dealing with questions.
- asking appropriate questions.

Assessment

This unit is centre assessed and externally moderated. In order to achieve this unit candidates must produce a portfolio of evidence showing that they have met all of the assessment objectives. Portfolios of work must be produced independently. They will need to be made available, together with witness statements and any other supporting documentation, to the OCR Visiting Moderator when required.

Centres must confirm to OCR that the evidence produced by candidates is authentic. An OCR Centre Authentication Form is provided in the Centre Handbook and includes a declaration for assessors to sign. It is a requirement of the QCA Common Criteria for all Qualifications that proof of authentication is received.

Guidance on Assessment and Evidence Requirements

This unit aims to develop candidate's knowledge and understanding of the role of the human resources department and its importance within the organisation. The unit also aims to develop the skills required to perform effectively in an interview situation.

This unit has links with Unit 4: Customer service and selling skills in travel and tourism, Unit 8:

Planning and managing a travel and tourism event, Unit 9: Living and working overseas, Unit 11:

Career planning for travel and tourism, Unit 12: Developing skills through work experience in travel and tourism, Unit 13: Working as an overseas resort representative, and Unit 27: Working as airline cabin crew.

Links with a selection of travel and tourism organisations are encouraged for the delivery of this unit. Centres may wish to establish these. Alternatively, candidates may be able to research organisations, either individually or in small groups, share information and make comparisons. Information may also be provided through a case study, visits, talks, work experience or alternative. Ideally, organisations from different sectors of the industry and different types of organisation will be used to highlight different procedures and practices.

It is envisaged that such links with organisations will highlight the fact that the role of the human resources department varies from organisation to organisation and that management techniques and recruitment practices vary enormously. Classroom discussion of the different practices should be encouraged. However, it is recommended that underpinning knowledge of all areas is provided prior to organisational visits.

This will enable candidates to make comparisons and comment on good practice. There is a wide selection of printed and video material available on all aspects of human resource management.

When developing candidates' understanding of management techniques, tutors should draw upon candidates' experience of being 'managed' at work experience, within a work place and even within the classroom. Where candidates have worked in teams, they should be encouraged to consider whether the teams worked well and if so why. Tutors may wish to use the Belbin questionnaire to demonstrate the different team roles and the fact that a range of roles within a team is important.

It is envisaged that this unit will be used to develop candidates' awareness of the recruitment practices and the necessary preparation needed to gain employment within a travel and tourism organisation.

Candidates should chart the stages of the entire recruitment process, with explanatory notes of each stage. Again, contact with organisations will highlight differences and possible 'short-cuts' taken by organisations. Candidates should be encouraged to discuss these and comment on good practice. An understanding of the recruitment process can be used to encourage candidates to consider the need for their own applications to be professional and the costs involved in recruiting one person.

When preparing for Assessment Objective 4, candidates should be encouraged to produce curriculum vitae and complete job application forms to a professional standard. They could collect and evaluate job descriptions and person specifications. The paperwork used to shortlist candidates should be made available to candidates. Candidates should develop an awareness of their own body language. Self-reflection on skills gained and those requiring further development should be encouraged. It is anticipated that the practical activities used to develop candidates' interview techniques both as an interviewer and interviewee will help their preparation for their own interview situations, on completion of the course. Candidates can work in pairs or small groups for the assessment of Assessment Objective 4, with each candidate taking a turn as the interviewee and interviewer or interview panel member. Tutors are encouraged to video these interviews and candidates should be encouraged to self-evaluate. This could be cross-referenced with Unit 11: Career planning for travel and tourism.

Candidates may provide portfolio evidence for all of the assessment objectives in this unit using a range of presentation techniques. This may include assessor testimony/witness statements logbooks, diaries, the use of video, audio and presentation software, posters/charts, written work. Where video and/or audio evidence is provided this must be supported by assessor testimony/witness statements. Where candidates demonstrate competence, centres should record skills demonstrated on appropriate recording documentation.

5

Employment of Hospitality Professions

Introduction

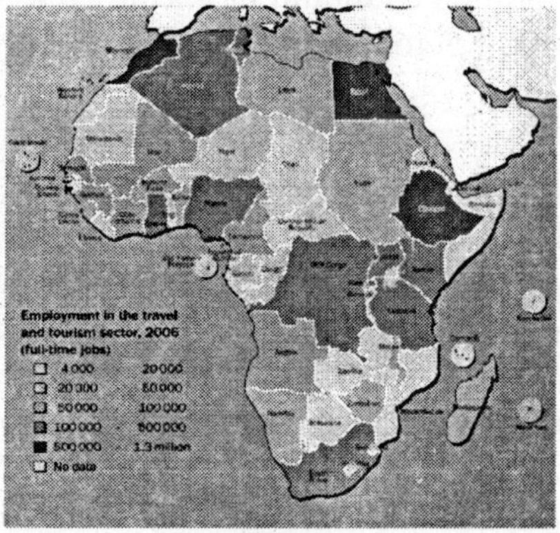

Employment in the travel and tourism industry in Africa

Employment in the travel and tourism industry in Africa. About 6.3 million people work in the travel and tourism industry in Africa, where tourism is highly dependent on natural and cultural environment. However, since travel & tourism touches all sectors of the economy, its real impact is even greater.

Preparing for Employment in Travel and Tourism

Activity

In the last session, work was focused on how recruitment and selection is used in organisations to attract effective people into jobs in the travel and tourism sector. Building on an understanding of how people in the real world make progress through their careers in the sector, you will have learned from completing work on a series of tasks:

- The stages involved in recruiting staff into jobs that you selected.
- That you can produce a flowchart of the process.
- The documents needed, such as a job description and person specification.
- The strengths and weaknesses of your chances of getting into the selected job.

Higher grades were available if you started an action plan for getting the job you want in the industry. In this session, you're going to start looking at the skills you will need to develop in order to promote yourself in a positive fashion during a job selection process. That means analysing someone's interview performance and then showing that you could do better by using self-selling skills. If you've made it through the initial pre-selection stage to be invited for an interview, you know you stand a chance of getting the job if you perform well at interview. Some people complain that interviews are too highly pressured situations for them to show themselves in the best possible light. But in truth, good interviewing skills are very rarely natural-they have to be learned and then sharpened by experience. Let's see how one individual handled a particular interview.

Can you help your career take off in the right way?

A Dream Job and a Nightmare Interview

Tarjani felt nervous. She had been looking at the email she had received from the airline, saying she'd got through to an interview for her dream job: member of cabin crew on the London to Singapore long-haul service. But she hadn't found out much about the airline or the country she would be visiting regularly. Her friend Murali had warned her that she had better be well prepared for the interview, as he knew that the company were pretty hot on getting the right people in as cabin crew. But Murali had gone off with his mates for the evening and Tarjani didn't really know where to start. Unfortunately, the interview was the next day and she still hadn't done much preparation, expect for rereading the job advert. She hadn't kept a copy of her application, or the documents the company had sent through-the job whatsit and person thingy-as she had been in too much of a rush to get the application sent. She was still going through her wardrobe, deciding what to wear for the big day tomorrow, when it occurred to her that she would have to catch the bus to the place where the interviews were being held. Murali wouldn't be able to give her a lift-he wouldn't be back at his place until well after she had to leave to get to the interview.

Suddenly, she remembered that she didn't have any credit on her mobile, so couldn't check the bus times or order a taxi if she needed one. That phone box down the road was still out of order, so she'd have to spend all her time this evening going through the timetables online. That took ages, because she always forgot to favourites the right Web site. She was in a right state and had to stay up really late, as there was no way she could sleep with all the stuff she hadn't done on her mind.

The next day was one that Tarjani would like to forget, but didn't think she would be able to for a while. Later, when she talked to Murali, the sorry tale emerged:

- She'd overslept and missed the bus that would have got her to the office where the interviews were happening.
- Although in the end she was just in time, she was so flustered that she barged into the wrong office, interrupting another interview that was going on. So embarrassing!

- She'd thrown on some clothes which would have been OK if they weren't so creased they looked like she was on her way back from a festival.
- The first question in her interview asked her to say what she knew about the company: doodly squit, as it turned out. She couldn't even get the name of the airline right.
- The other questions weren't much better. She hadn't realised that they would be so in-depth. "What would you do if a passenger was rude to you because for safety reasons you wouldn't allow him to see the flight deck?" She hadn't seen that one coming.
- She thought she was on firmer ground with her answer about her qualifications. But she'd forgotten the name of a couple of modules on her college course. Well, it was nearly a year ago. And surely they'd got it all on her application? That didn't go down too well.
- To cap it all, she caught her heels in the hem of her skirt as she got up at the end of the interview and nearly fell over. She felt such an idiot and the four interviewers all had a good laugh about that. She'd just scowled at them as she left.
- As she left the offices, it started to rain. Disappointed and soaked, she eventually got home after missing another bus.

Murali agreed with Tarjani's analysis: she wouldn't be hearing from them again. "Next time you'll be better prepared," he said. She couldn't help feeling angry with him for deserting her just before her big moment. I mean, if you can't count on your best friend to help you through that, who can you rely on?

Task

Using the experience of Tarjani, who quite clearly blew her big chance at the job of her dreams, write a script for an interview that goes somewhat better. Base the interview on your own choice of job, selected in an earlier session, or one that you have only recently identified. Track the progress of how you would prepare for the interview, making sure you cover the following important aspects of promoting yourself positively.

About the Organisation

- How is it structured?
- Where are the teams of staff located?
- How is the organisation presented in the media?
- Why do you want to work for them?

Practical Points for the Day

- Have as normal an evening as possible before the interview day.
- Don't stay up late the night before. If you've prepared well, you've got nothing to fear.
- Eat a meal before leaving for the interview.
- How will you get yourself ready for the interview?
- Prepare clean, ironed and appropriate clothes to wear.
- Plan your journey to and from the interview.
- Make sure you get to the interview with plenty of time to compose yourself.

It's your big day-don't miss the bus!

Revise Your Application

- Read through what you said about yourself in your application.
- This means always keeping copies of everything you sent.
- Interviewers only have this information about you, so make sure you know what you said.

Anticipate Questions

- Think about the likely questions you are going to be asked.
- How will you answer them?
- Ask someone beforehand to think up some really tricky questions and work out what you might say in response.

Practice What you will Say

- Practice your interview technique by writing a script of things you might want to say.
- Read these through (in private or with someone you trust!) and listen to how you come across.
- Make sure that you can make your key points fluently, by concentrating on practising them out loud.

Use the Opportunity

- Remember that an interview is not just about an organisation finding out about you.
- It's also an opportunity for you to find out if you'd like to work for an organisation.
- Think up some really good questions, which will show that you've really thought about the job and where it could lead you.
- Practice asking these out loud before the interview itself

Tourism = Employment: Is India Capitalising?

At several trade and global events over the years, the travel and tourism industry has been highlighted as an important economic employment generator. Veterans have voiced their opinion on the same. It is certain that travel and tourism, if properly encouraged can play an important role for economic stimulus and building consumer confidence. Travel fuels business growth, makes entertainment possible and sustains rural destinations.

It also strengthens trade by boosting income for the poorest countries, as well as for global suppliers. Taking all these factors into consideration we need to recognise the value of travel and most importantly its capacity to generate jobs. The tourism sector in India did witness an increase in employment numbers from 44.7 million to 51.1 million during the period 2004-05 to 2006-07 however, we need to cash in more on this potential. Taking India and its cultural diversity into consideration, we have diverse offerings and also the talent of the youth and artisans which need to be tapped. Every state has diverse tourism opportunities but still the focus is on the regular. This gives us an opportunity to augment the much talked about domestic tourism, which certainly needs a short in the arm. Apart from a few players in the industry who have tried to bring a new flavour to domestic tourism, this sector yet needs to be aggressively marketed.

Encouraging domestic travel is good for consumer confidence; international travel has the added value of strengthening trade flows. Action to boost trade promotion, simplify regulation, build infrastructure and rationalise taxes, in turn incites companies to invest, innovate and stimulate demand. This kind of public–private sector collaboration should be strongly commanded within and between all states, as it can help build resilience and buoyancy across economies.

Tourism Employment & Opportunity

CDS' innovative TEMPO model is a collaborative system organized to build the capacity of micro, small, and medium size enterprises to access new markets and B2B linkages, more fully participate in public sector planning, and more convincingly sell the assets they have to offer to the tourism industry.

TEMPO is an 'intrapreneurial' model, and programs that follow it focus on assisting local businesses to provide services demanded by tourists at market rates and international standards. The programs utilize donor funding to build capacity of local businesses and perform asset audits and value chain analyses to determine the goods and services on offer versus market demand from tourists. They then become collaborative nonprofit enterprises that link high-performing local businesses into international booking and reservations systems.

This combination of services that provides capacity building for businesses in the tourism industry and facilitates entry into real-time reservations systems is the stand out added value of TEMPO versus other tourism development programs.

Activities within the TEMPO model that create sustainable and sustaining tourism enterprises include:

- Demand Surveys,
- The CDS Inventory and Asset Audit System,
- The CDS Tourism Products Registry,
- Value Chain Analysis,
- Strategy and Action Planning,
- Capacity-building and Partnerships,
- Competitive Grants,
- Product Development,
- Digital Content Development for Marketing and Sales,
- Linkages to Wholesale and Retail Tour Operators and Other Channels.

Tourism Employment

Overall View

On average, 1.1% of persons employed in the EU work in the tourist accommodation sector.

In 2007, more than 9 million persons were employed in the hotels, restaurants and catering (horeca) sector in the EU; this equals 4.2% of all persons employed. The highest number of jobs in this sector was observed in Spain (1.45 million), followed by Germany (1.43 million). However, when taking into account the size of the labour market, the largest shares employed in the horeca sector were found in Malta (8.3%), Spain (7.1%), Greece

(6.9%), Austria (6.4%) and Cyprus (6.3%). About one out of every four persons employed in the horeca sector works in an enterprise providing tourist accommodation (hotels and similar accommodation, campsites, etc.), giving a total of 2.3 million employed in 2007. At the height of the tourist season, i.e. in the third quarter of the year, the number of persons employed climbs by an additional 10 percent to an estimated 2.5 million. In relative terms, this means that 1.1% of all the employed in the European Union work in the tourist accommodation sector.

The Member States showing the highest share of employment in tourist accommodation were Malta (5.3%), Cyprus (3.2%) and Austria (2.3%). Not surprisingly, these are also the top three Member States in terms of tourism intensity, i.e. the number of nights in collective tourist accommodation divided by the number of inhabitants. The sections which follow take a closer look at the pattern of employment in the tourist accommodation sector, compared with the horeca sector and the labour market as a whole.

By Gender

The share of female employment in the tourist accommodation sector is high at 60%.

The share of full-time employment in the tourist accommodation sector is not much different from the share in the EU-27 economy as a whole. About four out of every five persons are employed on a full-time basis. Looking at the hotels and restaurants sector as a whole, this is the case for only 72% of the persons employed (or 69% when excluding the tourist accommodation subsector). Only in the Czech Republic does part-time work tend to be slightly more common in tourist accommodation (8%) than in the horeca sector as a whole (7%).

Looking at the country data, big differences can be seen, ranging from almost no part-time employment in the tourist accommodation sector in Bulgaria or Romania to a rate of 60% in the Netherlands. In general, the figures for this sector reflect the full-time/part-time breakdown in the economy as a whole. Countries with a high share of part-time employment in short-stay accommodation, such as the Netherlands, Denmark (44%), Norway

(38%), Germany (32%) or Sweden (30%), also have around 25% or more part-time workers in the whole labour market, compared with the EU average of 18%.

The tourist accommodation sector is a major employer of women. On average, 60% of the EU labour force in this sector consists of female workers, who make up only 45% of the persons employed in all economic activities in the EU. In terms of creating job opportunities for women, the accommodation sector scores even better than the hotels and restaurants sector as a whole – where female employment stands at 56%.

The differences across the European Union are relatively small, although slightly more pronounced than for the economy as a whole, where in nearly every country the share of female employment deviates from the EU average of 45% by no more than a few percentage points. Among the countries for which data are available, more than two out of every three persons employed in the tourist accommodation sector are female in Romania (72%), Norway (71%), Poland (70%), Finland (70%) and Germany (69%). Malta (38%) and Italy (49%) are the only countries where women do not take the majority of the jobs in the tourist accommodation sector. But, together with Greece, these two countries also have the lowest female participation rate in the economy as a whole.

The analysis by gender with the full-time/part-time breakdown. The proportion of women working full-time is much higher in the accommodation sector (75%) than in the rest of the economy (68%) or, more specifically, than in the hotels and restaurants sector as a whole (64%).

Among men working in this sector, 90% have a full-time contract, which is slightly less than the overall average for men (92%). Only in the Nordic countries – Denmark (50% versus 36%), Sweden (51% v. 42%) and Finland (27% v. 19%) – are significantly more women working part-time in the tourist accommodation sector than in the economy as a whole. On the other hand, a significantly higher proportion of women are working full-time than in the economy in general in Austria (69% versus 59%), Portugal (96% v. 83%) and Switzerland (59% v. 41%). The lowest rate of full-time employment in the EU can be observed in the

Netherlands, for both male (59%) and female (28%) workers, but this Member State also registers the lowest overall average rate across the EU for both men and women.

The shaded/patterned sections of the pie charts, the share of part-time employment. In both the tourist accommodation sector and in the labour market as a whole, slightly less than 20% of persons employed works on a part-time basis, 19% and 18% respectively. In both cases, women account for around 80% of these part-time jobs. Out of 100 persons employed in the EU, 4 are part-time working men while 14 are part-time working women. For the tourist accommodation sector this is 4 and 15 respectively.

The situation with full-time employment is more pronounced. Women occupy 56% of full-time jobs in the accommodation sector. Indeed, out of 100 persons employed in this sector in the EU, on average 81 work full-time, of which 45 are women and 36 are men. On average in the economy women account for only 37% of full-time employment.

By Age

43% of those employed in the tourist accommodation sector are under 35 years old.

Both the hotels and restaurants sector as a whole and the tourist accommodation sector offer job opportunities to a young work force. Indeed, with 48% of persons employed in hotels and restaurants and 43% in the tourist accommodation sector younger than 35 years, both have a much younger age profile than the rest of the European Union labour market, where only about one in three of those employed is under 35.

This observation at EU level also applies to most of the Member States for which data on the age profile of employment in tourist accommodation are available. In most of these countries, the share of the two youngest age groups taken together lies 10 or more percentage points above their average share in employment in the economy as a whole.

Under-35s make up more than half of the employees in the tourist accommodation sector in Slovakia (58%), the Netherlands (56%), Sweden (56%) and Norway (56%). In all four countries, this share exceeds the average for the whole economy by around 20 percentage points. Cyprus is the only Member State where the age profile of employees in tourist accommodation is less young, with under-35s taking just 28% of the jobs in the tourist accommodation and 33% in the horeca sectors, whereas their share in the economy of Cyprus as a whole stands at 37%.

Only in Greece and Spain, two countries with a big tourism industry, does the age profile in the accommodation sector appear to be not significantly different from the age profile in all economic activities taken together.

At the other end of the age distribution, employment opportunities for persons aged 55 or more tend to be more limited in tourist accommodation (11%) than in the labour market (14%) overall. However, it must be underlined that reliable data are available for only a few countries, partly due to the low probability of including older persons employed in this sector in the sample for the survey used to collect the data.

By Education Level

The data in the previous sections revealed that tourist accommodation in particular employs younger and female workers. A third socio-demographic group strongly represented in this sector are persons with a lower level of education, i.e. persons who completed lower secondary education at most. That 36% of employees in the tourist accommodation sector did not complete upper secondary education, compared with a general labour market average of 25%.

For all countries where data on employment broken down by educational level are available, the conclusion that the tourist accommodation sector employs relatively more persons with a lower level of education holds true.

The biggest deviations from the average for the economy can be observed in Switzerland, where the share of lower educated persons in tourist accommodation is more than double their share in the whole labour market (36% versus 16%). Other countries where – compared with the entire economy – this sector offers jobs especially to less educated persons are Germany, Sweden, Norway and Denmark. Portugal (71%), Cyprus (24%) and Hungary (14%) are the only countries where there seems to be no noticeable difference (Portugal being the country with the highest share of employees with a low level of education in the European Union).

These findings are in line with the statistics on ICT use in enterprises, which indicate that the tourist accommodation sector does not require a high level of e-skills from most staff. Instead, only 36% of the employees in this sector use computers in their daily work, compared with almost one out of every two employees (49%) when considering all economic activities. Among the branches covered by the Community survey on ICT usage and e-commerce in enterprises, only the construction sector has a lower penetration rate for ICT at the place of work than the hotel and accommodation sector.

By Job Status

The accommodation sector does not differ significantly from the rest of the economy in terms of full-time/part-time breakdown. However, considering the duration of the jobs and the average stay with the same employer, the sector appears to offer less stable jobs than the rest of the labour market.

The proportion of those having a temporary job rather than a permanent job is more than twice as high in the tourist accommodation sector (where 30% of the jobs are temporary) than in the economy as a whole (14%).

In all the countries for which data on the duration of jobs are available, the accommodation sector performs relatively poorly. The largest discrepancies between this sector and the economy as a whole can be observed in Greece (59% permanent jobs v. 89% in the whole economy), Italy, Sweden and Bulgaria.

The more limited availability of permanent jobs can be linked to the seasonal nature of tourism. Indeed, Greece, Italy, Bulgaria and Malta also appear to have the largest variation in number of persons employed between the peak and the trough quarters.

The discrepancy in terms of share of permanent jobs between the tourist accommodation sector and the economy as a whole is particularly small – not more than 3 percentage points – in Hungary,

Finland, Denmark and Spain. The lowest shares of permanent jobs in the tourist accommodation sector can be found in Poland (58%), Greece (59%) and Sweden (61%). In the case of Poland, however, this is not exceptional, as this is also the Member State with the lowest proportion of permanent jobs in the economy as a whole (72%).

Another indicator of stability of employment is the average stay with the same employer. That staff turnover is much higher in the accommodation sector – with an average stay with the same employer of slightly over 6 years (76 months) – than in all economic activities taken together (121 months, in other words more than 10 years).

Comparing the accommodation sector with the rest of the economy at the level of the Member States, the average stay is less than half as long in Greece and Sweden. On the other hand, the discrepancy seems to be smallest in Portugal and Spain.

Seasonal Variation

Tourism activity varies strongly in the course of the year. In every Member State, occupancy in collective accommodation (expressed as number of nights spent by tourists) is at least twice as high in the peak tourism month as in the quietest month. Logically, the countries with a short tourist season have the highest seasonal variation in nights spent. In Greece and Croatia, the number of nights spent in collective accommodation is respectively 13 and 35 times higher in August than in the low season in January.

The quarterly data, that the number of tourism nights is 2.5 times higher in the third quarter (the peak quarter) of the year than in the first quarter (the trough quarter). With a ratio of "only" 1.2, employment in this sector tends to be far less affected by seasonal influences.

On average, the seasonal variation is only half as pronounced in the hotels and restaurants sector as a whole as in the tourist accommodation subsector. In only four countries (the Czech Republic, Denmark, the Netherlands and Norway) employment in the latter subsector seems to be less volatile over the year than in the horeca sector. In the economy as a whole, seasonal fluctuation is relatively limited– but this robust aggregate can, of course, hide strong seasonal variations in certain branches of the economy. Within the tourist accommodation sector, the highest seasonal fluctuations in employment are observed in Greece and Croatia.

In both these countries, the level of employment in the peak quarter of the year is nearly double the level in the trough quarter and 30% to 35% higher than the annual average.

At the other end of the spectrum, there is no significant seasonal variation in employment in Denmark, the Netherlands and Norway, although the number of nights spent by tourists is two to three times higher in the peak season than in the low season.

Based on data for ten Member States (accounting for 65% of employment in the tourist accommodation sector in the EU), the seasonal variation in employment separately for full-time and part-time jobs.

The two types of employment contract tend to have a different seasonal pattern. While both are relatively low in the first quarter, part-time employment seems to be the main contributor to the seasonal needs in the second quarter.

In the third quarter, full-time jobs appear to fill the additional needs on the tourist accommodation labour market (although it is not clear from the data whether these are additional full-time posts or an increase in weekly working hours to bring existing part-time posts up to full-time level).

By Region

Regions with high tourist activity tend to have lower unemployment rates. Tourist activity can have a negative impact on the quality of life of the local population in highly touristic areas. However, the influx of tourists can also catalyse the local economy, including the labour market.

The top regions (at NUTS 2 level) in the European Union in terms of number of nights spent by tourists per capita of the local population and takes a look at the unemployment rates in these regions. In order to take into account structural differences across the EU, the regional unemployment rate is compared with the unemployment rate at national level.

Although tourist activity will, of course, not be the only factor affecting the unemployment figures, That in all but three of the 20 most popular tourist regions listed, the unemployment rate lies below the national average. Two of the three regions where this does not hold true, namely the Canary Islands and Corsica, are island regions relatively remote from the mainland.

The Community statistics on tourism provide no data on occupancy of collective accommodation below the NUTS-2 regional breakdown.

However, at a more detailed regional level the number of bedplaces in tourist accommodation in comparison with the local population figures can be used as a proxy for the intensity of tourist activity in the region– assuming the capacity eventually accommodates tourist visitors.

That in most of these tourist areas the unemployment rate is lower than the national rate. Two of the most significant exceptions to this finding are the Greek islands Zakynthos (Zante) and Kerkyra (Corfu), both part of the Ionian Islands. As shown above, Greece tends to have a highly seasonal tourism industry.

This seasonal component possibly distorts the comparison as the unemployment figures are an annual average. In Rügen, Germany's number one region in terms of tourism intensity, the unemployment rate is nearly 10 percentage points higher than the German average.

In this specific case, the comparison is affected by the fact that Rügen is in Mecklenburg-Vorpommern, the Bundesland with the highest unemployment rate.

Total Employment

• The analysis in this paper mainly focused on the tourist accommodation sector, not on the entire tourism industry. In general, the breakdown into economic activities used in official statistics does not single out the tourism sector as a whole.

In particular, apart from a few core tourist activities such as tourist accommodation or the activities of tour operators and travel agencies, most tourist activities can be filed under sectors of the economy of a broader nature. For instance, restaurants can cater for both tourists and locals or transport companies can provide services to tourists but can equally well run freight or commuter operations.

To overcome this measurement problem, the European Union, together with international organisations active in the field of tourism statistics (the UNWTO, UNSD and OECD), has been fostering development of a framework that will allow accurate measurement of the tourism industry and comparison with other branches of the economy.

Taking the concepts, definitions and aggregates of the System of National Accounts as a starting point, this statistical instrument called "Tourism satellite accounts" (TSA) should allow valid comparisons with other industries and also between countries or groups of countries.

Part of these TSA cover employment in the tourism industry. Unlike the analysis in this paper, the TSA figures are not limited to the tourist accommodation sector, but also include tourism-related activities of other branches, such as the food and beverage serving industry, passenger transport or culture, sports and recreation.

Currently, national, non-harmonised data are available for a handful of Member States. These estimates for 10 Member States. The contribution made by the tourism industry to total employment ranges from 3.4% in the Czech Republic to nearly 10% in Slovenia. In Spain the tourism industry accounts for almost one out of every eight jobs (12.0%) in the economy.

Based on the aggregate data for these 10 Member States, the share of the tourist industry in total employment appears to be around 6.2%. Employment in the accommodation sector accounts for around 1.1% of the labour market, or approximately 2.3 million jobs. From the TSA estimates, total employment in the tourist industry can be estimated to be five to six times higher, with somewhere between 12 and 14 million employed in the EU. Once again, it must be stressed that these preliminary figures are based on non-harmonised national data from only 10 Member States.

China to Boost Tourism Employment to 100 Million by 2015: Report

China's tourism industry is expected to employ 100 million people by 2015, state media reported Thursday, meaning one in every 14 Chinese will work in the sector then. The government will introduce various policies to help the industry reach the goal, which marks a steep increase from the 60 million currently employed in the industry, the People's Daily said.

Authorities will adopt measures to facilitate job hunting and subsidise training of new staff, according to a statement posted on the National Tourism Administration's website Wednesday.

They also plan to launch a campaign to expand tourism infrastructure in less developed areas, the administration said.

Labour Minister Tian Chengping said earlier this year that the employment;

Employment in the Tourism Industries

- Two possible points of view on Employment.
  * from a perspective of supply (persons employed) and
  * from a perspective of demand (jobs),
- A person might have more than 1 job.
- A job might be occupied by more than 1 person.
- No one to one relationship between jobs and employed Persons.

Tourism Employment vs. Employment in the Tourism Industries

- Labour is a factor of production, and as such, related to a production process, not to a product, and even less so to the consumption of a product by certain category of consumers (a visitor);
- Employment in an establishment, and thus in an industry, can be observed and measured:
- Employment associated with tourism consumption can only be estimated via an explicit or an implicit model.

The basic recommendations: measuring employment in the tourism industries.

The units of measurement

* Number of jobs,
* Number of employed persons,
* hours worked (which should be included???),
* Equivalent full time job.

What do we want to know?

- For each tourism characteristic activity:
    * Number of jobs (monthly? Yearly? Peak and low?) by
- Gender.
- Status in employment.
- Qualification.
    * Number of employed persons,
    * "Quality of the job",
- Permanent.
- Seasonal.
- Direct contract/through an employment agency.
- With/without social insurance.

Sources for measuring employment in the tourism industries;

- From the supply side: household surveys; main difficulties.
    * Significance at the detailed level of activities,
    * Comparability of measurements overtime,
    * Geographical coverage; issue of rural area or small villages,
- From the demand side: surveys of economic activities; main difficulties.
    * Snapshot at a given moment in time,
    * Relationship of this snapshot with supply statistics,
    * Non permanent activities; seasonality,
    * Use of employment agencies.

Tourism Creates Employment Opportunities

Culture

Tourism creates opportunities of employment in the smallest and most remote communities. The Eastern Cape is one of the privileged provinces which has been awarded such an opportunity.

This task of alerting people to the possibilities is led by a non-government organisation called Fair Trade in Tourism South Africa (FTTSA) which is working towards a fairer, participatory and sustainable industry in South Africa.

One of its specific objectives is to contribute towards the Black Economic Empowerment programme and also to assist community-based and other emerging tourism enterprises to access niche markets.

Projects in the Eastern Cape include the Mehloding Community Tourism Trust in the northern Alfred Nzo District Municipality; Pondoland Community Trust and Tshezi Trust in OR Tambo District Municipality; the Kwam Emakana township homestays in Cacadu District Municipality, and the Nqileni Community Trust in Mbashe Local Municipality.

The Mehloding trust is one of the successful projects led by the NGO. The community owns the Mehloding adventure hiking trail and some homestays for tourists. This was an underprivileged community due to the lack of employment opportunities but FTTSA has sprinkled some nourishing water on the economic and social condition of the community.

Thozamile Xaki, a community tour guide, said: "We learn more about the environment and we gain entrepreneurship skills. This gives us as the community the urge to plough and preserve clean water for our tourists and it encourages us to start our own businesses." The projects have created job opportunities to impart skills to those who lack them and also recognition for Mehloding but above all the activities draw tourists to Mehloding.

The beautiful nature-preserving community has caught the attention of many tourists throughout the many years of its existence.

Nomthandazo Mnyameni, another community tour guide, said she has witnessed change in her community in terms of recognition and their knowledge on how to approach other NGOs when they need any kind of assistance. Even though this project is alive and advantageous, it does not really cover all the community's needs in terms of giving all of them suitable jobs, nor has it employed all the jobless.

Jabu Manyathi is not employed in this project. She said the project had given jobs to some and imparted skills for those in need. One still has to stand up and do something for oneself in order to survive. Jabu said she was not satisfied with the communication channels between the organisation and the community members that are not employed on the project.

6

Trends and Opportunity in Hospitality Industry

Introduction

The most widely used technique for analysing the macro-environment is known as STEEP analysis. STEEP analysis divides the influences in the macro-environment into five categories:

Socio-demographic—*social, cultural and demographic forces.*

Technological influences—*products, processes, IT, communications and transport.*

Economic influences—*fiscal and monetary policy, incomes, living standards, exchange rates etc.*

Environmental influences—*waste disposal, pollution and energy consumption.*

Political influences—*governmental, legal and regulatory influences.*

It is worth noting that in some texts the STEEP acronym is replaced by STEP with environmental influences omitted. In other texts the STEP acronym is turned around and presented as PEST. However, the framework for analysis is essentially the same in both cases.

It is this popular framework which is explained and explored in this chapter.

After studying this chapter, students should be able to:

- Explain what is meant by the macro-environment.

- Explain Ginter and Duncan's mechanisms of carrying out macro-environmental analysis.
- Describe the components of each of the four STEEP influences.
- Describe how the STEEP factors are interlinked and interrelated.

The Macroenvironment

What is the Macroenvironment?

We refer to the macro-environment as the broad environment outside of an organization's industry and markets, It is generally beyond the influence of the individual organization but can have significant impact on the macro-environment (industry and market) in which the organization operates. The macro-environment is sometimes referred to as the *far* or *remote* environment because it tends to exert forces from outside the organization's sphere of influence and the forces are usually beyond control.

Changes in the macro-environment can be of immense importance to an organization. They can bring about the birth or death of an entire industry, they can make markets expand or contract, they can determine the level of competitiveness within an industry and many other things. It is therefore essential that managers are alert to actual and potential changes in the macro-environment and that they anticipate the potential impacts on their industry and markets. In many ways analysis of the macro-environment is more difficult than internal analysis since it involves everything that occurs outside the organization. The problems when dealing with such a vast amount of information are, first, assessing what should be included and what should be left out and second, how the information should be organized in a rational and meaningful way. As Lynch (2000: 109) made clear, 'there are no simple rules governing an analysis of the organization. Each analysis [of the macro-environment] needs to be guided by what is relevant for that particular organization. This is to say that although analytical frameworks can be suggested for sorting and organizing pertinent information, the key issues are likely to be highly specific to each organization's circumstances.

Conducting Macro-environmental Analysis

Ginter and Duncan (1990) listed the following activities as components of macro-environmental analysis:

- *Scanning* macro—environments for warning signs and possible environmental changes that will effect the business.
- *Monitoring*—environments for specific trends and patterns.
- *Forecasting*—future directions of environmental changes.
- *Assessing* current and future trends in terms of the effects such changes would have on the organization.

The same authors went on to identify the potential benefits of macro-environmental analysis as:

- Increasing managerial awareness of environmental changes.
- Increasing understanding of the context in which industries and markets function.
- Increasing understanding of multinational settings.
- Improving resource allocation decisions.
- Facilitating risk management.
- Focusing attention on the primary influences on strategic change.
- Acting as an early warning system, proving time to anticipate opportunities and threats and devise appropriate responses.

Limitations of Macro-environmental Analysis

We should be careful to note that macro-environmental analysis has its limitations and pitfalls. At its roots, the macro-environment can be extremely complex and at any one time there may be conflicting and contradictory changes taking place. The pace of change in many macro-environment situations is increasing and becoming more turbulent and unpredictable. This degree of uncertainty has, to some extent, cast some doubt over the value of carrying out a macro-environmental analysis at all. By the time that an organization has come to terms with one major change in the macro-environment, another change may have occurred that requires even more attention and action.

Accordingly, managers that are concerned with strategic analysis must:

- be aware of the limitations and inaccuracies of macro-environmental analysis;
- carry out the analysis continuously (because it changes so frequently);
- constantly seek to improve sources of information and techniques for its analysis;
- use the information as one source of organizational learning;
- use the information to inform future strategy.

With these points in mind, macro-environmental analysis is a valuable mechanism for increasing strategic awareness of managers.

STEEP Analysis

The complexity of the macro-environment makes it necessary to divide the forces at work into the five broad categories we have already encountered. It is important to remember that the four categories are interrelated and constantly interact with each other. In the process of STEEP analysis (sometimes called STEP or PEST analysis) it is therefore important to explore and understand the relationships between the forces at work.

It is equally important to identify the relative important of the influences at work for the organization, its industry and its markets. Finally, because of the uncertainty of the effects of macro-environmental change on the macro-environment, it is essential that a range of possible outcomes of the changes are identified and considered.

In carrying out a STEEP analysis it should be pointed out that some of the factors may be generic in that they affect all industrial sectors, whist other are specific to travel and tourism, or a particular sector within the industry. Peattie and Moutinho (2000) provided a review of some of the major environmental influences in travel and tourism using an extended framework, which they termed SCEPTICAL analysis. In this case the acronym stands for:

- Social
- Cultural
- Economic
- Physical
- Technical
- International
- Communications and infrastructure
- Administrative and institutional
- Legal and political

Other texts such as Lockwood and Medlik (2001), Buhalis (2001), Vogel (2001), Cooper and Gilbert (1998) and Vanhove (2001) also give some interesting insights in discussing the key macro-environmental factors affecting the travel and tourism industry.

In her analysis, Auliana Poon (1993) pointed to the radical changes that were changing the travel and tourism industry. She suggested that a 'new tourism' was developing to replace the 'old tourism' based on mass tourism. The five key forces (consumers, technology, production, management and 'frame conditions') which had served to create mass tourism in the first place were themselves changing to create the new tourism.

Some text use the STEP or PEST acronym, thereby omitting explicit recognition of physical environmental influences but considering these as part of the other influences. The approach here, however, is to explicitly recognize the central importance of physical environmental influences in a tourism context by considering them under a separate heading. It is clearly the case that there can be few industries where the interdependence between the physical environment and economic activity is so clearly visible (Peattie and Moutinho, 2000).

In the following sections the component parts of STEEP are considered systematically. The approach adopted here is to list some of the generic factors and to provide illustrations of the industry specific factors by using the airline industry for purposes of illustration.

Socio-demographic Influences

Analysis of the social environment is concerned with understanding the potential impacts of society and social changes on a business, its industry and markets.

For most analyses, analysis of the social environment will require consideration of :

* *Social culture* (values, attitudes and beliefs)–its impact on demand for products and services, attitudes to work, saving and investment, ecology, ethics, etc.
* *Demography*–the impact of the size and structure of the population on the workforce and patterns of demand.
* *Social structure*–its impact on attitudes to work and products and services.

Social culture

The cultures of countries in which a business operates can be of particular importance. The culture of a country consists of the values, attitudes and beliefs of its people, which will affect the way that they act and behave (or, put simply, its 'personality'). There are important cultural differences between all countries. Culture can affect consumer tastes and preferences, attitudes to work, attitudes to education and training, attitudes to corruption and ethics, attitudes to credit, attitudes to the social role of a business in society and many other things.

Demography

Demographic trends are similarly improtant. Demography is the social science concerned with the charting of the size and structure of a population of people. The size of the population will obviously be a determinant of the size of the workforce and the potential size of markets. Just as important will be the structure of the population. The age structure will determine the size of particular segments and also the size of the working population.

The size and structure of the population will constantly be changing and these changes will have an impact on industries and markets.

Social Structure

Social structure is strongly linked to demography and refers to the ways in which the social groups in a population are organized. There are a number of ways of defining, social structure, such as by socio-demographic groupings, by age, sex, location, population density in different areas, etc. The social structure will affect people's lifestyles and expectations and so will strongly influence their attitudes to work and their demand for particular products and services.

Among the most important general changes in recent years in the social environment has been the change in people's attitudes to the physical environment. Increasing awareness of the problems caused by pollution and the exhaustion of non-renewable resources have caused travel and tourism organization to rethink (in many cases) the ways that they produce their products and the composition of the products themselves. Similarly, changes in social structure (upward mobility), lifestyle (increased leisure) and demography (ageing populations in developed countries) have significantly altered many market and industry structures.

Socio-demographic Influences—Airline Sector

A number of demographic factors point towards a greater use of air travel. Thus an increasing proportion of the population being relatively healthy and prosperous, increasing number of retired people, a decline in average family size, increasing amounts of paid holidays and larger numbers of double income families all point to higher usage of air services. Leisure travel (which accounts for about 80% of trips) has grown more rapidly than business based travel.

Other factors that might be considered are lifestlye trends and attitudes of society towards air travel and associated airport development. An increasingly mobile society where people take safe, reliable and affordable air transportation for granted is challenged by a critical society which assesses the contribution of air travel to air and noise pollution (Holloway, 1998). This dichotomy, in which the competing needs and interests of airline stakeholder groups need to be considered, represents a challenge to airlines, regulators and governments.

Technological Influences

Analysis of the technological environment involves developing an understanding of the effects of changes in technology on all areas of a business and its activities, including:

* Goods and services.
* Operational processes.
* Information and communications.
* Transport and distribution.
* Society, politics and economics.

Developments in information and communications technology (ICT), like the development of personal computers (PCs), networks, satellite, cable, Internet and digital communications together with rapid advances in software, have all contributed to revolutionizing the way that business in conducted in many industries. Activities are now better co-ordinated, research and development is speeded up, thus making businesses more flexible and responsive. For example, many activities previously carried out by middle layers of managers, which often involved collating and analysing data from operational activities and reporting to senior managers can now be more effectively carried out using ICT solutions. As a result, many companies such as British Airways have cut costs through reducing the numbers of people employed particularly at middle levels of the organization in a process referred to as *de-layering*.

Similarly, changes in transport technology have revolutionized business and have changed societies and cultures. It is possible to transport tourists as well as materials, components and products with far greater speed and at much lower cost as a result of developments in road, rail, sea and air transport. These improvement in transport have also increased the total amount of personal and business travel that people undertake and this has led to profound societal changes both in tourist 'exporting' and 'importing' regions. Increasing wine consumption and more varied culinary tastes in the UK are responses (at least in part), to wider participation in international travel.

As a consequence, it is important that organizations monitor changes in the technologies that can affect their operations or their markets. In most industries, organizations must be flexible and be ready to innovate and adopt new technologies as they come along. The way in which (and the extent to which) organizations do or do not employ the latest technology can be an important determinant of competitive advantage.

Technological Influences—Airline Sector

The Computer Reservation Systems (CRS) such as Sabre developed by American Airlines are powerful tools of travel marketing technology. The system developed largely in the 1960s and 1970s have attained global reach and hence they are now often referred to as Global Distribution System (GDS). The recent development of Internet search and booking engines developed by CRS providers allow for diversified distribution and communication channels to be utilized thus creating new opportunities for airline marketing. Allied to the use of CRS are the Revenue Management Systems that have been developed. These systems, which utilize the CRS accumulated databases, allow for the yield realized to be optimized by varying prices and altering the mix between classes of tickets that are issued.

In relation to the aircraft themselves, technological innovations continue to drive costs down and influence route structures. The 380 (*Megaliner*) currently being developed by Airbus Industries, for example, will have a capacity of some 550 passengers with operating costs about 17% lower than the Boeing 747 (Brown, 2001). Route patterns and airport infrastructures are two aspects which may well have to change in response to the aircraft's introduction. Additionally, a number of short to medium range jet aircraft models with twin fuel efficient lean burn engines have been introduced over recent years and further such developments are planned. Such aircraft allow the airlines to consider introducing routes which were previously considered to be unviable.

Economic Influences

Analysis of the economic environment will centre on changes in the macro-economy and their effects on business and consumers. It is important to remember that because governments intervene (to varying extents) in the operation of all countries' economies, many factors classed as political in this chapter will have important economic implications.

Broadly speaking, the regulation of a national economy is brought about by two key policy instruments—fiscal and monetary policy. These policy instruments, alongside influences from international markets, determine the economic climate in the country in which a business competes. From these, a number of other, vital economic indicators 'flow' and it is these that organizations experience–either for good or ill.

Concepts : Fiscal and Monetary Policy

Fiscal policy is the regulation of the national economy through the management of government revenues and expenditures. Each fiscal year, a government raises so much in revenues (such as through taxation) and it spends another amount through its various departments (such as on health, education, defence, etc.). The government is able to influence the economic climate in a country by varying either or both of these sides of the fiscal equation.

Monetary policy is the regulation of the national economy by varying the supply and price of money. Money supply concerns the volume of money (in its various forms) in the economy and the 'price' of money is the base rate which determines the interest rate that banks and other lenders charge for borrowings.

In the UK, the Chancellor of the Exchequer is in charge of fiscal policy whilst monetary policy is overseen by the Monetary Policy Committee of the Bank of England.

When the effects of fiscal and monetary pressure work themselves out in the economy, they can affect any or all of the following economic factors:

- Economic growth rates (the year to year growth in the

total size of a national economy, usually measured by gross domestic product).

- Levels of income in the economy.
- Levels of productivity (*i.e.* output per worker in the economy).
- Wage levels and the rate of increase in wages.
- Levels of inflation (*i.e.* the year to year rise in prices).
- Levels of unemployment.
- Balance of payments (a measure of the inter-national competitiveness of one country's economy against its international; competitor countries).
- Exchange rates (the exchange value of one currency against another).

Economic growth, exchange rates, levels of income, inflation and unemployment will all affect people's ability to pay for goods and services and accordingly, they can affect levels and patterns of demand. Similarly, levels of productivity, wage levels, levels of inflation and exchange rates will affect costs of production and competitiveness. All of these indicators must be monitored in comparison to those faced by competitors abroad to provide indications of change in international competitiveness.

Economic Influences—Airline Sector

The economic environment of the airline sector has been characterized by growth in relation to most key figures. Air travel demand has closely mirrored the cyclical pattern shown by gross domestic product (GDP) figures in that it responds to cyclical upswings and downswings. However, air travel growth has far exceeded GDP growth over the period. Between 1960 and 1995 the total world economy, measured by GDP, grew by a factor of just over three, while air transport, measured by tonne-kilometres, grew by a factor of nearly 20 (Hanlon, 1999). The airline industry also has a high level of fixed costs and consequently average load factors and revenue measures per passenger are crucial in maintaining profitability. Furthermore, fuel and aircraft prices are major expenditure items subject to fluctuations and the international orientation of the industry means that movements in foreign exchange rates can have major effects upon industry profitability. Holloway (1998) maintained that aviation managers face the need to pursue strategies capable of sustaining profitability throughout entire economic cycles.

Environmental Influences

The environmental influences here refer to the influence of concerns for the physical environment (both the natural environment and the built environment) on travel and tourism organizations. In recent years increasing concerns about ecology and 'green issues' has been an important social trend and this has changed people's attitudes towards the effects of products and operational processes on the environment. Issues such as global climate change, ozone layer depletion, deforestation, extinction of species, soil erosion, desertification, acid rain, toxic waster and water pollution have become important concerns with regard to the natural environment (Peattie and Moutinho, 2000). To such concerns regarding the natural environment might be added others concerning the built environment such as traffic congestion, deterioration buildings and historic sites, poor urban planning and visually inclusive buildings. The problems and issues identified have certain unifying characteristics. First, they all have international dimensions and second they are not exclusively tourism related but nevertheless have important implications for tourism managers amongst others.

Whereas twenty years ago most consumers showed little concern for the long-term effects of products and processes on the natural environment, today people are increasingly aware of the need to protect it. Following various developments such as the publication of the Brundtland Report in 1987 (WCED, 1987) and the Earth Summit in Rio de Janeiro in 1992, there has been increasing commitment to the principles of sustainable development in many industries, including tourism.

This has led to pressure on governments to introduce legislation and other measures to control pollution. The combined desire of consumers for products which are themselves environmentally friendly and which have been produced by 'green' methods has resulted in the realization by business that there are profits to be made by being environmentally friendly or at least appearing to be environmentally friendly. British Airways, for example, has developed a series of environmental awareness programmes for its managers and sponsored the 'Tourism for Tomorrow' awards in recognition of tourism organizations that have attempted to create products that have a positive environmental impact.

Scandic Hotels–environmental Programme as a Source of Competitive Advantage

Scandic Hotels (which is now part of Hilton plc.) is the leading hotel brand in Scandinavia, a region in which consumers traditionally are highly environmentally conscious. The group, which employs some 7500 people, has 155 hotels of which 133 are in the Scandinavian countries with others located around Europe. The brand, which positions itself as offering 'value for money', places great emphasis on continual competence development of employees at all levels of the organization and on its environmental programme.

Scandic's environmental programme was launched in 1994 following consultation with staff and the hotel group is an active member of the International Hotel Environment Initiative (IHEI). The programme involves the continuing education of all employees and includes initiatives such as:

- The introduction in 1995 of eco-rooms, which are 97% recyclable. More recently, the company has also developed 'eco-hotels', in which the entire construction of the hotels is guided by environmental principles. To date, more than 8000 eco-rooms and six eco-hotels have been built.
- The achievement of 'Swan' certification for four hotels. The Swan is the official eco-label in Scandinavia and verifies that the hotels have met stringent environmental standards.
- The abolition of individual soap and shampoo packages in 1994 reduced emissions of soap and shampoo by 40 metric tonnes and eliminated 10 million packages anuually.
- The introduction of the 'resource hunt', a programme promoting the efficient use of resources. Initially carried

out in the Scandinavian hotels between 1997 and 1999, the programme reduced carbon dioxide emissions by more than 15% and energy costs by 20%.

During 2000, Scandic also introduced, following staff consultation, a community involvement programme called 'Scandic in Society' which aimed to define the company's role in society by engaging in local issues that were important to each community in which Scandic hotels were located. Through such a programme the company aimed to demonstrate its corporate citizenship and contribute to societal changes and improvements.

The issues of the sustainability of tourism development for tourist destinations and attractions has been widely addressed in the tourism literature over recent years by authors such as Hawkins and Holtz (2001), Weaver (2000), Berry and Ladkin (1997), Clarke (1997) and Mowforth and Munt (1998). A number of authors have also traced the environmental impacts of particular sectors of travel and tourism.

Graham (2001), for example, traced environamental policies and practices at a number of airports including Oslo, Manchester, London Heathrow and Amsterdam. Cartwright and Baird (1999) traced the environmental impacts of cruising and reported on the ways in which attempts have been made to reduce the polluting effect of cruise ships. The traditional method of removing rubbish from ships was to dump it overboard. Now such practices are outlawed and large fines are imposed on shipping companies found guilty of such pollution, partly in response to consumer pressures. A modern cruise ship such as P&O's *Oriana* contains four sewage plants so that as much rubbish as possible is retained and disposed of safely into containers at ports. There is also a worldwide ban on the discharge of fuel oil into the sea (Cartwright and Baird, 1999).

Environmental in Influences—Airline Sector

Environmental concerns in the airline sector include the effects of noise and aircraft emissions and the impacts of developing airport and ground transportation infrastructure. Public tolerance of aircraft noise has been diminishing in spite of the reduction in noise levels due to the development of less noisy aircraft types

(Graham, 2001). The problems associated with aircraft noise have led to ever more stringent and sophisticated noise abatement measures being introduced at most major airports. Some of these gases emitted by aircraft in flight, primarily carbon dioxide and water vapour, are greenhouse gases which contribute to global warming and climate change. However, it is thought that aviation's contribution to global human-made carbon dioxide emissions amounts to only around 2% of the total (Graham, 2001). The infrastructure of creating airports and ground transportation to support airlines has often proved controversial. Thus the agreement to proceed with a fifth terminal for London's Heathrow Airport was secured only after ten years of public consultations, whilst Manchester Airport proceeded with building a second runway in the face of strong lobbying by environmental pressure groups.

Political, Governmental, Legal and Regulatory Influences

The political environment is defined as that part of the macro-environment, which is under the direct control, or influence, of the government. Governments have direct control or influence over:

- *Legislation and regulation*—this covers laws that influence employment, consumer protection, health and safety at work, contract and trading, trade unions, monopolies and mergers, tax, etc.
- *Economic policy*—particularly over fiscal policy. Governments usually set policy over the levels of taxation and expenditure in the country.
- *Government-owned businesses*—nationslized industries. Some governments retain control over key strategic industries (such as airlines) and the way in which these are controlled can have 'knock-on' effects to other parts of the economy.
- *Government international policy*–government intervention to influence exchange rates, inter-national trade, etc.

The objectives that a government may have towards the regulation of business will depend in large part upon the political leaning of the governing party. Most governments have, however, sought to construct policy over a number of key areas of business activity:

- Control of inflation (such as to improve inter-national competitiveness).
- Promotion of economic growth and investment.
- Control of unemployment.
- Stabilization of exchange rates.
- Control of balance of payments.
- Control of monopoly power, both by businesses and trade unions.
- Provision of public and merit goods like health, education defence, etc.
- Control of pollution and environmental protection.
- Redistribution of incomes (to varying degrees).
- Consumer protection.
- Regulation of working conditions.
- Regulation of trade.

To varying degrees, all businesses will be affected by political influences. Accordingly, it is important for managers to monitor government policy to detect changes early so as to respond effectively. Another important aspect of the political environment is *political risk* and its potential effects on business. Political risk is particularly important in international business. Whilst Western Europe and North America are comparatively politically stable, other parts of the world like Eastern Europe, South America, sub-Saharan Africa and parts of the Middle East have undergone periods of political instability. It is therefore necessary to monitor closely the political situation in these areas when trading with them, as the political risk are large. Even in more stable areas, political uncertainty can be higher at, for example, election times or when other political crises arise.

Political Environment—Airline Sector

The political environment of the airline sector has been characterized by an extended network of national and international rules and regulations, many of which date back to the Chicago Convention of 1944 and the Bermuda Agreement of 1946 (Sampson, 1984). Based on the acknowledgment of the sovereignty of nations over their airspace and of the equal right for every nation to participate in air travel, the so-called *five freedoms of the air* were established:

- *First Freedom*—The right to fly over another country without landing.
- *Second Freedom*—The right to make a landing for technical reasons (*e.g.* refuelling) in another country without picking up/setting down revenue traffic.
- *Third Freedom*—The right to carry revenue traffic from your own country (A) to the country (B) of your treaty partner.
- *Fourth Freedom*—The right to carry revenue traffic from country B back to your own country A.
- *Fifth Freedom*—The right of an airline from country A to carry revenue traffic between country B and other countries such as C or D on services starting or ending in its home country A. (The freedom cannot be used unless countries C or D also agree.)

The five freedoms were followed by a complex web of bilateral inter-governmental agreements that allowed national governments involved to maintain control over national interests related to air travel. A more liberal approach is reflected in the so called *open skies* agreements granting carriers of the states involved unlimited access to the routes between airports in these states. The concept of open skies reflects a development of major importance for the airline industry: liberalization unfolding around the globe (Doganis, 2001).

In the USA (which accounts for over 40% of the world's airline industry), the strict regulations governing the domestic air travel market were swept away by the Airline Deregulation Act of 1978. The act abolished regulations specifying the carriers that were allowed to fly on particular routes and impose controls on air fares. After deregulation many new carriers entered the market (and many subsequently folded), but most of the largest carriers, such as United, American, Dalta and Northwest, survived but undoubtedly competition in the US domestic market has increased in the longer term by the emergence of low cost carriers such as Southwest Airlines.

Subsequently, similar deregulation occurred in Europe. A different approach towards implementation was selected, however, owing to the complexity of achieving deregulation in the fragmented political landscape of the European Union. Consequently, a step by step process towards liberalization took place which culminated in 1997. Another major trend among European governments was the privatization (in whole or in part) of former state-owned carriers such as British Airways, Air France and Lufthansa.

Heavy regulation over the ownership of airlines remains, however. In many cases, such as the USA, airlines must still be 'substantially owned' or effectively controlled by nationals of the designated states. Thus airlines continue to be treated in a different manner to most other industries, reflecting its strategic significance and as Doganis (2001) pointed out, paradoxically the most internatonal of industries remains almost exclusively national in terms of ownership and control.

Bibliography

Airey, D. and Nightingale, M. : *Tourism Occupations, Career Profile and Knowledge*, Annals of Tourism Research, 1981.

Brunt, Paul: *Market Research in Travel and Tourism*, Oxford, Butterworth Heinemann, 1997.

Carl H. : *Internet Distribution of European Travel and Tourism Services*, Research Centre of Bornholm, Denmark, 1999.

Cukier, J. : *Tourism Employment in Bali: Trends and Implications*, London: Thompson, 1996.

Donald E. : *Public Personnel Management: Contexts and Strategies*, Upper Saddle River, NJ: Prentice Hall, 1998.

Douglas C: *Practical Tourism Forecasting*, Oxford, Butterworth Heinemann, 1996.

Eberts, Marjorie: *Careers in Travel, Tourism, and Hospitality*, Lincolnwood, VGM Career Horizons, 1997.

Harrison, Lyndon: *Tourism Means Jobs*, Chester, Lyndon Harrison, 1996.

Judi Radice: *Restaurant & Food Graphics*, Glen Cove, PBC International, 1994.

Klein, S. : *Information & Communication Technologies in Tourism*, Springer-Verlag, Wien-New York, 2000.

Kotler, Philipl: *Marketing Places: Attracting Investment, Industry & Tourism etc*, New York, free press, 1993.

Madhukar Manoj : *Hospitality Industries in Next Millennium*, Rajat, Delhi, 2001.

Marjorie, E.: *Careers in Travel, Tourism, and Hospitality*, Lincolnwood, VGM Career Horizons, 1997.

McNicol, B.J. : *Views of Residents, Developers and Government Planners About Tourists and Tourism Resort Developments in Canmore, Alberta*, The University of Galgary, Alberta, 1996.

Morrell, J. : *Employment in Tourism,* London: British Tourist Authority, 1985.

Murphy, P.E. : *Tourism: A Community Approach,* London: Methuen, 1985.

Nancy, N.: *Choosing a Career in Hotels, Motels, and Resorts,* New York, Rosen Pub. Group, 1997.

Norman G.: *Hotel, Restaurant, and Travel Law: A Preventive Approach,* Albany, Delmar Publishers, 1993.

Paajanen, M. : *Assessing Local Income and Employment Effects of Tourism: Experience using the Nordic model of tourism,* Wiley, 1999.

Richards, G. : *Culture, Crafts and Tourism: A Vital Relationship,* Tilburg: Atlas, 1999.

Robert C.: *Cases in Hospitality Marketing and Management,* New York, John Wiley, 1997.

Rue, Nancy N.: *Choosing a Career in Hotels, Motels, and Resorts,* New York, Rosen Pub. Group, 1997.

Sabharwal Rajiv : *Tourism and Hospitality Management in Liberalised Era,* Pacific, Delhi, 2011.

Sharma Sunil : *Planning and Development of Tourism and Hospitality,* Rajat Pub, Delhi, 2007.

Simmons, D. : *Community Adaptation to Tourism: Comparisons between Rotorua and Kaikoura,* New Zealand. Tourism Management, 2002.

Slinn, Judy A: *Tourism: Management of Facilities,* London, Pitman: M & E, 1993.

Smaoui, A. : *Tourism and Employment in Tunisia,* London: Oxford University Press, 1979.

Smith, G. : *International Tourism and Hospitality Careers through Education and Training,* CHRIE Annual Conference, Washington DC, 1996.

Spartidis, A. : *Employment in the Tourist Sector and its Socio-economic Implications. In: Economic Commission for Europe,* New York, 1976.

Swarbrooke, J.: *Marketing Tourism, Hospitality and Leisure in Europe,* London, International Thomson Business Press, 1996.

Index

A

Air Transport, 61, 62, 63, 65, 66, 69, 234, 237.
Airline Sector, 233, 235, 237, 240, 242.
Approach, 52, 59, 70, 106, 132, 150, 169, 174, 180, 185, 226, 231, 243, 244.
Assessing Training, 157.

C

Communication, 33, 60, 69, 72, 76, 90, 93, 101, 112, 113, 154, 180, 201, 203, 226, 235.

D

Developments, 51, 52, 53, 57, 78, 122, 130, 145, 185, 234, 235, 238.
Dining Room Attendant, 8, 10.
Doorkeeper, 11, 12, 13.

E

Economy, 35, 55, 56, 57, 61, 67, 72, 74, 75, 80, 82, 83, 85, 122, 126, 155, 164, 165, 172, 174, 177, 178, 182, 190, 191, 198, 206, 214, 215, 216, 217, 218, 219, 220, 222, 236, 237, 241.
Employment, 1, 4, 6, 8, 10, 11, 12, 15, 16, 17, 20, 22, 23, 25, 27, 34, 35, 37, 39, 40, 42, 50, 51, 52, 54, 55, 56, 67, 68, 81, 87, 99, 121, 122, 125, 130, 152, 165, 166, 167, 168, 171, 172, 177, 178, 179, 180, 181, 182, 183, 184, 186, 190, 195, 196, 197, 198, 204, 206, 211, 212, 213, 214, 215, 216, 217, 219, 220, 221, 222, 223, 224, 225, 241.

F

Fast Food, 13, 14, 15, 16, 174, 186.

G

Global Industry, 57, 128.
Globalization, 50, 51, 52, 61, 66, 67, 70, 73, 77, 80, 81, 82, 83, 150, 191.
Governments, 50, 54, 62, 63, 123, 124, 125, 150, 152, 153, 157, 190, 193, 234, 236, 238, 241, 243, 244.

H

Hospitality, 21, 22, 23, 32, 33, 34, 36, 38, 43, 45, 61, 69, 70, 72, 76, 81, 121, 122, 123, 125, 126, 127, 128, 129, 130, 161, 162, 164, 166, 167, 169, 170, 185, 191, 192, 193.

Hospitality Institutes, 129.
Hotel Bellhop, 23.
Hotel Industry, 25, 35, 49, 72, 77, 82, 83, 123.
Housekeeper, 26, 27, 28, 94, 95, 96, 98, 112, 113, 114.
Housekeeping Department, 92, 93, 94, 95, 97, 99, 100, 104, 107, 108, 113, 114, 115.
Housekeeping Management, 33, 90, 125.
Human Resources, 30, 31, 51, 52, 67, 69, 70, 74, 77, 80, 82, 126, 127, 128, 129, 130, 150, 151, 152, 154, 156, 164, 167, 168, 200, 201, 203, 204.

I

Institutes, 33, 123, 124, 125, 126, 127, 128, 129, 130, 151.
International Tourism, 56, 57, 67, 69, 79, 82, 125, 130, 168, 173.

J

Job Outlook, 17, 28, 40, 42.

L

Languages, 46, 47, 154, 155.
Laundry Management, 135.
Lodging Managers, 29, 32, 33, 34, 35, 37.

M

Marketing and Sales, 70, 213.
Monetary Policy, 227, 236.

O

Organization Chart, 94.

P

Programme, 50, 51, 124, 143, 144, 152, 153, 154, 161, 162, 225, 239, 240.

R

Restaurant, 8, 9, 11, 12, 13, 14, 15, 23, 32, 33, 34, 40, 41, 42, 44, 53, 67, 124, 137, 148, 149, 177.

S

Services, 6, 12, 24, 26, 28, 29, 30, 31, 35, 36, 43, 52, 53, 54, 55, 57, 59, 60, 61, 62, 63, 64, 65, 66, 67, 68, 69, 70, 72, 74, 75, 76, 78, 79, 87, 88, 89, 90, 94, 95, 107, 116, 117, 118, 123, 124, 126, 130, 131, 135, 136, 149, 150, 155, 156, 159, 160, 161, 164, 165, 166, 171, 174, 180, 183, 190, 191, 193, 194, 195, 197, 198, 199, 212, 213, 222, 232. 233, 234, 237, 243.

T

Tourism Industry, 56, 58, 59, 60, 61, 68, 70, 71, 73, 78, 81, 122, 123, 124, 125, 130, 150, 155, 156, 176, 180, 181, 190, 191, 192, 206, 211, 212, 213, 217, 221, 222, 223, 231.
Travel and Tourism, 25, 60, 61, 65, 68, 122, 128, 200, 201, 203, 204, 205, 206, 207, 211, 230, 231, 233, 238, 240.

□□□